G000242751

KEN CAMPBELL
The Great Caper

Michael Coveney

KEN CAMPBELL
The Great Caper

The Authorised Biography

Foreword by Richard Eyre

NICK HERN BOOKS
London
www.nickhernbooks.co.uk

LANCASHIRE COUNTY LIBRARY	
3011812110833 0	
ASKEWS & HOLT	27-Apr-2011
B CAM	£14.99
NLA	7|11

Ken Campbell: The Great Caper
first published in Great Britain in 2011
by Nick Hern Books Limited,
14 Larden Road, London W3 7ST

Copyright © 2011 Michael Coveney
Foreword copyright © 2011 Richard Eyre

Michael Coveney has asserted his right
to be identified as the author of this work

Cover design by Ned Hoste, 2H
Cover photograph (of Ken and Doris)
by Eamonn McCabe

Typeset by Nick Hern Books, London
Printed and bound in Great Britain by
CPI Antony Rowe, Chippenham, Wiltshire

A CIP catalogue record for this book
is available from the British Library

ISBN 978 1 84842 076 2

MIX
Paper from
responsible sources
FSC
www.fsc.org   FSC® C013604

Contents

Foreword

Ken once adapted a German play called *School for Clowns*. It was written for children and consenting adults and is the best of its kind I've ever seen. Set in a classroom, the play ended in total, glorious, unqualified anarchy as the clowns took over the class and, with the assistance of the audience, evicted their teacher. In performance at Nottingham Playhouse several hundred schoolchildren bayed for the expulsion of the Professor – played by Ken. He straightened his wig – a plastic dome with carrot-coloured Mao-style hair stuck to its sides – dusted off the chalk from his academic gown, stepped down into the auditorium with the words 'Clowns, I am unable to continue in the circumstances' and made his exit through the rioting schoolchildren, into the foyer, past the box office and onto the street.

I feel desperately sad that Ken has been unable to continue in the circumstances. He enriched all our lives by being consistently original, inventive and funny. He made you think, see and hear the world differently. There are few days that I don't think of his notion of 'panging' to other worlds or fail to remember him hurling an actor against a wall and screaming in his all-too-imitable voice – like a whining exhaust pipe with a broken silencer – 'Act PROPER!' Or recall his description of a certain kind of hyper-realistic performance as 'tie acting'. Or ponder his indictment of much of what happens in our theatres as 'brochure theatre'.

It wasn't always a joy to be woken by Ken on the phone at one o'clock in the morning to share his latest enthusiasm, but when the calls stopped I felt a loss. And I still feel that loss now. I have never known anyone who seized the moment with quite so much enthusiasm – and who was quite so relentless in wanting to share it with others. His evangelism for Gerry Webb of Space Consultancy and Interplanetary travel, EST, Max Wall, Spike Jones, Ian Dury, Charles Fort (the visionary not the hotelier), Robert McKee the script doctor, the Royal Dickens Theatre, the Bournemouth aqua show, the underwater play in the Liverpool swimming pool, the office on Walthamstow marshes, Werner the dog, the School of Night…

Ken once graphically displayed to me the two sides of his character, holding a hand in front of each half of his face in turn: the pirate and the char. The pirate was wild, sometimes savage, sometimes bullying, ambitious, brazen, loud and brilliant. The char was mournful and melancholic, and sometimes, though not very often, quite tender.

In 1900, in Paris, there was a prize called the Guzman Prize: 100,000 francs for anyone who could communicate with an extraterrestrial being on another planet. (The planet Mars was excluded on the grounds that it was too easy to communicate with Martians.) I think Ken should, belatedly, be offered this prize. He once told me of an encounter he'd had with the Venusian Consul in London. I suspect he was talking about himself: he was on a mission here to shake up our ideas about theatre. I told him that I didn't think I knew any Venusians. 'That's because you're always staring in the gutter looking for sixpences. Look up and you'll see them all the time.' I'm looking up now and I hope he's looking back.

Richard Eyre

Acknowledgements

The author and publisher gratefully acknowledge permission to quote extracts from the following:

Skungpoomery by Ken Campbell, *Impro* by Keith Johnstone, *theatre@risk* by Michael Kustow, and *99 Plays* by Nicholas Wright, all published by Methuen Drama, an imprint of A&C Black Publishers Ltd; *Memories, Dreams, Reflections* by C. G. Jung, published by Fontana Press, an imprint of HarperCollins Publishers; *Peter Hall's Diaries: The Story of a Dramatic Battle* by Peter Hall (edited by John Goodwin), and *Spy for Love* by Neil Oram, both published by Oberon Books Ltd; and *A View from the Bridge* by Arthur Miller, by permission of the Wylie Agency.

Illustrations

Family photos (courtesy of Margaret Robinson, Daisy
    Campbell and Prunella Gee)
The Happy Marriage (courtesy of Yvonne Cooper)
Spotlight photo*
Old King Cole (© Nobby Clark/Arenapal.com) and *Old King
    Cole* programme
The Ken Campbell Road Show (courtesy of Jane Wood)
Walking Like Geoffrey and *Bendigo* programmes
*School for Clowns**
The Great Caper (© Mick Rock 1974, 2011 / V&A Theatre
    Collection, Victoria and Albert Museum) and *The Great
    Caper* programme
*Illuminatus!**

Family photos (courtesy of Daisy Campbell and Prunella Gee)
Fawlty Towers (© BBC Photo Library)
In Sickness and in Health (© BBC Photo Library)
*The Warp**
Portrait*
*Recollections of a Furtive Nudist**
Pigspurt (© Mark Douet/Arenapal.com)
*Jamais Vu**
*Violin Time **
The Pidgin *Macbeth* (© Colin Willoughby/Arenapal.com)
Nina Conti (© Claes Gellerbrink Photography)
Ken and Fred (© Martin Argles/Guardian News & Media Ltd)

* *indicates source unknown*

Every effort has been made to trace and acknowledge the owners of the various pieces of material in this publication. Should the publishers have failed to make acknowledgement where it is due, they would be glad to hear from the respective owners in order to make amends.

Prologue

There had never been a funeral like it. Warren Mitchell, heroically prising his frail eighty-two-year-old body from his wheelchair, told a Jewish joke. An actor recited a speech from *Macbeth* in Pidgin English. And a distraught former colleague rushed the coffin, tearing off the lid. The corpse could be briefly glimpsed, wrapped in dog blankets. The dead man's daughter declared that her father used to make her learn poems whenever she asked for a pair of new shoes.

Ken Campbell – actor, director, provocateur, and one of the true great originals of the post-war British theatre – was buried on 9 September 2008 (he had died, suddenly of a heart attack, on 31 August) in the heart of Epping Forest, in Essex, removed to his silent resting place among tall trees on a sled drawn by his own three black mongrel dogs and followed by several hundred mourners and a clarinettist in a kilt. Tears were shed and handfuls of Essex earth thrown. Luckily, our distressed fellow mourner did not jump into the grave – 'I don't want him to be dead,' he had screamed while being bundled from the scene – but no one would have been remotely surprised if he had done so. Things like that happened with Campbell around. His being dead didn't seem to make much difference.

Before the ceremony, friends and family gathered in the reception area, drinking coffee and exchanging stories. Peter Cheeseman, now shaking dreadfully from Parkinson's, reminisced about Campbell's early association with his theatre in Stoke-on-Trent. In fact, we had a concert of reminiscence.

Campbell's voice spewed out his own material, one speech reminding us that 'funeral' was an anagram of 'real fun'. His first Road Show colleagues, a breakaway commando group of actors telling real-life myths and mysteries in pubs and clubs while banging nails up their noses and shoving ferrets down their trousers – Bob Hoskins, Jane Wood, Andy Andrews and Dave Hill – recounted Ken's arguments *for* stopping all Arts Council grants for five years and *against* banishing the Lord Chamberlain in the bad old days.

Jane Wood read out a letter Campbell had written to Lindsay Anderson in 1970 declaring that he was increasingly drawn towards 'soppy acting, or acting how your uncle used to act'. Chris Langham, a subsequent Road Show performer, and co-author with Campbell of the *Illuminatus!* epic which opened the National Theatre's Cottesloe auditorium in March 1977 – with a recorded prologue spoken by John Gielgud as a computer named FUCKUP, the First Universal Cybernetic Kinetic Ultramicro Programmer; the best anarchist joke ever perpetrated at the heart of the National – evoked the Campbell method by saying that there was no reason to do *Hamlet*; Ken was only interested in telling stories that really *had* to be told.

Nina Conti recalled asking Campbell what he thought about life after death. 'I'm all for it,' was the gleeful reply. And he was obviously right. Never was the spirit of a man so present in his suddenly bereft friends. Nina Conti is a good example of someone whose life Campbell changed in an instant. She was marking time in small roles at the Royal Shakespeare Company when he delivered a large dog puppet, with full instruction kit, to her stage door and suggested she have a go at ventriloquism. She's now one of the top vent acts in the country.

Jim Broadbent told a story that summed up Campbell's way of theatricalising every minute of his life. Broadbent was staying on the top floor of a hotel in Amsterdam with a group of actors led by Campbell. They all squeezed into the lift whereupon Campbell instructed them to get down on the floor with their legs in the air. When they arrived at ground level, legs up, the doors opened in front of an astonished group of wannabe ascendants: 'Cor, that came down at a hell of a lick!' rasped Campbell, rather like one of Lord Snooty's pals in the *Beano* magazine he cherished in his early years.

Prunella Gee, Campbell's former wife, actress and mother of their daughter Daisy, explained there was no hierarchy of grief on this occasion: we all had our own Ken. We learned that Gertie, the eldest of the three dogs, was being taken on by Daisy, and that the other two, Max and Bear, were going to Roy at the Essex Dog Training Centre. Doris, the African Grey parrot to whom Ken had been teaching her own autobiography while collecting her feathers and droppings in a remarkable collection of artwork, had acquired a new perch in Hornsey, sharing it with a fellow squawker called Groucho.

The stories and memories flowed on as we trooped back from the grave and improvised a mass picnic. Oh, and there was another unhappy Campbellian incident. The actor Chris Taynton, who had gone across to speak to the dogs and give Bear a biscuit while a Leonard Cohen song was being played, had his nose nearly scratched right off for his trouble. That explained the bevy of paramedics in the corner.

Two or three weeks later I was asked by Prue and Daisy if I would consider writing a book about Ken. He had been on the point of writing his own autobiography and had lately been warning his friends and family to watch what they said, or else they'd be 'in it'. I demurred, but only briefly, and then only at the prospect of failing to do justice to such an extraordinary and inimitable spirit of our theatre, a true one-off who reminded you, in whatever he did, why you liked going to the theatre in the first place.

Ken Campbell was a writer, director and unique monologist, a genius at both producing shows on a shoestring and inculcating the improvisational capabilities of the actors who were bold enough to work with him. An Essex boy who trained at the Royal Academy of Dramatic Art (RADA), he never joined the Establishment, though his official posts included a brief spell as Artistic Director of the Liverpool Everyman in 1980 and a professorship in ventriloquism at RADA. Even more remarkable than *Illuminatus!* as a project was a ten-play, twenty-two-hour hippy extravaganza, *The Warp* (1979), a sort of 'acid *Archers*' written by the poet Neil Oram, in which the protagonist's search for his own female consciousness took him from fifteenth-century Bavaria through Soho in the 1950s, on to stories of UFOs and transcendentalism and a flying-saucer conference in 1968, soon after the Paris *événements*.

Campbell, an irrepressibly jovial elf, with a thin streak of malicious devilry – both Puck and hobgoblin – was in recent years most widely known for his wild and wonderful one-man shows. These embodied the quality of 'friskajolly younkerkins' that Kenneth Tynan, quoting John Skelton, ascribed to Ralph Richardson's hedonistic, twinkling post-war Falstaff. It was a word, and a Campbell quality, he might have invented himself in one of his clown plays. He gave up 'serious' acting – although he was never less than serious *about* acting – when he realised he was enjoying what everyone else was doing too much, although he did appear in a take-over cast in Yasmina Reza's *Art* at the Wyndham's Theatre in 2000 alongside War-ren Mitchell, his old friend from his early days as a West End understudy, who was to become both his mentor and leading champion; Mitchell would read everything Campbell wrote from the day they first met and bonded on tour, rewarding him with free meals and criticism in perpetuity.

On television, Campbell appeared memorably as a bent lawyer in G. F. Newman's *Law and Order* series; in one episode of *Fawlty Towers*; and as Warren Mitchell's neighbour, Fred Johnson, in the sitcom *In Sickness and in Health*. He popped up bizarrely in films such as *A Fish Called Wanda* and Derek Jar-man's *The Tempest*, very much the same persona, bursting at the confines of a role and never quite fitting any other scheme of show business than his own.

With a gimlet eye and a pair of bushy eyebrows that had lately acquired advanced-canopy status, outgrowing even those of the Labour grandee Denis Healey, Campbell was a perennial reminder of the rough-house origins of the best of British theatre, from Shakespeare, music hall and Joan Littlewood to the fringe before it became fashionable, tame and subsidised. When Richard Eyre presented Campbell's *Bendigo*, a raucous vaudeville about a legendary prizefighter, at the Nottingham Playhouse in 1974, he thought it was one of the most enjoyable things he had ever seen in a theatre (so did I). 'Most of Campbell's capers,' said Eyre, 'look as if they are going to be follies and turn out to be inspired gestures of showmanship.'

Campbell later pursued improvisation as a goal in itself, and at the Edinburgh Festival of 2008 – his last gig – he supervised the improvised performances of shows that had no previous existence except as fictions in the columns of 'pretend' reviews written by several critics on national newspapers. One of these on-the-spot musicals was set inside Ken Campbell's head and, while it didn't beggar belief, it did challenge an audience's powers of credulous concentration; inside Ken Campbell's head was not always an easy place to be.

My last sighting of Campbell, an unexpected one, had been on the late May bank holiday of that same year, before he went to Edinburgh. The rain was sheeting down. It was a really horrendous afternoon. As work in the garden was out of the question, and we craved some fresh air, my wife and I decided to go for a walk on Hampstead Heath, pretty sure that nobody else would have the same idea. A few hundred yards in, on the pathway on the Parliament Hill side, between the running track and the Italian café, we made out a dim figure surrounded by dogs; also, emerging from the mist, his ex-wife Prue and their two grandchildren. Ken leered at me through the pouring rain as we approached and said: 'Oh... as it's *you*, we'd better put on a performance!' He brought out his whistle while Prue, Dixie and little buggy-bound Django were hustled to one side. His three black dogs proceeded to run and caper as he put them through their training paces and outdid them in their own specialities of yelping and barking. Suddenly, several other dogs, then more, raced into the improvised arena and joined in, madly, while their gradually materialising owners formed an expanding huddle of witnesses to what was suddenly... what was it, exactly... a dog circus, a canine charivari, a dream?

The whole experience was weird and unforgettable, like most of Campbell's shows, which came about through the sheer force of his imagination and willpower – certainly not through subsidy or sponsorship – and which were mostly a celebration, above all, of his own interests, enthusiasms and delight in strangeness. 'I have a desire to be astounded,' he once said (echoing Diaghilev's famous entreaty to Cocteau, '*Étonne-moi!*'). And that desire governed how he lived his life, as much as the work he achieved.

Where did all this energetic hooliganism come from? I now knew I wanted to learn more about both Campbell's life and his relationships at work and in private, which often, though not always, amounted to the same thing. I rang the actor Bill Nighy and asked if he would speak to me for an hour about his association with Campbell. He refused point-blank: 'I'll speak to you for ten hours about Ken,' he said.

Prue and Daisy made available to me, without condition, all of Ken's scripts, six dozen file boxes and the same number of notebooks, a huge, rowdy assemblage of work-in-progress, unpublished material, cuttings, letters and articles. Jane Wood and Dave Hill loaned me material pertaining to the Road Show, and then sat in their kitchen with me for two long sessions. Neil Cameron, Mitch Davies, Nick Hern, James Nye, Antonia Owen, Ian Potter and BBC radio producer Robyn Read were unstintingly generous in sharing material, DVDs and suggestions.

Sheridan Thayer made sure I viewed her excellent film about Ken, *Antic Visionary*, more than once. The British Film Institute dug up an archive copy of *The Madness Museum*. I'm grateful to all of them, and to Jeff Merrifield and Ian Shuttleworth, as well as James Nye, for allowing me to quote from their extensive writing on Campbell and his associates. Campbell's friends in Toronto and St John's, Newfoundland – Andy Jones, Paul Thompson and Ed Riche – spoke to me by telephone, as did Neil Oram from Scotland. Ken's cousins Maureen

Robinson and Christine Van Sickle loaned me invaluable material and photographs, and Christine posted me Ken's father's short, unpublished autobiography from Dayton, Ohio.

The following also spared time to share experiences with, and memories of, their friend and colleague: Richard Adams, David Blank, Claudia Boulton, Mike Bradwell, Jim Broadbent, Simon Callow, Roger Chapman, Nina Conti, Yvonne Cooper, Josh Darcy, Russell Denton, Ayanna DeVille, Bill Drummond, Bob Eaton, Sir Richard Eyre, the late John Ezard, Chris Fairbank, Tim Fiddler, Jacqueline Genie, Bob Hoskins, Terry Johnson, the late John Joyce, Richard Kilgour, Sarah Lam, Chris Langham, Mike Leigh, Sean McCann, Sylvester McCoy, Chris Martin, Adam Meggido, Warren Mitchell, Hla Myat Saw, Bill Nighy, Boo Oldfield, Cindy Oswin, Sean Phillips, Tony Porter, Irving Rappaport, Camilla Saunders, Oliver Senton, John Sessions, Anna Steiner, Nicki Stoddart, Mavis Taylor, Chris Taynton, Susan Tracy, Lucy Trodd, Maureen Vincent, Thieu-Hoa Vuong, Glen Walford, Colin Watkeys and Harvey Webb. I'm also grateful to my wife Sue Hyman for her advice and good company, and to Caradoc King and Elinor Cooper at A P Watt Ltd for their good offices.

I have aimed for accuracy and full acknowledgment of all sources without clogging the text with footnotes. Needless to say, any errors in detail or chronology are my own. I owe a lot to Nick Hern for his keen-eyed and creative editing. As for truth: everything here is true, or should be if it isn't. And if it isn't, let's at least follow Ken Campbell's example and suppose that it is. It's the 'supposing' that really counts. One of Campbell's favourite books was *Dreamwatcher* by Theodore Roszak, a psychological thriller which deals in the power to observe the dreams, fears and sexual fantasies of others and to enter those dreams and reshape them. He made a note of the heroine's state of mind as he prepared a new show: 'These are not my dreams... these things are not inside of me. Who can say how they come?' It was his job, he said, 'to keep folk distracted, entertained... and deceived about the true state of things.'

1

Ilford Calling

Kenneth Victor Campbell was due to be delivered at home by a stroppy midwife, a Jehovah's Witness, who caused a fuss and demanded her own chamber pot. 'The more I saw of that woman,' said his father, 'the happier I was in the knowledge that men were rarely, if ever, pregnant.' In the event, there were complications unrelated to the midwife, and Mrs Elsie Campbell was delivered of her first and only child by a Caesarian operation in nearby King George's Hospital on 10 December 1941.

The family home was a comfortable three-bedroom detached house in the Gants Hill district of Ilford, which also straddles Barkingside. Number 2 Haigville Gardens is one of several strikingly designed properties in a quiet street off the busy Cranbrook Road. These houses were part of an extensive building programme in the late 1920s and are termed, architecturally, 'chalet bungalows', even though they have an upstairs level. Young Kenneth's future primary school, Gearies Junior, was only a ten-minute walk away; the Gants Hill Library, so deliciously evoked in his later monologues, just across the main road; and there was a twenty-foot garden where he would keep books and records in his own little shed. Sheds were his favourite buildings, always. His dad built this one, and also ran a path through the garden for children's bicycles. During the war, his mum kept chickens, all of them with names beginning with 'V' – for Victory.

By the time he was three or four, little Kenneth was interviewing himself in his own ground-floor bathroom, finding a jungle world of animals in the patterns on the linoleum floor. He had an imaginary friend called Jelp and created outlandish stories of flying doodlebugs and rampaging wild beasts with toilet-roll eyes. These infant solo performances would leak out under the door, and passing relatives – though not his vaguely disapproving father – would say, 'You should go on the stage.' Years later, in 1964, his first performed play, *Events of an Average Bath Night*, was indeed set in a bathroom, as well as in three streets and a shed. Ken Campbell was never much given to fancy theorising; his idea of 'good' acting was the dynamic opposite of whatever it is they do at the Royal Shakespeare Company, and he first defined it as 'Uncle Fred' acting, the sort of attention-seeking showing-off your relatives did at family gatherings. The thing that appealed to him most about the comic actor and impressionist John Sessions, to whom he gave a first big break, was that he'd been utterly true to his bathroom.

There was an interlude, though, between birth and bathroom: aged one, he was evacuated with his mother to his paternal grandmother's house in Eastham in the Wirral and then went to stay with an aunt half a mile away. He was suddenly surrounded by cousins on all sides in an area of Britain not spared in the German bombing raids; the city of Liverpool, across the Mersey, would always play an important part in his life. He used to say that 'to get things done' you had to go to Liverpool. Ken's mother, Elsie Handley, was an Ilford girl, and his father, Anthony Colin Campbell, traced his line through landowners in the North West to seafarers in the port of Liverpool. Colin (he never used his first name) was the eldest of eight children whose father, Robert Campbell, a purser in the Merchant Navy, and later employee of the naval outfitters Wheatley and Lewis in Liverpool, had turned, after the General Strike in 1925, to mining spar from disused lead mines in North Wales, grinding it down and selling it to local builders for pebble-dashing cement facings on houses.

The Campbell clan lived in a solid suburban house in Wallasey. Robert was president of the Egremont Cricket

Club and organised dances where the children, who all played musical instruments, were pressed into service. Colin was born in 1903, and left school in Liverpool in 1919, the year in which he opened the batting for Egremont in Wallasey Park; he was a good tennis player, too. He wanted to go to sea but was packed off instead to the Commercial Cable Company – a rival to Western Union – in Liverpool to serve a fifteen-month training apprenticeship. He worked for the transatlantic CCC for fifty years. His job entailed listening on headphones to extremely high-speed Morse code and typing it out in blocks of six, the fixed length of an average word; the pricing was based on that statistic.

During his retirement in Croyde, Devon, Colin Campbell (who died in 1977) wrote an unpublished memoir called *M-I-M* (the international Morse signal to indicate laughter and appreciation – and a private signal between the operators on either side of the Atlantic to get back to work after using company time to exchange pleasantries and family news). He subtitled it with an oratorical, Pooterish flourish: 'Being an account of the lighter side of a cable telegraphist's life in the pioneer days of international communication before, and after, automated printer signals superseded the Morse code: when news agencies were the sole purveyors of local and world news; when a red sky at night or morning foretold the weather prospects; when radio and television programmes existed only in the realms of fantasy; and when party political broadcasts were undreamt of – HAPPY DAYS!'

Colin was a small, quiet, dapper man with a surprising fluency in after-dinner speaking. He recounts how in 1921 he was posted with the company to Waterville in Ireland, where a colleague was John Moores, a fellow Liverpudlian full of embryonic plans for the football pools company of Littlewoods which he founded two years later; Colin notes the ongoing local struggles between the Black and Tans and the Irish Republican Army, but he comments more ruefully, with hindsight, on his mistake of refusing Moores's invitation to join him in the new enterprise. He was transferred to the London head office in Wormwood Street in the City in 1924 and lived in digs in Goodmayes and Seven Kings – about forty minutes away on the new railway line into Liverpool Street – before settling with two colleagues in three different addresses on the south side of Valentines Park in Ilford. At the tennis club in the park, he met his future wife, Elsie (and, indeed, his second wife, Betty). Although his prowess had been in cricket – he had opened the batting for Wanstead and the South Essex second eleven – Colin now concentrated on his tennis, and on Elsie, who was one of three sisters.

In one of Ken's early television plays, *You See, the Thing is This*, Walter, a tennis player in a Barkingside bedsit whose father was a founder member of the Gants Hill Tennis Club, is visited by his much younger female playing partner who has been 'nicked' by a male friend for the mixed doubles. Walter is eaten with despair at losing his partner. Not only was this an imaginative rejig of what had actually happened to his father, but the part of Walter, the Campbell character, was played by Ian Holm, ten years older than Ken, and a fellow Ilfordian and Old Chigwellian (Ken went to Chigwell School in 1952). Holm's father was a doctor in charge of the Barley Lane mental hospital in Goodmayes, on a site which now incorporates King George's Hospital. Colin's world, like Walter's, was turned upside down when Elsie died in 1954. His work was a reserved occupation during the war, so he had continued commuting to the City while serving as a warden with the Home Guard. He had become secretary of the newly formed Valentines Tennis and Social Club in 1946, but took a promotional vacancy as a travelling rep so he no longer had to work late-night shifts, although he did drive all over the southern counties (claiming sixpence a mile on his expenses).

Ken missed his mother – although he never spoke about her much in later life – but happily inherited his father's talent for both magic tricks and do-it-yourself carpentry. His older cousins, Christine Van Sickle and

Maureen Robinson, recall that his gusto for messing about and enjoying the company of relatives and friends continued unabated after Elsie's death, however much he was hurting inside. There were family holidays in the cottage at Llanarmon in North Wales (now Denbighshire) once owned by Colin's parents, or with his cousins in Ireland, or on the Manchester Shipping Canal – and many big family reunions. And there was the cinema and there were comics. Three years before he died, Ken recalled his love of the cinema as a child in a programme note for a revival of his classic children's play, *Old King Cole*. His mum, he said, loved the pictures and used to take him at least once a week from the age of five: 'Usually we'd go to the State Barkingside or the Gants Hill Odeon. Occasionally we'd go two stops up the Central Line to the Wanstead Kinema. And it was in the Wanstead Kinema I saw the best film ever. It was 1948, and I can remember saying to my seven-year-old self: "There's never going to be a better picture than this." I begged Mum to take me back again, but it had only been on for that one night. And it was never shown again. The film is *Helzapoppin'*.'

Interestingly, *Helzapoppin'* is a cinematic version of a long-running, completely bananas American vaudevillian stage show and is often quoted as a forerunner of, and influence on, the British surreal humour of *The Goon Show* and *Monty Python*. Ken knew he couldn't successfully recreate the whole madcap film in stage terms, so he listed the other enthusiasms he had as a seven-year-old child which fed into the writing of *Old King Cole*: 'Laurel and Hardy, Abbott and Costello, The Bash Street Kids, Captain Marvel (but not Superman – Captain Marvel had a sense of humour, but Superman was too grim and proper), Sid Millward and his Nitwits, Spike Jones and the City Slickers, Tony Hancock, *Educating Archie*, Kenneth Williams, *Doctor* and *Carry On* films, James Stewart westerns (*Winchester '73* and *Where the River Bends*), *Journey into Space*, Max Wall, Whitehall farces, evil geniuses, potty professors, Billy Bunter and Just William.' (It's equally instructive to learn that he really disliked Hans

Christian Andersen, the Brothers Grimm, *Aesop's Fables*, the *Children's Newspaper*, Enid Blyton, the *Eagle* comic and 'all cream-bun handsome noble British sportsmen'.)

Maureen Robinson, a retired nurse now living in Buxton, then a teenager, remembers staying in Haigville Gardens in order to visit the Festival of Britain: 'In the presence of adults, Ken was the perfect little boy, always very well-spoken, but otherwise he could be a real monkey. I had arranged to meet a secret boyfriend at the Festival, and Ken wasn't allowed to come along with me. He threw a "paddy" and told Colin and Elsie that I only wanted to go there to meet my boyfriend – dear child!' Elsie, who never smoked, was developing a bad cough during this period. She went to the hospital for a check-up and was detained there for two weeks. When Colin collected her in the car, he was told she had five months, if that, to live. He kept this news to himself, never telling anyone, not even Elsie herself. He described in *M-I-M* how, occasionally, when driving the car, 'It crosses my mind that it was in my power to put a quick end to the misery of us both. However, such intentions were readily dispelled when I remembered the plight in which any such actions would place my son.' Colin was knocked sideways by Elsie's death of throat cancer exactly five months after the diagnosis, and 'this sorry chapter ended'. It's amazing how little he says about her, or his loss; there's not a smidgen of self-pity.

For the subsequent eight years, throughout Ken's secondary schooling at Chigwell School, and his two years at RADA, father and son rattled around together in Haigville Gardens. The loss of his mother before the onset of adolescence explains, for many of his friends, his deeply romantic approach to women: he definitely put them on a pedestal and treated them with such intensity he was incapable of sustaining a permanent relationship. 'On our own,' Colin wrote, 'Kenneth was no trouble at all, and his demands on me were practically negligible.' Until the summer of 1959, when he was in his eighteenth year, Ken left for school at 7.45 a.m. every day, taking a bus towards Epping Forest.

He'd be home by 6 p.m. and the two of them would have an evening meal. It was only when Ken was about to leave RADA that Colin contemplated a second marriage: he and Betty Keates, a widow and a friend of Elsie's, and fellow tennis player, were spliced in June 1961.

Ken was a diligent pupil at Chigwell School, where he'd won a scholarship as a day boy after passing the eleven-plus exam. His A-level subjects were English, French and German. He seemed destined for Cambridge University and was awarded a place there to read English that he never took up. Other 'interests' intervened. He loved carpentry and swimming, but was averse to most sports. Compelled to take part in an inter-schools cross-country race, he puffed his way home in 145th place, not quite last, but not far off. Mostly, though, there was the theatre. His contemporaries, Tony Porter, a vicar's son who became a teacher, and the *Guardian* journalist John Ezard, testify to his outstanding performance as Faustus, selling his soul to the Devil in exchange for power and knowledge, an utterly Campbellian conceit. Porter was Mephistopheles, only second-choice casting, he says, because Ion Alexis Will, another friend with whom Campbell kept in lifelong touch (and his collaborator on his 1974 play *The Great Caper*) had decided he couldn't stand Chigwell any longer and left to pursue a career as an international entrepreneur.

John Ezard also recalls 'how superbly and movingly this fifteen-year-old caught the quality of simple baffled goodness of the seaman Billy Budd' in a stage version of Herman Melville's novel. 'I can still see and hear him, on the stage. Not a twitch of an eyebrow then. Next cast as Quince in Shakespeare's *Dream*, he conspired with the producer [and Head of English] Parry Davenport to reinvent the rustics as modern TV clowns, reducing audiences to helpless laughter [thirty years later Campbell would direct a *Waiting for Godot* with the tramps played as quick-fire television impressionists]... Then came Canon Chasuble in *The Importance of Being Earnest*, uproariously successful but with numerous twitches. Reviewing the production for the school magazine, I wrote that his Canon "came up from the crypt rather than over from the vestry" and said he needed more disciplined outlines. Ken always knew when to reject advice and – mercifully for his career – he rejected that.' Ezard was a member of the Valentines Park gang which Ken memorialised, he says, rather in the manner of Beckett's *Watt* or *Molloy*, in a sustained piece of purple prose, now lost. What did the gang do? Scratch each other's spots, mostly, says Ezard, but Valentines – the best park for miles around, with a seventeenth-century country mansion that has been splendidly renovated – was rich in opportunity for messing about on the boating lake, watching cricket (it was a county ground for Essex for one week of the summer for many years), chasing through shrubbery and wide open spaces, or just hanging out.

The Latin master at Chigwell was George Harvey Webb, whose connection with the professional theatre and general intellectual inquisitiveness were to have a profound effect on Campbell. Harvey Webb was a champion fiddle player and had been a member in the band of socialist folk singer Ewan MacColl, the great innovative theatre director Joan Littlewood's first husband, co-founder of Theatre Workshop and author of the beautiful song 'The First Time Ever I Saw Your Face' as well as 'Dirty Old Town'. Harvey Webb was a member of various think tanks and had a registered IQ of 250, one of the highest ever recorded (an IQ of 100 guarantees you membership of MENSA). He had also been a member of the Hitler Youth ('When it was still all right to be one,' said Campbell) and, after he left Chigwell for a post at William Ellis School in Camden, North London, he and his Canadian wife, Pamela, who was independently wealthy, funded and co-founded the East 15 Acting School with Margaret Bury, Joan Littlewood's wardrobe mistress. The East 15 School grew out of Littlewood's work at the Theatre Royal, Stratford East, where Theatre Workshop had been based since 1953. Although MacColl had not approved of the move from Manchester to London, and had left both the company and Littlewood, Harvey Webb remained in touch with Joan, researching and appearing in productions and even doing Littlewood's bidding as a minder for Brendan Behan when he came to London to work on *The Hostage* in 1958. He helped hustle Jean Genet through customs on the occasion he came to see Littlewood. Asked if he had anything to declare, Genet replied simply: '*Moi, je suis pédéraste.*'

'Harvey Webb taught Latin violently,' Ken told Dominic Cavendish in a *Theatre Voice* podcast interview in 2004; the great challenge was apparently to get him off that subject and on to other things. Much later in life, Harvey Webb was crucial to Campbell's whole Science Fiction Theatre of Liverpool enterprise, but at Chigwell it's clear he gave Ken a glimpse of what riotous fun a life in the professional theatre could, and should, be like: Ken had seen him onstage, playing his fiddle, in *The Hostage*, and became a regular visitor to the Harvey Webb household in Theydon Bois. He must have seen other Theatre Workshop productions. He certainly soon knew all about Joan Littlewood. Harvey Webb's son, confusingly named Harvey Harvey Webb, also attended Chigwell School, much later, but reckons that Ken 'was sort of ostracised' by the other boys on account of being both cockney and common, not to mention a scholarship boy: 'I think the experience made him not want to go to Cambridge. He started off meek and mild and, as he went through puberty, he became much more difficult and cantankerous. In the end, he became a bit of a handful for the teachers.' Harvey Webb Junior identifies another key meeting Ken had at this time: with Joy Tomson, a vivacious, enthusiastic and wealthy New Yorker who had lived on the same street in Montreal as his mother's grandparents and who had attended the same theatre-school classes in Manhattan as James Dean, Marlon Brando and William Shatner. Joy came over to negotiate with Joan Littlewood about taking the Theatre Workshop to New York – where she owned two or three theatres – and, according to young Harvey, Ken was entranced 'and changed his path right there'.

Without talking about it too much with his father, Campbell was determinedly going about his theatre learning process while still working hard for his A-levels. He joined a local amateur drama group, the Renegades, in the summer of 1958 and by Christmas had appeared in no fewer than four productions with them: as a juvenile in both Kaufman and Hart's *You Can't Take It With You* and N. Richard Nash's *The Rainmaker*; as an older man (sporting a bushy RAF-style moustache) in Leslie Sands's *Intent to Murder*; and as Toothache, a pain in the neck, a variation on the traditional broker's man, in *Cinderella*. The Renegades was run by an extraordinary man, James Cooper, son of a Barking brush manufacturer, who had worked in the theatre in Nairobi just after the war and subsequently on the south coast as a dancer. In 1947 he had founded the Renegades with a performance of *Hamlet* in the Ilford Town Hall which was acclaimed by Alan Dent – 'a worthy pioneer!' – in the *News Chronicle*; this was in the same year as Paul Scofield and Robert Helpmann alternated in the role at Stratford-upon-Avon. Dent had seen eight Hamlets in 1947. Cooper's was 'by no means the worst of them'.

Cooper was the kind of wilful maverick and one-man band – he waged a constant war of words with local councillors – that Ken admired all his life, and indeed he remained close friends with Jimmie, as he was generally known, until the latter's death in 1987. Cooper produced and directed ten or eleven shows a year in Ilford, always playing the lead as well as designing the set and the lights, arranging the music, manning the box office and, if need be, tearing the tickets, for almost forty years. You can see why Campbell, who came to believe that doing the impossible in the theatre was the only thing worth doing, admired him so much. Cooper was a polished comedian and a fine pantomime dame – I saw a lot of his work and was indeed a member of the Renegades myself in the mid-1960s – and he thought subsidy was the enemy of popular art. In a converted Scout hall known as the Little Theatre behind the old Harrison Gibson building in Ilford High Street, Cooper presented world premieres not only of comedies by Philip King (author of *See How They Run*, one of the great British farces of the twentieth century) and Duncan Greenwood, but also the first ever stage version, in February 1959, of Reginald Rose's *Twelve Angry Men*, originally a television play, in which Ken appeared as Sherman L. Segal, Juror Number Two – 'a surprisingly mature performance,' said the *Ilford Recorder* – with Cooper himself in the Henry Fonda film role.

Shortly after joining the Renegades, Ken wrote to Cooper from Austria, where he had hitchhiked from the Dutch frontier during the summer holidays of 1958. Among the people who'd given him lifts, he said, were a Fascist priest, a mountain doctor and a variety artiste who was coming to the London Palladium in October. He had slept in a Cologne lunatic asylum and was expecting to 'enjoy their hospitality' on the return leg. And he had twice faced the alternative of paying an on-the-spot fine or spending two hours in jail for walking and hitchhiking on a German Auto-bahn, though it is not known which alternative he plumped for. I bet it was the two hours in jail.

The *Ilford Recorder*, sensing a 'character' in their midst (Cooper had shown them the letter), interviewed him before his third appearance at the Little Theatre – they had already noted that 'good-looking young Kenneth Camp-bell proved popular with audiences' – and suggested that the actor, in his answers, was providing a very good idea of his writing style: 'I find that one of the greatest stimuli for lively thought is a book in which I am not interested. For instance, last night, while my eyes were following the words of Gibbon's *Decline and Fall*, my mind was having a most spectacular and poignant debate on girls, atomic fall-out and the French sewerage system. Definitely one must have a gimmick for solitudinous thought. Our gardener strums a ukulele. My aunt drinks whisky.'

These are not the musings of an average seventeen-year-old. They betray a propensity to be funny in public and do not sound at all unlike the Ken Campbell of twenty or thirty years later. This was a side of himself he'd kept hidden at home, at least when his dad was around. James Cooper's widow, Yvonne Haesendonck, who appeared in leading roles with the company over many years, says she never recalls Ken talking about his father or bringing him to the theatre. Which explains why Colin, fully expecting his son to go to Cambridge, was 'staggered' to be informed that Ken 'had been in touch with the Essex education people and they had agreed a grant for a place at RADA'. He was prostrate with disappointment: 'To me,' he wrote in *M-I-M*, 'the theatrical profession has always appeared somewhat promiscuous and lacking in security, but he made it so very definite that it was what he clearly wanted to do, my opposition was negligible, and I could not but remember how very disappointed I had been when my own father put the hoodoo on my going to sea, as so many of my school pals had done.' Campbell started at RADA in the same week as he appeared with the Renegades in the role Emlyn Williams had written for himself, Morgan Evans, in *The Corn is Green*. Morgan is an illiterate boy from a coal-mining town who is given a chance of bettering himself through an education by a strong-willed local teacher. Campbell knew how much he owed his Chigwell friends and teachers, and James Cooper, and he gave a performance, said the *Recorder*, 'that topped all previous achievements with his portrayal of the budding young genius'. He was on his way. But he would never forget where he'd come from.

2

RADA to Rep

A cademe's loss was theatre's gain. 'Cambridge saw nothing of him,' remarked Colin ruefully in *M-I-M*, 'except for his disreputable character appearance in *Fings Ain't Wot They Used T'Be* on tour at the Arts.'

The next decade was a pell-mell progress through training, repertory theatre, writing and launching himself as a director. One of the most distinctive things about Campbell was his love of the craft of acting. Not the sort of acting that is usually thought of as good acting these days – seamless, decorous, unflashy, internalised – but the sort of acting that is probably more often thought of as bad acting. In this, he joined hands with the old-school Victorian and Edwardian managers and audiences in admiring an actor – the nineteenth-century tragedian William Macready, perhaps, or in our day Laurence Olivier – who got his effects by theatrical rather than natural methods. And Ken understood that you could only achieve such effects by good technique and a full heart.

He hated inaudibility in the theatre, and laziness, and lateness, and lack of preparation. One actor was once stuttering in a rehearsal room and apologised to Ken by saying that it would be all right on the night. 'All right on the night?' rasped Campbell, 'All right on the night? What about NOW? I once knew an actor who was always saying that it would be all right on the night. And do you know what? IT NEVER FUCKING WAS.' He loved the practical wise saws of the actor-manager Sir Seymour Hicks, who published two books about acting in the early years of the last century. He often photocopied pages and gave them to actors with his favourite bits underlined: 'Technique in acting is more than half the battle, given that the artist is a good one, for technique is the conjuror performing his tricks with deftness and certainty.'

It must have been in some ways a strangely unreal hiatus, RADA – with its theory classes and high-minded workshops – in his progress from the pragmatic, old-fashioned Renegades to the knockabout world of weekly rep. James Cooper, rather than one of his RADA teachers, would certainly have approved Ken's liking for Seymour Hicks's description of the Macready pause – so called 'because of the length of time that fine actor took to get on with the next sentence, while he made effects with looks and noddings of the head, assisted with exclamations such as "Ah!", "Oh!" and "Humph!"... he had a trick of talking under his breath during the progress of a scene, and often at the end of his own lines.'

Campbell may have gone straight from school to RADA, but he did lots of other things as well, such as holiday jobs and writing. When they were digging up Ilford High Road he took a temporary job with a firm called Craddock and Finnegan as a tea-boy and putter-outer of the red danger lights at night-time. His duties included phoning through the workmen's bets on the horses and greyhounds, and he made such a mess of this one day (getting his tips muddled and losing the ganger, or chief digger, £38) that he was fired. Before he left, he purchased a large tube of extra-strength laxatives and mixed them in with the tea bags in one last round of liquid refreshment served in mugs on a tin tray. The fall-out was catastrophic. He reported the scene in his notebooks: 'By three o'clock next day, chaos at the Craddock and Finnegan section of the Ilford High Road hole: a sort of relay race between the excavations and the convenience up the road. And none of the men could face the pneumatic drill till the following Saturday.'

Immediately after their final term at school, Ken and Tony Porter both took supply-teaching jobs at a secondary modern school in nearby Romford, for just two or three weeks: 'an illuminating experience after the sheltered world of Chigwell,' said Porter, who was bound for Cambridge. They read Edgar Allan Poe to their classes, as well as James Thurber and G. K. Chesterton's Father Brown fiction. The experience filtered through. It is clear from the volumes of unpublished plays and stories that he filed away in cupboards and folders that Ken was writing from a very early age. Why was this? Not just because he was good at English at school, and always read voraciously and adventurously – his choice of books for prizes in the sixth form at Chigwell were Ezra Pound's *Cantos* and James Joyce's *Ulysses* – but also because, as he said, typing was in his blood. Colin Campbell could type at such an incredible rate, said Ken, 'that you couldn't differentiate the individual sounds of the keys hitting the paper'. His son inherited this talent, keeping his dad busy keyboard company in Haigville Gardens. Among the reams of typescripts and letters in Ken's box files, it is rare to find a typo, an error, a score-through or a rewrite. His spelling is perfect, so is his punctuation.

The skill paid off years later, in 1978, as he typed out great wodges of one of his two great cornerstone epics, as the poet Neil Oram recalled: 'I was contracted to do a ten-play cycle called *The Warp*. Ken said, "How good's your typing?" I told him it wasn't that good but I did have a new typewriter. He said, "I've got an *electrical* typewriter and I type really *fast*! We could work together in my garden shed. You dictate and I'll type." So we began at the end of June: him sat in the shed... me standing outside dictating one scene after the other. He'd say, "What about that scene about the prostitute... or the tramp..." etc. And I'd dictate the whole scene with all the theatrical instructions.'

Stories and first drafts of plays and sketches piled up in the Barkingside back room as he pursued his RADA course, training in voice, mime and fencing. 'When I look back on it,' he told his friend and occasional researcher James Nye, 'I was singularly awful at all of them. There were these extraordinary exercises, and once you'd developed this "voice" you were encouraged to use it at all times – on the bus, in the pub and so on.' He rebelled and was called in by the principal, John Fernald, who frankly, and kindly, told him that he was a comedian, really, 'And we don't do enough for comedians here.'

His contemporaries at RADA included the film director Mike Leigh, the playwright David Halliwell, the actors Peter Rocca, Naomi Buch, John Hurt and Alan Lake (who later married Diana Dors). Leigh was one year behind Ken, but he does remember him giving an extraordinarily grotesque performance in, he thinks, Dylan Thomas's Jekyll and Hyde play, *The Doctor and the Devils*: 'He was definitely part of the scruff minority at RADA, "on" to other things than boulevard theatre. He was also quite straight in the sense that he always dressed with a tie and spoke well, in an Ilford suburban way. He certainly could "do" voices, but he hadn't yet invented the character we know as Ken Campbell.'

One or two of his RADA contemporaries kept him company at the Renegades. Larry Linville, the American actor best known for playing the inept surgeon Major Frank Burns in the television series *M*A*S*H*, was one of only three transatlantic students in Ken's RADA year, and he trekked out to Ilford to play Rodolpho in Arthur Miller's *A View from the Bridge*. Ken was cast as the lawyer Alfieri, drawing the audience's attention to the tragedy of James Cooper's Eddie Carbone in a Miller speech you can imagine him delivering with an awe-struck concern: 'I looked in his eyes more than I listened – in fact, I can hardly remember the conversation. But I will never forget how dark the room became when he looked at me; his eyes were like tunnels. I kept wanting to call the police, but nothing had happened. Nothing at all had really happened...' In the Road Show, and his later improvisation pieces, Ken would operate as a 'goader' or ringmaster to the action, perforating the fourth wall between stage and audience. This was his true *métier* as a performer, and he must have first discovered it while playing the confidential Alfieri, a man at once struck by a sort of horror and compelled to share it with an audience. It's significant that the *Ilford Recorder* gave him a Best Supporting Performance prize, his only theatre award until, many years later, he won an Evening Standard Best Comedy gong for one of his solo shows.

Before his last term at RADA, in April 1961, he appeared for the last time with the Renegades as Gratiano in *The Merchant of Venice* (Cooper was Shylock), and brought three more RADA contemporaries to keep him company: Bernard Gibbons (later RSC associate Bernard Lloyd) was Bassanio, Madeline Blakeney played Jessica, and John Alderton – who later met his wife, Pauline Collins, in Ken's first television play, *One Night I Danced with Mr Dalton* (1968) – played Launcelot Gobbo. And, for good measure, school chum Tony Porter turned up as the Prince of Aragon. It was as if, under Jimmie's auspices, Ken was starting to form his own company for the first time. But he was in no position yet to start calling the rehearsals and shouting the odds. He left the drama school in mellow mood, reciting an affectionate poem of farewell on Sunday 16 July 1961 that namechecked not only John Fernald, but also his fellow students Larry Linville, Bernard Gibbons, Naomi Buch (with her 'suggestive looks'), Rosemary Martin, Stanley Lebor and Diana Barrington:

> Stay here all night dancing
> On the sofas loaf and lurk
> Drink up, be merry, s'not as if
> Tomorrow you must work
>
> We'll see no more the fire escapes
> We'll see no more Bob's log
> Or Reginald carrying coffee
> And biscuits for Yat's dog
>
> We'll see no more John Fernald
> Or John Fernald's gins and ports
> Larry Linville looking happy
> Bernard Gibbons in his shorts.

And so on, for sixteen more stanzas. His first professional engagement was at the Colchester Rep, an Essex gig that kept him based in Gants Hill where he could carry on writing. He recalled his time there in a National Theatre Platform conversation with Michael Billington in December 1991: 'The director was a two-bottle-of-whisky-a-day man, Robert Digby, out of whom you could only get any sense before nine o'clock in the morning. I became a great admirer of an actor there called Stuart Pearce, who, too young to serve in the war, had joined the Tod Slaughter touring company – they revived all the old "blood and thunder" Victorian melodramas – where he used to do all his performances, whatever the accent, whatever the character, absolutely through the nose. I used to collect little technical tricks. Hugh Hastings, who wrote the great comedy *Seagulls Over Sorrento*, was in the company, too, and he taught me how to play third-act inspectors. You could steal the show by the simple expedient of learning your lines – instead of just reading them from the notebook, as was the tradition. Hugh told me to learn the lines – and then *start looking for clues*! Well, the theatre went up! The director, Ted Webster, went mad and threw the fire bucket at me: "Thanks for the note, Ted," I said!' The only way he found he could stop the audience laughing – and not annoy old Ted – was to 'dry' after his first line and make sure the whole audience heard the prompt. By the end of the week, the leading lady congratulated him on slipping back into 'dull inspector' stereotype: 'We were all very worried at the beginning, but it's got so much strength now,' she said.

Possibly as a punishment he then 'got lumbered' with the small role of Angus in *Macbeth*. His lifelong fascination with this mysterious supernumerary, who has only nineteen lines spread over eight scenes, began because a Canadian director arrived in Colchester to do a 'Method' production of the tragedy and sent the actors off to write an essay on their characters. In Ken's case, he got a bit more than he bargained for; Ken was determined to be the definitive Angus. He notes in his essay that once Angus has entered with Ross in the second scene, Ross gets mentioned by Malcolm but Angus is overlooked. Are they ignoring him? Has he committed a social gaffe? Is he, in fact, literally overlooked because he is a dwarf? During rehearsals, Ken tried to argue that Angus hangs around in scenes, silent and ignored, possibly because he is 'hooked on haggis' – his mouth is always full. The idea of an ostracised, undersized haggis-muncher unable to speak for fear of spitting out bits of old meat and onion did not impress the director (his response was, 'It's not a bloody pantomime!'). But Ken turned his absence from the banquet into a positive, having Angus join the resurgent army of Malcolm and Mac-duff, and lavish his last nine lines on his two new friends Menteith and Caithness before he 'exits marching'.

'The last glimpse we have of Angus is quietly dressing up as a tree with the other boys (presumably as a bonsai): unless of course we take the penultimate stage direction to include Angus: "Flourish. Enter, with drums and colours, Mal-colm, Old Seyward, Ross, *the other Thanes, and Soldiers.*" If we *do* take this to include Angus, the play is then rounded off with an unprecedented mellowness – whimsy, even. For it is com-forting to learn that under Malcolm's new liberal regime, the smelly little midget will at last be accepted.' As Shakespearean criticism, this is as persuasive as anything in A. C. Bradley or Harold Bloom, certainly more inventive and funnier. And it started a curiously fruitful relationship Campbell would main-tain with 'the Scottish play' in a future acting assignment at Stoke and much later in his career with what became known as the Pidgin *Macbeth*.

While racking up his credits at the Colchester Rep he caught a local showing of a new film starring Anthony Newley, *The Small World of Sammy Lee* (1963), and was much taken by the actor who played Newley's brother and ran a delicatessen in the East End. In an extraordinary twenty-three-page letter he wrote in 1985 to the actress Sarah Lam, he recounted the impact made on him by this actor: 'I went to see the film again that week to learn the delicatessen man's performance. It was undoubted in my mind that a chance would soon come up to "do" that characterisation, or a characterisation based on it, or inspired by it; so when I say learn it, I mean something like taking in the essence of it so I could do it with a different text.' Campbell wasn't appearing in the next week's play at Colchester, he recounted to Sarah Lam, so he had a Monday off in the West End and joined 'the merry band of theatrical drunks who at that time used to crawl from the Salisbury to the Cranbourne to Some Other One, and then back again, whiling away the afternoon closing time in the Kismet Club.' Outside the Salisbury, he bumped into the producer Bob Swash, for many years the right-hand man of the Australian impresario Robert Stigwood, who had set up the *Fings* tour. Swash asked him if he was doing anything. Ken said, not much, so Swash asked him to come up to the office and read for a particular role in a play he was touring briefly before bringing it into the West End; Swash didn't think he'd get the role, but 'I might give them some sort of lead to what they were looking for'.

In the event, Swash said he wasn't quite right, but would he accept, there and then, the understudy duties for the role and a five-line walk-on at the end of the play? ' "Yes, great," I said. They gave me the script. I got straight on the train to Colchester to go and tell them face to face how I was dumping them in the shit and collect my things, and on the journey I read through the play. What a fool I'd been! It came to me EXACTLY how to do that part. Every line of it fitted to a tee, like gloves, the way Warren Mitchell, for that is who it was, had performed the brother in *The Small World of Sammy Lee*!' When he got home he rang the office to beg to have another go at it. Swash's assistant said, 'That's so sad, we've just cast the role two minutes ago.' 'Who have you got?' asked Campbell. And the reply: 'His name's Warren Mitchell.'

The play was *Everybody Loves Opal*, a 1961 Broadway heist comedy of three crooks trying to murder the eponymous Opal (for the insurance). It was written by John Patrick, the American author of such well-known potboilers of the day as *The Hasty Heart* and *The Teahouse of the August Moon*. In New York, it had starred Stubby Kaye and Eileen Heckart. In London, apart from Mitchell, the cast included Liz Fraser, Betty Marsden and Lee Montague, who was replaced on the short tour by James Villiers. Ken's girlfriend at the time was an older actress called Yvette Rees, who had been at RADA with Mitchell, so she charged Ken with passing on her love at the first read-through. This he did, and on adding a fulsome appreciation of the delicatessen performance in the Newley film, Campbell was promptly adopted by Mitchell as his new best friend. The director Toby Robertson then announced that, as Mitchell was signed up for an episode of *The Avengers* on television, the understudy, Ken, would be reading in and taking down the first week's blocking, or moves. The other actors stuck to their scripts, and there ensued a routine, rather boring week.

'Then, on the next Monday,' Ken told Sarah Lam, 'the Return of the Man from the Delicatessen. "Hello," I said, "I've got all your moves and everything written down." "It's all right," said my Hero, "I know them. Or at least I know what they ought to be." Rehearsal began, Liz, Betty and Lee still nose in script. But Warren, NO SCRIPT AT ALL! Although he'd been absent all the preceding week HE KNEW ALL HIS LINES PERFECTLY! AND HE KNEW WHAT HIS MOVES OUGHT TO BE! Jesus, that was a landmark in my life that day. On the tour, Warren seemed to prefer my company to that of his co-stars, and on the beach in Bournemouth, during a lull in the tech, I gave him the script of my first play, *Events of an Average Bath Night*, and he read it there and then in his deckchair and said he'd like to direct it.' And he did, later that year, and Yvette Rees was in it.

Before he left London on tour with *Opal*, Ken booked two tickets for the first Saturday performance at the Vaudeville in April 1964 for his father and stepmother Betty. It had opened on the Wednesday to the opposite of selling reviews. Nobody loved Opal. 'There must be a frightful graveyard where truly terrible plays are buried and laid to rest,' sneered the *Evening News*. Bob Swash's assistant, Arnold Taylor, gave Ken the money back on his parents' tickets, saying, 'I don't see why you should be the only one forking out tonight.' The notice was already posted. So Warren Mitchell was available to direct *Events of an Average Bath Night* earlier than expected, and did so at the RADA theatre, the Vanbrugh, later in the year, with a professional company formed from recent ex-RADA students. It was the first, and last, show Mitchell ever directed.

Campbell never talked about the play, and it's certainly a bit of a mess, but it's a very lively mess, stamped through with his trademark verbal ebullience and nuttiness, and it marks the stage debut of the bungling idiots Faz and Twoo, who re-emerge in full glory in *Old King Cole*. Mitchell's theory about the names is that he settled on them because he wanted

Faz to be able to say, 'You're a twit, Twoo,' which he did. In *Old King Cole*, the pair are crazy fixers, or broker's men, Faz very much leading his feeble-minded assistant by the nose in a mock-royal scenario once described by one of its American producers as '*Ubu Roi* for children with Benny Hill playing Ubu'. In the earlier *Events*, they're a couple of bungling robbers, whose lost bank-robbery dosh ends up funding a poor people's sick-animal centre, the dream of an Old Woman whose horse Wordsworth has died eating daffodils and who extracts the loot from the susceptible Twoo – 'Et tu, Twoo?' exclaims the fazed phrase-maker Faz. This adventure is part of a larger scheme dreamt up in Boddle's bathroom with his friend Jelp (the name of Ken's invisible 'friend' from his own lino visions in Haigville Gardens), and the action lurches into some fairly unfunny, misfired torture scenes involving the Old Woman, a snapped chain and a floppy sword; she's their granny and she's tied up with hiccups, Faz and Twoo tell a passing policeman. There's something here of the cranky British comedy tradition of people like Spike Milligan and Ivor Cutler, and you can see Campbell grappling with elements of vaudeville, pantomime and the absurd – the show ends back in Boddle's bathroom, a package of money (the lost dosh) plops through the letterbox, a large jungle beast reappears (Jelp had previously gone off to fight him) and the curtain falls on the stage direction: 'Exit pursued by elephant.'

Next, Ken answered an advert which asked for actors who could swim for an aquatic version of *Treasure Island* in Bournemouth Baths. For two summer seasons, either side of his first engagement at the Victoria Theatre, Stoke-on-Trent, and sharing a flat with two dwarves, he played first Long John Silver, going in off the deep end, you might say, and then various roles in *Gulliver's Travels*. The key element here was that he was also put in charge of the 'shallow-end acting bits', a credit on his CV that did not lead to any immediate subsequent engagement. In between the Bournemouth summers, he also joined that national tour of Lionel Bart and Frank Norman's *Fings Ain't Wot They Used T'Be* so disdained by his father. This was the revised version of the 1959 Stratford East musical with which director Joan Littlewood followed her two smash hits of 1958, Shelagh Delaney's *A Taste of Honey* and Brendan Behan's *The Hostage*.

Campbell never spoke with any great affection for the show, and a brush with Frank Norman a few years later at the Royal Court, an unhappy experience, would send him decisively in the direction of his real vocation. *Fings* was probably too cute for his taste even then, with its fashionable Soho underworld of spivs, ponces, tarts and doxies, and he would have been immune to the charm of Bart's title song and the plangent instant nostalgia of the rest of the score; he was never all that musical at the best of times. The fact that Littlewood was clearly a great influence on his subsequent career wasn't a factor here; it wasn't she who rehearsed this touring cast.

He then joined another tour as a comedy stooge to Dick Emery, an immensely popular television comic of the 1960s, but blotted his copybook when he got a laugh one day at the first house. The sketch was a dinner-party send-up of a television 'talking heads' programme of old farts, and Emery tottered on as a decrepit waiter just as Campbell delivered the scripted line, 'Ah yes, that reminds me of a story I once heard about a bishop...' and continued, off script, 'He was sitting on a Tube train with a load of choirboys...' and Emery came sharply out of character and said, 'What was that, Ken, what happened next?' At the second house, Emery shuffled onstage and poured a scalding cup of coffee into his (Ken's) lap: 'I'm the comedian around here,' he hissed under halitotic breath.

This hectic series of engagements did little for Ken's professional acting profile, but probably pushed him even more certainly towards writing. He thought Warren Mitchell had made a brilliant job of directing *Events*, but the reviews, he said, could only be challenged in the history of that discipline by those for *Everybody Loves Opal* in their loathing. 'Only Clive Barnes, then the second-string critic for the *Daily Express*,' Ken said in his letter to Sarah Lam, 'had a moment of hope for me: "Mr Campbell may one day write a good play, but not last night." "Back to the drawing board," said Warren, and I became his pet writer-protégé-cum-babysitter.'

From that moment, Ken was a regular guest at Mitchell's home in Highgate, North London, where he would show the senior actor anything he had written, and Mitchell would read every word, offer comments and encouragement. Mitchell (real name, Warren Misel), a brilliant character actor whose later stage career would include King Lear and Willy Loman in Arthur Miller's *Death of a Salesman*, had also trained at RADA and had been a professional actor since 1950, after appearing for a few seasons with the influential left-wing amateur Unity Theatre in North London. He knew talent when he saw it, and he knew what it was like to struggle. He was nothing at all like Alf Garnett, the hilarious loudmouth bigot he played in Johnny Speight's 1966 hit comedy series *Till Death Us Do Part*. Theirs was a remarkable friendship that would last the rest of Ken's life. It got to the stage, Mitchell cheerfully admitted, that his three children would be disappointed when he came home from work and he wasn't Ken: 'They'd get very excited and say, "Ken's here"; and I said, "I don't get that kind of reception when I come home!" He built a worm sanctuary in the garden, and he taught them how to make clay models, which they would then put up on the fence in the front garden and try and flog them to passing members of the public.'

No doubt Mitchell cast an approving eye over a couple of short stories that in the autumn of 1964 found their way into print in the unlikely outlet of the fashionable *Town* magazine owned by Michael Heseltine, the self-made Tory politician and businessman and future Deputy Prime Minister to John Major. *Stirred for a Bird* is an obsessive story of a drama-school student lusting after an unobtainable beauty, Melissa Parton, to whom he writes postcards; the hero sleeps with a lock of her hair and finds an Oriental simulacrum of her in a Mile End pub – who turns out to be a bloke. A romantic letter-writing obsessive with a taste for Oriental ladies is not a character too far from its author, and Ken would indeed one day write a play about a search for the Perfect Woman shortly before he fell in love with one of the most beautiful actresses of the day, Prunella Gee.

Interestingly, his file copy of the story was clipped to a rejection letter dated 4 June 1962 from the avant-garde publisher and entrepreneur John Calder. The story, Calder said, 'has many virtues but, we have decided, is not quite good enough for publication. Nevertheless, it shows considerable promise... it could be rewritten and tightened up... we feel you have genuine talent...' He then offered to look at any other work Ken might care to submit. This has to count as a critical green light, and a very important one, and it's surely not fanciful to suppose that Ken was following Calder's advice when he rewrote the article and submitted it to *Town* magazine – with a successful result. Robert Graves had a short story published in the same edition. In the very next issue of *Town* in September 1964, there is another, shorter short story by Kenneth Campbell entitled *Norbett*, a 900-word vignette of a mysterious, grand old actor in a repertory company where he is known as the Duchess of Brighton. He has two Jaguars – no one knows where his wealth originates – and two friends called Ambrosine and Lamborne. His sex life is thought to be non-existent but, when drunk, he asks the narrator ('myself') and the leading lady to strap him to a bed and tickle him with a feather. It's like a mini-glimpse of Ronald Firbank with a dash of Joe Orton (whose *Entertaining Mr Sloane* was the hit play of that summer), written with a pleasing dryness and throwaway wit: 'Bed-strapping is not all that uncommon, after all.'

A rather dull article about life at RADA was published in the *Weekend Telegraph* magazine in 1965, and in June of the same year Ken received a rejection letter from Joy Matthews, the fiction editor of *Nova* ('a new kind of magazine for the new kind of woman'), addressed to him in a flat in The Triangle, Bournemouth, presumably the one he shared with the two dwarves. In another unpublished first-person story, Ken recycles his supply-teaching stint: *My Most Unforgettable Character* features a thirteen-year-old boy in a Romford secondary modern, Chase Cross (today, the school is Bower Park Comprehensive), who doesn't wear school uniform, doesn't read or write, but runs the classroom and eventually responds to the supply teacher; a little like a lower-class version of Terence Rattigan's *The Browning Version*, there are clear early signs of *School for Clowns,* Campbell's inspirational subversion of a classroom comedy. None of his juvenilia is without interest, though a gusty farce, *The Vicar Comes to Tea*, with a cast list including two spinster sisters (one dipsomaniac, one nymphomaniac), a vicar called Purejoy, a policeman who wears a dress after wetting his trousers, a Shavian dustman and a lady from Oxfam, betrays more rowdy irreverence than structural control.

Much better was a play called *Just Go, Will You Harry*, which would find a home with the next great encourager in Campbell's life, Peter Cheeseman, the Artistic Director of the Victoria Theatre, Stoke-on-Trent. It's a one-act play of just forty-five pages in which Harry, a jilted boyfriend of Judi, pesters her for friendship in a late-night hamburger joint. He then harangues a friend of hers who tries to put him off the scent. Judi agrees to see him again in a year's time and to remain 'acquainted'. There's so much that is personal in this little play, and so much that is characteristic of Ken. It's not a side of him that would declare itself in his work, but in his secret life of relationships – not something he ever talked about – he had the rare gift of retaining, and indeed nurturing, the friendship of women who had not actually been his lovers, however much he might have wanted them to be. Most importantly of all, he remained close to Prunella Gee, 'the Perfect Woman', long after their five-year marriage had ended in divorce.

The theatre was changing, and Ken's career, always reactive to what was going on around him, was about to change with it. He had relished being a part of the last days of the old-style repertory theatre, and had learned invaluable lessons that would stand him in good stead for being authoritarian with the less technically correct actors emerging from the drama schools and the universities into the 'Swinging Sixties'. But he was also serious about himself as a writer, and a not very conventional one at that. He carried his Essex background with him wherever he went. He loved stories of highwaymen, lunatics, clowns, actors and landladies, and he wanted to make some kind of combustion out of his seething talents and the influential examples of James Cooper, Joan Littlewood, his father, his favourite films, Warren Mitchell and the new writers at the Royal Court. He'd found his voice but not yet his launch pad.

3

Stoke Fire and Bolton Blues

What needed to happen? Ken was ready for a place where he could operate on three fronts: as a writer, a director and an actor. The man who made it possible was Peter Cheeseman, one of the unsung heroes of British theatre in the mid-twentieth century (he died in April 2010), who took up the banner of in-the-round, community-based, repertory theatre advocated by Stephen Joseph, the son of publisher Michael Joseph and West End revue star Hermione Gingold. Joseph had formed his Studio Theatre Company in 1955, based in Scarborough for the summer months, then touring for the rest of the year. One of his regular dates was in Newcastle-under-Lyme in North Staffordshire, where his theatre manager was Cheeseman, who shifted the base to a converted cinema, the Victoria, in nearby Stoke-on-Trent, in 1962. Stephen Joseph's best-known protégé is Alan Ayckbourn, who took over at Scarborough, but Cheeseman was no less formidable an advocate for Joseph's ideals of a renewed intimacy between stage and audience, not only in the new configuration of in-the-round but also in the matter of creating a vibrant relationship between that audience and a permanent company of actors.

That old 'weekly rep' theatre world Campbell had experienced on tour and at Colchester was rapidly becoming a thing of the past, swept away in the new tidal wave of contemporary playwrights at the Royal Court, the new permissiveness, the accent on regionalism in drama (as opposed to tacky West End reproductions) and the idea that the lower-middle and working classes were a potential new theatre audience. Outside London, Cheeseman was quickest off the mark in all this, and he had fierce ideas of how things should be done, so fierce in fact that, towards the end of 1966, he had a blazing row with Stephen Joseph, who sacked him and installed another manager, Terry Lane, in his place. But the actors started a petition to reinstall Cheeseman – a bigger petition, they claimed, than was once raised to keep the great footballer Stanley Matthews at Stoke City. After six months, the council bought the theatre and reinstated Cheeseman as Artistic Director on 1 July 1967.

One of those vociferous petitioners was Dave Hill, an ebullient and no-nonsense actor from Skipton in Yorkshire, who had stayed in Stoke during the Lane period, working night shifts at a local bakery. Hill and his wife Jane Wood, daughter of a business executive and a teacher, whom he had met while training at Rose Bruford College, were stalwarts of Cheeseman's early years and both would become founder members of the Ken Campbell Road Show, along with Bob Hoskins, whose first professional job was at Stoke after he'd somehow slipped into acting at Warren Mitchell's old stomping ground, the Unity Theatre in London. It was a different game then for an actor. There were not so many options in film or television when you came out of drama school, and you had to have worked forty weeks in theatre before you were allowed on television, anyway. Dave Hill had served nine months in Perth Rep before Stoke, and on the way home to London, he and Jane decided to stop off at Stoke and see a play. A friend of theirs, Edward Clayton, was in the company. 'Stoke was the most adventurous theatre at the time, with a policy of new plays and classics,' says Hill, 'and we decided we wanted to work there the most.'

Cheeseman had first hired Ken as the Porter in *Macbeth* in 1965, and he rejoined the company in the following autumn of 1966 – along with newcomers Dave Hill, Mike Leigh, James Hayes and Shane Connaughton. The future RSC Associate

Director Ron Daniels was already there. Cheeseman wanted Ken for *Twelfth Night* but also, more importantly, as an occasional playwright. Over the next three years Cheeseman produced not only Campbell's *Just Go, Will You Harry* but also a Brechtian, piratical romp, *Jack Sheppard*, that Campbell had first written for the Bolton Octagon; a one-act play especially written for Bob Hoskins, *Christopher Pea*; and his children's classic, *Old King Cole*.

On the Scottish play, there's a story, probably true, possibly anecdotal – with Campbell, the question was never one of 'was it true?' but one of supposing that it had been – about his riotous Porter. Ron Daniels was playing Macbeth with a fair amount of seriousness – Ken used to say he went on to have an 'extinguished' career with the RSC – and was unhappy about the Porter's scene going on for too long and getting too many laughs. To combat this, Daniels would appear upstage towards the end of the scene, well before he was due to arrive, hoping to dilute its effect. One night, when, finally, Lennox and Macduff came on to ask of the Porter, 'Is your master stirring?' Campbell looked up, saw that Ron was already on – in fact he'd been there for ages – and said, 'Yes, there he is; he's stirring you right in the face!'

When it came to *Twelfth Night*, poor old Ron got another bad review from Mike Leigh, who said that his Malvolio was 'undoubtedly the unfunniest Malvolio ever seen in the history of the British theatre'. Ken, on the other hand, made almost as much of the tiny role of Valentine as he had of Angus at Colchester. Leigh, who played Fabian, still relishes his rasping, fruity one-line account of Olivia's mourning state: 'And water[ed] once a day her chamber round / With eye-offending brine.' Ken doubled as a soldier in the scene where Antonio, played by Dave Hill, was confronted in the street by Viola/Cesario (Gillian Brown, who would later be instrumental in launching Ken's career as a monologist) and then arrested by Orsino's men. On opening night, Hill was alarmed to find himself hustled off the stage, into the stalls and out the exit, all the while being and poked vigorously in the stomach by Ken and his halberd. In the corridor outside, an astonished Hill asked him why he'd done this. 'Well,' said Ken, 'you don't think, as I'm arresting you, that I'd stand around while she and him carry on making long speeches, do you?' It was an improvisation, but one he'd been saving up for the first night.

More significantly, perhaps, Mike Leigh recalls that Cheeseman dispatched a small cadre of the company to old folk's homes around the place with a vaudeville pot-pourri. Leigh's contribution, he says, was to play 'Beautiful Dreamer' on the kazoo, 'while Ken did some kind of bizarre juggling. Dave Hill and Gillian Brown were also involved. He was always very well turned out, Ken, usually wearing a tie, but there was no question he was also turning into Ken Campbell. I now realise, in fact, that he was directing the show, and that this was probably the embryonic start of his Road Show. He used to drive around in a blue, three-wheeled Reliant Robin motor car.' Several of the actors lived in flats in Sackville Street. Anjula Harman, who played Olivia in *Twelfth Night* and subsequently married Ron Daniels, was lodged in one upstairs from Ken's; his place, she says, was oddly furnished with hundreds of china dolls, some of them four feet tall. 'One day, he set them up in an entire scene in the garden and got us improvising around them. It became a regular thing: after the show, he'd say, "Let's play with the dolls." It was spooky and bizarre, but unforgettable. And we never broke any of them.'

Jack Sheppard came out of Campbell's wide reading of accounts of piratical enterprise and rough justice in the early eighteenth century, and included not only the Macheath-like aspect of Sheppard's life – he stole and pilfered, escaped from prison and was finally hanged – but also the character of Jonathan Wild, the thief-taker general, and Daniel Defoe's colourful account of Jack's hanging. There is one basic setting, The Black Lion Tavern, and a tumult of petty crime, ribaldry, pub talk and games, arrests and chases. Ken turned up at rehearsals with a full set of bound copies. 'It'll be a sorry day if we ever have to open these,' he said, and proceeded to rewrite the entire show around the actors' personalities.

Cheeseman was once asked by an archivist researching censorship on the British stage if he could remember an instance which indicated a shift in the level of public tolerance for outlandish or antisocial theatrical behaviour. He cited a big row in the neighbourhood over *Jack Sheppard* – 'a brilliant piece of theatre,' he called it – at the moment when a glamorous doxy in the cast turned to the audience and tried to conduct a poll as to whether or not one of the characters should take his trousers off. The Chairman of the lawn tennis club, Mr Plum (whose wife really was called Victoria), an accountant, wrote a long letter to the local newspaper complaining about this 'disgusting' scene. Cheeseman used the example to show how things taken for granted in London in the 1960s would still shock a North Staffordshire audience. Ever the diplomat when the livelihood of his theatre was at stake, Cheeseman quelled the brouhaha and even became fast friends with the Plums.

The short play Campbell wrote especially for Bob Hoskins, at Cheeseman's behest, *Christopher Pea*, featured an ugly, feeble-minded resident of Ilford 'who lived only on the fringe of our world', and who was another of Campbell's romantic fantasists. He falls in love with Brenda, an usherette in the ABC cinema on the Cranbrook Road, but can't even articulate a simple request for toffees in the corner shop: 'Can I have some teefees please...? Teefee taffee toodle tooly splaggly worldly blum.' Hoskins saw Christopher as a mental retard but reckons it was an inoffensive portrait as the character was so loveable and funny. Brenda owes rent to a nasty married landlord who confiscates her belongings. After a series of snapshot scenes in various Ilford locations, including Fairlop Tip and the Labour Exchange ('lunatics are all part of a day's work at the Ilford Labour'), where Christopher loses his job and his bike, there's a happy reunion with Brenda in the unreal cosiness of the cinema.

And best of all, and first of all, there was *Old King Cole*, which combined the elements of romance in *Just Go, Will You Harry* and *Christopher Pea* with an even stronger element of the vivid Stanley Unwin-style gobbledygook in the latter – in the scene where Faz and Twoo, the quick-change double act, are disguised as 'international wedding guests' in Buck Palace and in the final company song of 'Parapher-nalia'. The show was written at Cheeseman's express command for Christmas 1967. As part of the triumphant reopening season after the managerial hiccup, it was in very good company: Peter Terson's *The Ballad of the Artificial Mash*, an absurdist satire (with songs by Gillian Brown) on artificial foodstuffs and back-to-nature faddism, had been followed by a revival of the company's successful 'railway in the Potteries' documentary-drama, *The Knotty*, Arnold Wesker's *Roots* and Shakespeare's *Henry V*. Cheeseman's one condition was that, apart from appealing to kids, the Christmas show should be called something famous. Camp-bell riffled through the *Oxford Book of Nursery Rhymes* and chose Old King Cole because a) he was a merry old soul and b) the story didn't have a plot. 'As long as some geezer call-ing himself Old King Cole turned up some time or other and there was some mention of fiddlers,' said Campbell, 'we'd seem to be in the clear as far as the Trade Descriptions Act was concerned.'

In his introduction to the printed text, Campbell further traced the show's genealogy to his touring role of Redhot, an eighty-year-old kleptomaniac nutter in a huge old army greatcoat who appears in *Fings Ain't Wot They Used T'Be*. Omitting to mention Faz and Twoo in *Events of an Average Bath Night*, he claimed that, on that tour, he and fellow cast member Tony Rohr assumed the identities of the evil genius Faz and his feeble-minded assistant Twoo in devising collaborative squibs of literature designed to amuse only each other. He also noted that the theatre-in-the-round at Stoke, when stripped of furniture, looked more like a mini sports stadium than a theatre. *Old King Cole* is a unique fairytale that prospered initially in that in-the-round Stoke setting with a mock Olympiad of a pentathlon competition: water pistols and squeaky ducks and an egg-and-spoon-race decider were served up between Faz and Twoo launching their campaign to save the Princess Daphne from the obnoxious Baron Wadd. Campbell harnessed elements of pantomime with the theatrical properties of an all-action game show like *It's a*

Knockout and suffused it all with the sheer linguistic glee of nonsense-speak and comic-strip yuckiness of bottom jokes, dancing sausages, wet underpants, and green-jelly-and-gravy sandwiches.

The first performance, said Campbell, given to an audience of seven-, eight- and nine-year-olds, was amazing: 'They didn't just like it, they went bananas... Dave Hill as Baron Wadd had to leave the stage for half a minute to steel his nerve to continue the circus. Peter Cheeseman, however, was alarmed – he feared the mass hysteria that the play was creating could be dangerous – so we quickly reworked bits so they weren't quite so panic-inspiring... in fact, little was lost and, thanks to the Cheeseman wisdom, all audiences and casts have survived the experience ever since.' The play took children's theatre into a new dimension of knockabout, irreverent and gloriously disreputable comedy, and it soon entered the repertoire around the country. Significantly, it was chosen by the Unicorn Theatre as their farewell production at the Jeanetta Cochrane Theatre in 2004 before moving into their new purpose-built home by Tower Bridge.

'We were all absolutely obsessive about theatre,' says Jane Wood. 'Night after night we'd sit around in Stoke, all of us, talking about what we should do and how we should go about it. There was no thought of combining theatre with television or film. I was offered a role in the Karel Reisz movie of *Isadora*, starring Vanessa Redgrave, and I turned it down. Chris Martin, a hot actor at the time, was offered a major role in *Decline and Fall* on television and was told by Cheeseman not to accept it! The difference then was that everyone came up from London to see our work. Irving Wardle of *The Times* was always there. Bill Gaskill and Lindsay Anderson of the Royal Court would often come and see what was going on. The trouble today is that a young director would rather work for nothing at the Gate on the London fringe than run a theatre in Bolton or Stoke, because they know they won't get any real kudos for doing so.'

✧

There was a sense in which the changing theatre was all about what was happening *outside* London, because the new subsidised monoliths, the RSC and the National, were yet to find their feet after being inaugurated, respectively, in 1960 and 1962. It was a transition period between the new dawn and the explosion of the fringe at the end of the decade, and theatres like Stoke and Bolton were indeed the pioneers; a building programme of major new reps in Coventry, Nottingham, Sheffield, Derby and Manchester would soon follow, as the Arts Council were led by the nose (and not before time) by artistic imperatives and civic demand.

The Bolton Octagon, which opened in 1967 under the artistic directorship of Robin Pemberton-Billing, who also designed the auditorium (which could operate in the round, as an open stage, or thrust), was indeed a complementary counterpart to Stoke, and Campbell was prominent in both. *Jack Sheppard* figured in the opening season of the Bolton Octagon, where Robert Powell played the lead, as well as Mr Pat in Brendan Behan's *The Hostage* and Doolittle the dustman in Shaw's *Pygmalion*. Campbell came across from Stoke to direct *Jack Sheppard*. The company included not only Powell, who had recently completed a season with Alan Ayckbourn at Scarborough, but also Russell Denton, destined to play the lead in *The Warp*, who arrived in Bolton with experience of children's theatre with Brian Way and a season as leading man ('I think the director fancied me!') in weekly rep at Great Yarmouth. Denton remembers thinking how 'grounded' Ken was in the theatricality of theatre: 'He'd say, "Stop pretending that you're not on a stage... I don't want people who are pretending that they're not there! If you want to do that, go and join the RSC, because you're no fucking good to me!" And at that moment in my life I got it: I thought that if what I was doing was no good to him, it must be the absolute opposite... and I remember him telling someone else that they were making a scene too "neat" when he wanted a mess. "I'm not interested in trickery-dickery stuff," he'd say, "go and work with the Trevor Nunns and the Peter Halls: they're the conspirators!"'

Throughout the 'hiccup' period in Stoke, Ken, Dave Hill, Jane Wood and others were meeting regularly, every day almost, to work on improvisations, with no very clear end in sight, although out of this self-imposed work in 1967 came the television play *One Night I Danced with Mr Dalton*, broadcast on ITV in June 1968. Again, Campbell's supply-teaching experience paid off in the story of a nervous young English master whirled through a series of mishaps that begin in a doctor's waiting room and end with his dismissal from his job. Sylvia Clayton, writing in the *Daily Telegraph*, said the fresh and funny dialogue was never facetious because it was based in genuine observation. Referring to the encounter between Donald Churchill as the timid English master, and Pauline Collins as a friendly, uneducated waitress, as a stock Hollywood scene 'but lively and full of movement', she noted Collins's 'sly and original touch for comedy'. The setting, again, was Ilford, with namechecks for Gants Hill Library and the Cranbrook Road. Although Clayton found the thread of Campbell's jokes about Spenser's *The Faerie Queene* too elaborate – we should be so lucky to have such a thread in a television drama today – she applauded 'a very promising play'.

Susan Tracy, the future RSC actress, who became Ken's girlfriend, was playing a small role. During the filming of *One Night*, she would drive him home to his London flat above a shop in St John's Wood High Street, North London, and quite often stop over. Ken told her that if she intended becoming a serious actress, she had to work with Peter Cheeseman. So she auditioned for him, successfully... which is how Ken came to be lodging occasionally in the seven rooms she occupied in the east wing of Horsley Hall, a nineteenth-century mansion in Eccleshall, twenty miles south-west of Stoke. 'He was the most delightful, unspoilt man in those days,' she says, and their time together was idyllic; she driving back from rehearsals in her Mini to grill him a fish dinner before rushing back for that night's performance.

One significant side effect of Ken's time in Stoke was a developing interest in ferrets. He started with gerbils. The stage designer Anna Steiner – she had designed the *Twelfth*

Night and had got Mike Leigh to help out with the scene-painting – had a room in the Eccleshall mansion. She noticed that, when Ken came in from work, the first thing he did was see how his gerbils were coming along in their cage in a little room off the corridor. Wanting one for herself, she noticed some strange-looking creatures in a pet-shop window in Newcastle-under-Lyme. They were palpably not gerbils. She asked Ken about them. He knew immediately: they were ferrets. So they went back to the shop together and bought two ferrets: a yellow one with red eyes called Princess, who was distinctly vicious, and a polecat ferret with white eyes. Anna took them back to London with her and made a home for them in her Swiss Cottage apartment. It was not long before the bright lights and the trouser legs beckoned...

In London, commuting from Eccleshall, Ken stayed in St John's Wood, while Dave and Jane set up home in a studio flat on Haverstock Hill, Chalk Farm (they live there still). Ken wrote to Susan Tracy from London several times, taking stock of his career to this point and saying that she had made him care about people more in his work: 'Instead of orbiting the Earth and looking down on all the lesser people who weren't me, you've brought me down. I'm no longer on the exhilarating, one-eyed race for glory. I discovered one day that I really did care what happens to you, what becomes of you... in short, I found I was more bothered about somebody else other than myself.'

This short period of self-assessment is marked, too, in how he suddenly recalls a friend he'd never mentioned before, an actor called Roger Stephens to whom he was close, and with whom he flat-shared during the Colchester Rep days: 'He was in the last performance at Stoke before the company disbanded. He was keen to get on, had a lovely girlfriend, expert fencer, dancer and gymnast, and he died in hospital with a kidney disease last May. I can remember getting the news from his parents on the phone one morning. And I can remember going upstairs to carry on typing, I was in the middle of *One Night I Danced with Mr Dalton* at the time, and I cried like a baby. And finally, it sounds a bit corny but it's how it happened

– I said, "Right, Roger, you haven't gone in vain, mate, I shall be great." Life suddenly seemed very short indeed. But I think now that I cottoned on to the wrong aspect of the sad business. I was thinking about how successful he might have been. But in fact the thing about Roger was his enormous honesty and integrity, in his ordinary life and his work... It's his rock-hard honesty I want to be part of. Anyway, the thing is I have changed a lot. And I hold you totally responsible. I've sort of been made to review the worth of things. So thank you. Thank you very much. Thank you for being you, really.'

Ken and Jane Wood attended classes with Doreen Cannon, an exponent and disciple of the Method Acting craze in New York, in a room above The Enterprise pub opposite the Roundhouse. Ken had come across her work before, but he was still looking for a way to properly focus his creative energy. Like many people, he was blown away by the Living Theatre of New York when they visited the Roundhouse with their theatrical hippy-lifestyle statement, *Paradise Now*. And he discovered finally and decisively in 1969 that his future did not lie within the big companies. Above all, like many in his generation, he had craved recognition at the Royal Court. A chance encounter with Lindsay Anderson, one of the directors there, led to a conversation about Brecht and how he might try and write an epic in the Brechtian style. Sensing an *entrée* to Sloane Square, Ken showed Anderson *Jack Sheppard*. Was that the sort of thing he meant? No, it most certainly wasn't. But Anderson liked Campbell, probably because he was nothing like the other fringe tyros hanging around the place with their (to him) unstylish socialist prescriptions and antipathy towards star actors. In this, Anderson was slightly at odds with his fellow directors William Gaskill and Anthony Page, and he was instrumental – partly, perhaps, to cock a snook at them – in employing Ken as a director of a new play by the *Fings Ain't Wot They Used T'Be* writer Frank Norman, opening in November 1969.

Norman's *Insideout* was a prison play with all the usual ingredients of the genre: a serial inmate befriending a 'new boy', bent screws, male prostitutes, smuggled cigarettes and bullying. The new boy loses his girlfriend and leaves prison to resume a life of crime. Norman knew what he was writing about – he'd done time himself and became an overnight literary sensation when Raymond Chandler wrote a foreword to his prison novel *Bang to Rights* – but the play proved beyond Campbell's directorial capacity at the time. He wasn't comfortable. Even more hurtfully, to him, he fell out badly with Bill Owen, the leading actor he much admired, who was, like Warren Mitchell and Bob Hoskins, a Unity Theatre lad. Lindsay Anderson took over the production in its later stages of rehearsal but left (considerably) Ken's name on the credits. It was time to strike out in a totally new direction. And to live by the promises he had made to himself in that letter to Susan Tracy. Their affair dwindled, hastened by Susan taking up with another actor in the Stoke company, though a larder full of gerbils and ferrets was, she says, a sort of beginning of the end... Ken was devastated, but not for too long.

A mutual friend of Ken's and Jane Wood's, John Roche, who had also been at Stoke, was working temporarily in London as a cab driver and was looking for a placement as an Arts Council trainee director. He got one at the old Hornchurch Rep but wasn't happy and transferred to Robin Pemberton-Billing at Bolton, where Jane had just joined the company. In a faint premonition of the Road Show, Pemberton-Billing had taken a leaf out of Cheeseman's book and instigated a tradition of local documentaries; in the first, *Crompton's Mule* in 1968, Jane Wood joined the folk singer and actor Bernard Wrigley in a song of apprentice weavers. It was fairly anodyne stuff. Even though Bolton now presented *Old King Cole* (directed by Roger Chapman) as their Christmas 1969 show, the audiences needed a boost, so, in January 1970, the Chairman of the Octagon Board, Tom Markham, stumped up £500 to promote the theatre around the town. John Roche was deputed to hatch a plan, and he co-opted Ken to help out, without realising that if you want to run something yourself, says Dave Hill, the last person you want anywhere near you is Ken Campbell. Thus it was that John Roche unwittingly launched the Ken Campbell Road Show. Ken took over the outreach project (in the days before the word 'outreach' existed), which was labelled the Octagon Roadshow, and brought in Dave Hill, who had temporarily adjourned to the Lincoln Rep where he'd been working with Philip Hedley, later Joan Littlewood's successor at the Theatre Royal, Stratford East. Tom Markham's money was spent on sending this Octagon commando force out into working men's clubs and women's knitting circles, pubs and shopping precincts, to spread 'the idea' of the theatre, publicise its wares, and draw folk into the shows. But it didn't quite work out like that. The audiences in the community were very happy with what Ken and his actors provided, but showed little sign of wanting to visit the Octagon for 'proper' theatre. And if they did, they much preferred what they had already seen, and then they didn't bother. There was a huge row in the Octagon foyer between Pemberton-Billing and Ken, who was sacked on the spot, he said, 'for refusing to keep a civil tongue in his arse'.

4

On the Road Show

Robin Pemberton-Billing had simply wanted a travelling advert for his Octagon theatre. Campbell, on the other hand, envisaged an independent sort of Fred Karno's Army, a group of slapstick clowns performing modern-day music-hall sketches but without red noses or buckets of water. He saw Bob Hoskins as the new Dan Leno, the greatest star of Victorian music hall and pantomime. 'He was a bit disappointed when I couldn't come up to that,' says Hoskins. 'I wanted to be an actor. He was absolutely convinced I'd be a reincarnation of the great man, but he was wrong, though I think I understand what he meant. You have to remember that Fred Karno made Chaplin a star when he took him to America... The thing about Ken,' says Hoskins, who has seen every side of show business from the fringe and West End to Hollywood in a charmed career, 'is that he tried to use every element of the stage. If there was a heckler, you used it. A hole in the wall, you went through. He was tough, and in some ways he was a bully, but you never wanted to stand up to him because you were always interested in what he had to say.'

Once the Road Show moved more into stunts, and Sylvester McCoy came along, Hoskins left, even though the two of them were brilliant comedy partners for a while. 'What I came away with,' Hoskins adds, suddenly passionate, 'was what has lasted me my whole career, a certain attitude towards work. That attitude is "Fuck 'em": an absolute joy in the work but not the celebrity bit. I find that hard to deal with, still, today. It was all so simple with the Road Show: mostly, it was dramatised dirty jokes.' The point about the Bolton break-up, which simmered quietly as the Octagon Roadshow hit the town, was that Ken realised that the pub and club people weren't a potential theatre audience; they were another audience altogether. And this led him to consider what material he might use that would be nothing like a theatre audience expected.

At a festival of children's theatre at the Octagon in the summer of 1969, Ken had met Simon Hoggart, the *Guardian* journalist then based in the Manchester office. Hoggart told him about Stewart Sanderson, director of the Institute of Dialect and Folk Life Studies, which had been founded at Leeds University in 1964. Ken went along to see him. Sanderson was collecting stories of the kind that would be known nowadays as urban myths and can often be gleaned from the inside pages of the broadsheet papers. One I snipped several years ago from the *Telegraph* was about a depressed poet in Canada who had resolved to kill himself. He drank a bottle of whisky, fed his cats and left a note, then climbed the steps of his ladder to the noose he'd carefully arranged on the beams of his garage. Halfway up, he fell off the ladder, broke his neck and died. After visiting Sanderson, Campbell now knew what he was after, and he and his colleagues started to collect such stuff from newspapers, friends, correspondents and general hearsay, with a view to animating it in a performance.

Having split from Susan Tracy, he was now lodging – on his forays up north – in a house in Anneline Street, Chorley, owned by Alistair Rattray, a mature student at Chorley College, whom Ken had first picked up as a hitchhiker and who became both a performer and road manager with the new break-out group, the Octagon Roadshow. In the first instance, Jane Wood, John Roche, Bob Hoskins and a chap called Dave Miller answered the call, and Bernard Wrigley was on hand to write songs and play the guitar. The material was accumulating, much of it described by Ken as FOAFs, or Friend Of A Friend stories. He gave an example of one such item to James Nye: 'My brother, well no, a friend of his at work. Well, anyway, his cousin. Well, not him, but a friend of his went on a camping holiday. And they'd taken their grandmother with them, and she died, and they were miles from anywhere in Spain. So they stick the corpse in the back with the kids. But the kids got very upset by it. So they wrapped her in the tent and stuck her on the roof rack. They got to a little town, put the kids in the café to have a lemonade, and found a policeman. But no one could speak English, so they had to mime what had happened. And when he seemed to understand, they went out to show him the stiff. But somebody had stolen the car...'

The very first Octagon Roadshow, directed by John Roche, was given in The Wheatsheaf, a modern pub in the town centre, and the first playlet – the sketches were usually mini-dramas punctuated with snappy one-liners and songs – was 'The Hitchhiker': a lorry driver picks up a pale young girl, goes for a comfort break behind a convenient tree, and she vanishes. He tracks down her father and reports her disappearance, whereupon the father tells him that the girl died eight years ago... If that item went down well, as it did in the Bolton pub, they'd follow it with another, more Chaucerian hitchhiker sketch: a girl jumps up into the lorry driver's cabin and complains about the heat. Each time she removes an item of clothing, the driver sniffs and leers, until she asks him if he can manage to drive with one hand... he leers, sniffs, says he can... 'Well, blow your nose, then – all that sniffing's driving me mad!'

After the bust-up in the foyer, which happened a few weeks after the Wheatsheaf date, the first performance of the newly ejected and newly reconstituted Ken Campbell Road Show was given in The Yew Tree pub on the outskirts of Manchester. The hat was passed round and once they'd made fifteen bob each, they all drank up at the bar until closing time. It was a type of superior busking. This slightly altered company comprised Wood, Hoskins, Campbell, David Miller, Bernard Wrigley and Michael Robinson. They had forfeited the weekly £15 salary from the Octagon in exchange for living off the hat collections in the pub. They trained for their thirteen-hour days of rehearsal and performance, according to a newspaper item, by running across the moors for ninety minutes. The same item, commenting on the informal atmosphere of the project, reported Hoskins as saying: 'Look, there are a lot of my mates down the East End who'd like a night out at the Aldwych. But they're too bloody embarrassed by the bloody gin-and-tonic set in the bar afterwards.' An eighty-year-old local drinker said that he'd had the best laugh he could remember since 1914.

A tour of Pennines pub back rooms followed, booked by the late Ian Watson of the Mid Pennines Arts Association. And the writer and director Jeff Merrifield, who was to become a lifelong friend, offered Ken rehearsal facilities at Chorley College, where he was doubling as one of the first B.Ed. students in theatre in the UK and as social secretary. They had a fair show on their hands, but it wasn't fixed, or watertight, and it became less so when Wrigley left after a few weeks to return to the Octagon and participate in another documentary, this time about the local football team, Bolton Wanderers. Wrigley's decision was probably justified in the light of a highly successful subsequent career in television plays by Alan Bennett and Victoria Wood, and a string of appearances in all the major television soaps. Andy Andrews was soon recruited. He was a fine guitarist with long blond hair, a big moustache and a pleasant personality which suggested he was being cheeky and acerbic at the same time; and he didn't mind gooning around in his underpants. He was known to Ken because he was living in the Stoke designer Anna Steiner's house in Swiss Cottage. Once he joined, the group dropped Bernard Wrigley's songs and Andrews started writing musical material with Dave Hill.

The style was set in the first two shows, *Modern Myths* and *Bar Room Tales*. The two different titles only indicated that the programme included either the more philosophical sketches for the students' unions, or – in the pubs and clubs – concentrated on the knockabout stuff. Over eighteen months, the Road Show played in prisons and colleges, and was even booked, after a time, in theatres in Leeds, Liverpool, Manchester and Shrewsbury. Some of the tales were ingenious displays of plastic theatre, demonstrating impossible physical concepts: a red car is squashed by an elephant in a passing circus parade because the beast has been trained to sit on red tubs; or, had you heard the one about a DIY man who blew off his own balls when he lit a cigarette while sitting on a lavatory into which his wife had tipped his leftover paint thinner? The ambulance men laughed so much when told what had happened that they dropped the poor bugger down the stairs and broke both his legs.

Others were performed to a simple sketch/black-out formula, such as 'The Man on the Monument' (later known as 'The Man Who Tossed Himself Off'), in which two tramps, on finding a heartbroken suicide on top of a building, parlay his clothes and money off him in order to give him a purpose in life, by which time, stripped to his underpants, the fellow is changing his mind. He's lost the urge. 'I can't do it,' he says. 'Don't be a tit,' says one of the tramps, and gives him a helpful push. Or there was 'The Man Who Disappeared Up His Own Arsehole', with a husband and wife attempting to spice up their love life with a long band of knicker elastic, stretching it across the roomful of punters, Bob Hoskins holding it in his teeth, waiting for Jane Wood to let it go, into his face. 'Are you ready?' 'Yes,' says Hoskins, involuntarily opening his mouth, and the elastic travels at fifty miles an hour in the wrong direction... Even more alarming was 'Victim' in which a wife who's been raped is driving along in a car with her husband when she points out the window at another car: 'It's him,' she cries. Her husband gets out the car and beats the other driver to death, and they carry on. At the next traffic lights, another car pulls up: 'No, it's him...' says the wife, pointing.

Rehearsals were held every single day, performances became tighter and tighter, there was never any laxity or faffing around. Ken just didn't allow it, by all accounts. He skulked at the back at every single show – the company was indivisible – signalling maniacally if he couldn't hear, jotting down new stories, rushing up between sketches to scream abuse, altering the running order. It may have looked fun, and it was – and there was always a lot of drinking afterwards – but the Road Show was run like a boot camp. And there was hardly any money at all. Jane Wood says that they used to share out 'what there was' at the end of each week. Bob got the first £5 because he had a wife and a child in London. 'You couldn't give any large amount of money to Bob, or he'd go in the pub and buy everyone a drink, so we used to give him a pound a day. The gigs started rolling in: we'd do one at Leeds for Bill Hays to promote the new Playhouse, and then we had a job for Tetley's the tea people, and Richard Eyre would always invite us to do a show in the foyer wherever he was.'

By March 1970, the Ken Campbell Road Show was truly up and running. On 5 May, Ken wrote a long letter to Lindsay Anderson explaining its genesis. Most significantly, he declared his switch in ambition: 'I think I've done a happy thing: I'm convinced now that I haven't got the stamina, commitment or even interest to follow the path of yourself or Anthony [Page]... Since Christmas, with a group of six of us, I've written and directed about five hours' worth of material... We are constituted as a variety act and, apart from a lump-sum direct-aid grant from the Arts Council of £15 (which still hasn't arrived), we live entirely from our bookings.' He went on to explain to Anderson that the art of popular acting was lost: 'Soppy acting, or acting like your uncle used to do, goes down better.' And he defined something called 'prejudice acting', which entailed a Scotsman coming on in a kilt and doing a lot of throat-clearing, or an Italian ogling girls and throwing a lot of spaghetti bolognese around the place. Their correspondence was in advance of a major fringe festival that the Royal Court was planning for later that year, in which Anderson was obviously sounding Campbell out about participating. Anderson wrote encouragingly ten days later, saying that he had mentioned the Road Show to William Gaskill, the Artistic Director (Anderson, Anthony Page and Peter Gill were Associate Directors), and that he would pass on Ken's letter to Nicholas Wright, director of the new Theatre Upstairs: it would be necessary to create a convivial atmosphere in the Upstairs room, Anderson said, 'and not just have a stiff audience of Sloane Square avant-gardists sitting there expecting cultural enlightenment'. By the end of May, Nicholas Wright was on board, and Dave Hill was writing to Dick Linklater, the drama officer at the Arts Council, asking for suits: 'We are keeping ourselves and the office ticking over, but there is one problem which is becoming very serious – our suits are dropping to pieces!! This might not seem serious to you, but they are an essential part of our show... Although we do not expect a grant to continue our work, is there any chance of a capital grant to buy the five lads a suit and Jane a dress? The situation is critical...' £200 was duly forthcoming.

Campbell himself was becoming more messianic by the week. In an article in a Liverpool arts paper, he advocated a five-year closure of the Arts Council, despite the suits. Charity, he argued, robbed one of all dignity. What would happen? Theatres would close, no bad thing, and no real loss, because they were all museums, mostly, anyway: 'Actors who really wanted to act would act. In streets, pubs, fish-and-chip shops, canteens, transport cafés. And I guess that their standard of acting would improve. They would earn their bread only if they took those people there, at that time, on a real journey. They would become masters of the fading arts of contact with an audience... Instead of being the safe, subsidised, castrated toys of the middle class and the bourgeoisie, actors, once again, would be the outcasts, the outrageous, the rogues, the vagabonds, the gypsies. What I mean is – they would once again have dignity.' This was the voice of Joan Littlewood reborn, and it defined Campbell's unique status in relation to the rest of the fringe, which was impoverished, certainly, but actively seeking as much subsidy as it could lay its hands on while at the same time setting itself up in opposition to the political and cultural systems that would accommodate them. Whether or not state subsidy in the long run castrated or at least intimidated the fringe theatre movement is an argument still worth having. There's no doubt that the growth of studio theatres was something to do with tidying it all away as much as it was with providing situations of informality and intimacy in which most of the work found its truest voice.

At the time, it didn't feel like that to those on the inside. There had been the most enormous explosion of activity in the drama schools, art colleges and universities at the end of the

1960s, and it sprouted into a profusion of small touring companies like David Hare and Howard Brenton's Portable Theatre, Mark Long and Mike Figgis's People Show, Nancy Meckler's Freehold and John McGrath's 7:84 (so called because a statistic in the *Economist* claimed that seven per cent of the nation owned eighty-four per cent of its wealth). Those four groups represented four strands of the fringe: alternative literate prescriptive; art-school pictorial jazz-oriented; American-influenced physical; and Marxist political activist. These were just some of the proliferating categories, but the Road Show belonged to none of them. As Lindsay Anderson correctly intuited, Campbell and his storytellers didn't really belong in theatre spaces at all, despite being more rooted in the vaudevillian traditions of British comedy than any of their contemporaries.

The Royal Court festival in October and November of 1970 called 'Come Together' brought all of this into sharp focus. It was the brainchild of William Gaskill who, in an unprecedented act of innovative generosity, threw open the doors in Sloane Square to 'showcase' the work of new companies and help them build a bridge to the Establishment outlets. The festival ran for twenty days and nights in the main auditorium (and the upstairs studio), which was completely reconfigured, as were the expectations of an audience that might not have ventured into the extreme fringes of the avantgarde at that time. The American composer John Cage ran a musical evening made up of strange, incomprehensible guttural noises. A performance artist – a rarity in those days, not a job description – climbed to the top of a scaffolded structure and vomited into the auditorium below. Chickens were let loose in the stalls; a high priestess of happenings administered the last rites to a dead fish in a large coffin; and personnel from the People Show accosted the public on the street outside and accompanied them into the nearby telephone booth where they offered them 'dirty photos'.

Not all the programme was as deliberately provocative or interventionist. Peter Cheeseman's Stoke-on-Trent company was the sole regional-theatre representative with Peter

Terson's *1861 Whitby Lifeboat Disaster*, a documentary-drama that could have served as a template for all the documentary-dramas to come later, from Nicolas Kent's portfolio of tribunal plays at the Tricycle in Kilburn to David Hare's anatomies of the Iraq War, the British railway system and the financial meltdown in banks and big business. Gaskill himself directed three Beckett short plays in the Theatre Upstairs, David Hare directed Howard Brenton's powerful and disturbing *Christie in Love* for Portable Theatre and, importantly for Ken, Nicholas Wright directed Heathcote Williams's landmark *AC/DC*, a play in which, as Peter Ansorge said, 'the characters share a view that their lives are being ruled by electrical impulses passing between people and machines'. One of them is aggressively paranoid about stemming the flow of electricity emanating from other characters and the television screen. He's a personality living entirely off other people's voltage and the images of selfhood transmitted by the mass media. Another suffers from 'media rash', overloaded with 'false feedback', and his designated exorcist sets out to expel the media demons of pop singers, philosophers, film stars and television newsreaders. This fight against 'psychic capitalism' and the play's drug-enhanced obsession with the information explosion and 'celebrity fucking' was not only timely and prophetic, it laid out an area of theatrical investigation that would haunt Ken Campbell for the rest of his creative life. Many of the practitioners in 'Come Together' represented the new London underground culture that lay beneath the seismic upheavals in the arts and society of that time; Campbell was soon to be at its epicentre and, for him as for many, Heathcote Williams became both a symbolic genius and a talismanic comrade-in-arms.

Another key influence on Campbell was also part of 'Come Together'. Keith Johnstone's Theatre Machine – which had been formed at the Royal Court as early as 1962 to investigate comedy and mask work, and had evolved techniques that were already in widespread use in education everywhere – created an evening of improvisation based on suggestions and prompts from the audience. Johnstone's actors were rigidly trained in a post-*Commedia dell'Arte* style which allowed them maximum physical freedom to cope with unpredictable material content. It was this serious application of essentially traditional methods of clowning – which embraced silent movies, *The Goon Show* and the Marx Brothers – that appealed to Campbell; an appeal that is evident in all his subsequent work, right through to his final phase with the new improvisation crowd. Theatre Machine played on the Royal Court's main stage in the first week of 'Come Together', while the Road Show played late-night gigs Upstairs, with the venue transformed into a bar, and customers seated at small round tables.

The company for the Court was Ken, Dave and Jane, Andy Andrews and Alistair Rattray, with Tim Stern deputising temporarily, and more than adequately, for Bob Hoskins. This was my own first experience of Ken Campbell onstage: once seen, not easily forgotten. It was as if some kind of lunatic behaviour had been classified, without anyone's permission, as proper theatre, with an extraordinary current of licentious mayhem flowing at a rate of knots between performers and punters, or 'seekers' as we would become in Ken's own terminology. It was the violence of certain sketches that commended them. I remember thinking how cleverly, and disturbingly, serious psychiatric problems were glossed in brutal comedy. In 'The Man Who Thought He Was a Chicken', a mother harangued her son for being lazy, hitting him quite violently with a plastic dustpan. He starts clucking and lays an egg. Mum phones the doctor, and two men in white coats come round, ready to take him away; but as they arrive he reverts to being 'normal', so they take away the mother instead: 'Come on, Mrs Mott, we're off to the happy land where everyone's a chicken.'

There were elements of political incorrectness before anyone was politically correct, and sexist, masochistic black comedy long before such stuff was current in television programmes like *The Young Ones*. Dave Hill played a dwarf by kneeling and wearing shoes on his knees. He goes to the doctor for free contraceptives on the NHS. The doctor asks about his current method. Dave says he stands on a biscuit tin and, when his wife sees him going red in the face, she kicks the tin away. And one of the most popular sketches, 'Russian Roulette', was played in guttural gobbledygook: two men in fur coats and big hats are fighting over a woman, who stands between them. Each in turn holds the gun to his head and fires, until we have heard five clicks. The last one will be a bullet. One of them shoots the woman and the men link arms and mince off together.

The critic Vincent Guy, writing in *Plays and Players*, the theatrical monthly magazine, rejoiced in the Road Show's infectious mood of vitality and enjoyment after having endured the politically committed animadversions of C.A.S.T. (the Cartoon Archetypal Slogan Theatre, darling of political meetings and student unions); C.A.S.T. had made him want to crawl into a corner and die. Instead, he stayed for Ken Campbell and was rewarded with a splattering of broken eggs and chocolate cake on his trousers and shoes. The most notable response among the critics came from the *Observer*'s Ronald Bryden – the man whose *New Statesman* review of *Rosencrantz and Guildenstern Are Dead* had first brought Tom Stoppard to the attention of the National Theatre. He was, first of all, knocked sideways by the People Show with their combination of smoke bombs, verbal aggro and symbolic equations of consumer goods with imperialism (a brassiere filled with baked beans). 'Best of all,' said Bryden, 'I enjoyed Ken Campbell's late-night Road Show... six lewd young clowns who travel the pubs of Lancashire like a theatrical pop group, extending the art of bar-room tale into instant drama... If you believe, as I do, that the only new theatre worth having is one with a new, majority audience, they're the most hopeful thing on show.'

The Road Show broke out of the incestuous confines of so much else in the festival, aiming for the national audience that had been disenfranchised with the death of variety and the music halls and condemned to television entertainment in perpetuity. Such a campaign of audience inclusion was not on the agenda of any of the other 'Come Together' artists. Poignantly, of course, Ken ended his life touring draughty arts centres and small venues with his masterpiece monologues, but there was always a time for supposing that his brand of theatre, as first fully developed in the Road Show, would become as popular as bingo, pub darts or television talent contests. Alone among the critics, Bryden – who was arguably the most intelligent and courageous writer on theatre since Kenneth Tynan – stood firm, and he warmed to his theme over the next few years. Bryden had identified the Road Show, he said, as the most interesting company to spring up in the steps of the Living Theatre, La MaMa and Joan Littlewood. Once the festival was over, he wrote to the office in Chorley requesting a date for an interview and a photograph to be taken. And he even offered his own 'folklore' item about a young man who persuaded a girl to go on a first date with him to Mexico City, unmindful of the fact that one of the effects of altitude on the newcomer is difficulty in getting it up: he never could, or did.

Although Ken had an idea that the Road Show had run its brief course after 'Come Together', Gaskill wrote him a letter on 28 October, in the week after the last performance Upstairs, saying that 'breaking up is probably the right thing to do' but issuing him an open invitation to 'come back and do something' in the new year. The company had found its audience and there was renewed demand for performances on the touring circuit. Ken got down to work with Bob Hoskins on *Stone Age Capers*, which he described as 'a sort of Three Stooges meets *The Flintstones* pub play'. It was presented, again in the Theatre Upstairs, in April 1971, as well as a new *Bar Room Tales* with a cast of Dave, Bob, Andy, Jane and three newcomers: Chris Martin (an old friend and leading actor from the Stoke days, who would become a member of the National Theatre), Susan Littler (who would become Ken's next important girlfriend) and P. K. Smith (who would become Sylvester McCoy). Chris Martin was anxious about his inability to be as unbuttoned as the others. 'Don't worry,' Ken told him, 'you're the lines man,' thus boosting a fragile ego and making him feel at home. Similarly, Martin was having a minor confidence crisis when doing his Mick Jagger turn alongside Bob Hoskins as

Queen Victoria in a loud boozer on tour. 'Ken called me to the back of the pub where he had a row of whiskies lined up. He told me to shove two or three of them down me at once, and I went up on the stage and didn't care any more. It was a moment of inspired direction, because once you've broken through like that, you've always broken through.'

On the other hand, back in Sloane Square, Bob and Dave were already finding new outlets at the Royal Court. Both took part in a Brecht double-header featuring Tim Curry, Georgia Brown and Mark McManus, and consisting of *The Baby Elephant*, directed by Bill Bryden in the Upstairs, and *Man is Man* directed by Gaskill on the main stage, in February and March 1971. Dave Hill would progress into becoming a fixture in the great Bill Bryden companies both at the Court and at the National Theatre, while Bob Hoskins was soon launched on an illustrious stage and film career. Campbell would be hurt by what he saw as defections to the enemy, almost. But both men had always seen themselves as actors primarily, not lewd clowns, and there always came a point, says Jane Wood, when you wanted not to be consumed in Ken's life any more and live your own. Indeed, Andy Andrews left London eventually to go and live in Lancaster in order not to ever have the chance of bumping into Ken again and being dragooned once more into his exhausting full-on craziness: 'But there was always something unbelievably loveable about him,' says Jane, 'despite everything, all the rows and all the shouting. He was very loyal and generous and always the most incredible company.' Ken remarked in later years that Bob, who had so much talent, could have been the greatest comic since Jerry Lewis or Abbott and Costello, but that he chose to go and be 'gangsters' instead: 'And he's been rather successful at it, so I can't knock the decision.' In March 1972, Bob gave a breakthrough performance at the Court in Charles Wood's *Veterans* opposite John Gielgud. Did Ken see it? 'Yes,' says Bob. 'He liked it. But he said it would have been much better if he'd directed it!'

The snaring of Sylvester McCoy, or Kent Smith to give him his real name, or Percy James Patrick Kent-Smith to give him his full one, was a little more complicated. Where did he come from, this rubber-limbed eldritch jackanapes with the reflective lilt of Stan Laurel and the deviant wit of a gypsy mischief-maker? He remains best known as a long-serving Doctor Who on television (he was the seventh in the series), but in Road Show folklore he was the man who put ferrets down his trousers – and lived. And he threw himself around a lot. Still known offstage and to his friends as Kent, McCoy was born in Dunoon, trained to be a priest in Aberdeen, changed his mind, worked in the City on computers for five years and trained again to be an insurance salesman. He soon dropped out of that and was working as a box-office assistant at the Roundhouse – very much a hippy destination in the capital at that time; drugs were openly available in the long bar – when Ken Campbell came looking for a replacement for Bernard Wrigley. On the day Ken poked his head through the door, he spotted Brian Murphy, a regular Joan Littlewood actor, who was tearing tickets between jobs. He told Brian that he had this 'mad' show that he was due to open in two weeks and that he was desperate to find someone. Brian, who thought Sylvester (or Kent, as he still then was) was an actor (though he wasn't – 'I just never said whether I was or I wasn't'), pointed Ken in the direction of the box office and said, 'Try him: he's out of his head.' So, as Kent tells it, Ken stuck his head through the box-office window and said, ''Ere, you, I've got this Road Show starting, do you wanna be in it?' And Kent thought, and said, 'Yeah, why not, what an adventure.'

'I didn't know much about acting,' says Kent, 'so I got myself a blazer and a silk cravat and set off for Manchester by train, where I was met by Ken bedecked from head to foot in blue denim, not a good look, not even then. He didn't suit denim. We got into a funny little van. He'd gone and told them all that he'd found this amazingly mad hippy at the Round-house, and there I stood looking like Francis Matthews, except for the long hair and the moustache. He loved that even more; it was all part of the madness.' In the kitchen in Chorley, still disguised as Francis Matthews, an actor well known for his smooth, leading-man demeanour on television, Kent found Bob, Jane and Dave and the company manager playing Risk;

Bob was shouting that he'd just taken over Asia and Dave was saying that he couldn't do that because he had Russia, and Jane was just laughing – 'And these were supposedly the actors,' thought a bemused Kent. 'This was not what I thought of as actors, so I slowly lost the silk cravat and I don't know what happened to the blazer. I'd only borrowed it, anyway. I had no idea what to expect, but I took to it like a duck to water and soon realised how blessed I was to have fallen in with this bunch of people. Whatever Ken told me to do, I just did it, because I knew no better.'

An occasional Road Show participant and stand-in for Andy Andrews – because he played guitar – was Mike Bradwell, who had trained at E15 Acting School and would later found the Hull Truck Theatre Company and run the Bush Theatre. He remembers Bob coming and going a bit, depending on the fee. 'Every time Bob went off, he'd grow a full beard and, when he came back, Ken would say, "You can't play Queen Victoria with a beard." Bob said he'd shave it off for a tenner, so Ken would give him a fiver and he'd shave half of it off. Then Ken would say, "Don't be a cunt, you can't play her with half a beard, either," so he paid him the other fiver.'

In the summer of 1971, Road Show personnel merged with other fringe actors to join in 'a crazy musical magical show' on Southsea Common, near Portsmouth, called *Hirst's Charivari*. This was, in effect, the first alternative circus, precursor of Archaos and Circus Oz, and the brainchild, or rather brainstorm, of Mike Hirst, a huge toothless Yorkshireman (he looked like a cross between Jimi Hendrix and Dracula) who had been master carpenter at the Colchester Rep in Ken's days there, a stage manager for Joan Littlewood, and lighting designer for the legendary Isle of Wight rock festivals between 1968 and 1970. The show was a mixture of modern myths, clown acts and stunts, with a cast of ten, a pantomime rhinoceros, a swimming pool, a ballet sketch, a comedy chase on motorbikes and a seven-piece band playing the music of the great film composer Nino Rota. The Road Show nucleus of

Ken, Kent, Dave and Bob did their stuff, as well as Mike Brad-well who doubled as the back legs of the rhino and a sadly inefficient underwater escapologist: he nearly drowned sev-eral times, and diluted his considerable daily intake of local ales with half the contents of the swimming pool.

Charivari, a French word of unknown origin, is vari-ously defined as the spirit of the god Pan, and 'a serenade of rough music with kettles, pans, tea trays and the like'. Hirst's merry band of hippy mercenaries also included the forbidding and hirsute figure of Marcel Steiner, no doubt Central Casting's idea of the Wild Man of Borneo. Steiner had featured in the 'Come Together' festival with the Brighton Combination, one of the first Arts Labs, and he also ran the Smallest Theatre in the World – a sidecar on a motorbike with an audience capac-ity of two people. On a press night outside the Royal Court, he invited aboard two critics – one was me, the other Charles Lewsen, then of *The Times* – drove off down the King's Road and dumped us at World's End before driving back to continue larking about with people on the pavement. In my review I reported, without fear of contradiction, that at least half the audience thoroughly enjoyed the show. Samuel Beckett was working at the theatre at that time and when he saw the motorbike and sidecar said that he would like to write a play for it. Sadly, this masterwork never materialised.

The second Road Show in the autumn of 1971 (and returning to the Theatre Upstairs at the Royal Court in December), partly derived from *Hirst's Charivari*, was planned almost exclusively as a showcase of stunts featuring Kent in his now increasingly familiar alter ego and stage name: Sylveste McCoy (the final 'r', as in Sylvester, came later). So, as 'Sylveste McCoy, the Human Bomb', he appeared alongside a fluctuating per-sonnel of Andy, Judith Blake, Susan Littler, Marcel Steiner, the 7:84 Theatre Company regular Gavin Richards and the play-wright Terence Frisby, an old friend of Ken's from repertory days who had hit the West End jackpot with his 1966 sex com-edy *There's a Girl in My Soup* (subsequently filmed with Peter

Sellers and Goldie Hawn) and who needed a break from a debilitating divorce procedure. Frisby recalls the telephone call he received from Ken in Frankfurt in his compelling book, *Outrageous Fortune* (First Thing, 1998), about his disasters in the courts: ''Ere, listen, Tel, I've lost me spieler for me Road Show and I need someone over here tomorrow who can go onstage and talk without knowing his lines. I thought of you.' Frisby dropped everything and took the next plane.

In the course of the evening, Kent as Sylveste drove a three-inch nail through his nose, went an energy-sapping round with an all-in wrestler, allowed two volunteers from the audience to try and strangle him with a rope, took fifteen feet of brassiere elastic full in the mouth, released himself, Houdini-like, from chains and padlocks while trussed inside a mailbag, and went outside in the yard to explode a bomb on his chest. The *pièce de résistance*, though, was the 'live ferret down the trousers' act. This turn, like all the turns, was meticulously, even exaggeratedly, prepared and set up by the show's compère – really a sort of fairground barker, or spieler, or goader, played by Ken, or Gavin Richards, or Terence Frisby – and it used to reduce an audience, every single night, to a state of frenzied hysteria.

The act started, once the ferret was inserted, with Kent/Sylveste undoing his flies and allowing the ferret to pop out, like an inquisitive willy, and have a look around. He would drop his trousers and get a girl up from the audience to inspect him for any protection, signs of stiffening (sic) and so on, chase her back into the audience and tie up his trousers with string to stop the ferret escaping. The original plan was that Ken would have trained these ferrets to run up the ferret handler's arm and 'disappear', at which point, as compère, he would have announced that the ferret had escaped and get all the ladies to stick their legs in the air in case the ferret attacked them. But the ferrets were having none of this in rehearsal, so Kent/Sylveste had to stick them down his trousers and have done with it. 'The trouble with that,' he elaborates, 'was they'd just go to sleep, because it was nice and warm and cosy down there in that dark place, so I had to invent a ferret running around inside my trousers. Nothing we did was actually in the *Guinness Book of Records*, we just made that up. Ken had got the joke from some barman in Stoke who had been bet by a pal that he couldn't keep a ferret down his trousers, and he couldn't, so he lost ten shillings.'

In November, the show played in Kirkby, Liverpool, in a string of rough pubs where people were killed on a regular basis. The mini-tour was supported by the Merseyside Arts Association, and the *People* newspaper sent along a reporter whose article was headlined 'Does art to you mean a ferret down your trousers?' But the moral outrage misfired, and folk all over Britain started putting ferrets down their trousers. Soon, they were doing it on television. The *People* changed tack and joined in, finding a chap in Cornwall who broke another chap's record of thirty-six seconds by keeping one of his own ferrets down his trousers for a full minute. You have to be sharp about it with ferrets. The sign that they're about to bite is that they start to lick, but not for very long. In all his ferret-baiting, fun-raising escapades, Kent/Sylveste never once suffered an unwanted nibble, though he came close when he went to the limit, usually about forty-nine or fifty seconds.

It was around this time that the big name-change came for Kent. Several London critics identified him only as Sylveste McCoy in their reviews, hardly surprisingly given that the Royal Court programme contained a fictional biography recounting Sylveste's departure from Dunoon Grammar School at the age of fifteen to go and study with gurus in India, where he had learned all he now knew about nails up noses and ferrets down trousers. He had, to all intents and purposes, become the thing he played. The name, in the first place, had been taken from a popular music-hall song they'd all heard in one of the pubs in Chorley: 'That was my brother Sylveste; he's got a row of forty medals on his chest.' Dave Hill recalls an almighty row in which Ken persuaded a weepily resistant Kent that he only got good reviews, or indeed got noticed at all, as his alter ego, so he might as well live with it. He also had to admit that it was a better name than Kent Smith. Some time afterwards, in the late 1970s, when appearing in a play about Stan Laurel, Sylveste discovered that Laurel had worked for the first part of his career as Stan Jefferson, his real name, until a girlfriend pointed out that the name had thirteen letters in it. So did 'Sylveste McCoy', so he added a final 'r' and became Sylvester McCoy.

Reconciled for now to 'Sylveste', Kent's daredevilry grew by leaps and bounds, quite literally. If there were stairs in a theatre, he would tumble down them; if there was a balcony, he would swing from it by his fingertips; if there was a route to the stage from the back of the room, he would clamber over the audience as an acrobatic drunk; and if there were people sitting round minding their own business, he would disrupt their reverie and usurp it with revelry. He was a slapstick wonder of the age, a madcap little monster seemingly programmed by Campbell's malevolent Frankenstein.

The human-bomb show rolled into Dublin in April 1972, with two important and highly significant consequences. The venue was the Peacock, the smaller auditorium at the Abbey, Ireland's national theatre, and they weren't quite ready there for the quick flash of nudity that often accompanied Sylveste's escape from the mailbag, attired only in underpants. As he tells it: 'It was at the Peacock that my pee-wee cock popped out', an unremarkable enough occurrence at that time on the London stage – nudity was by now virtually de rigueur on the fringe – but an act of public obscenity in Catholic Ireland. The actors were informed that they had insulted the national flag, committed an act of sacrilege and that W. B. Yeats was almost certainly turning in his grave with Lady Gregory. The question of male nudity was raised in the Irish Parliament, the Dail, by Patrick Cooney of the Fine Gael Party, between other questions about a rape in Killarney and teenage pregnancy. The Abbey had been inundated with complaints about Sylveste's privates on parade, following a glimpse of some male nude buttocks the week before in an Adam Darius mime show. One front-page story was headlined 'Abbey Nude Scene Brings

Walkouts'. But there was no police raid. The upshot, of course, was that the Road Show became the instant talk of the town and, although only booked for a week – the Peacock at this time was operating a stop-go policy of one week booked, one week dark – the group was invited to play a season of nine weeks at the nearby Baggott Inn, which had recently opened a cabaret room. Once again, they packed out.

The second big upheaval in Dublin was the split between Ken and Susan Littler, with whom, according to Sylveste, Ken was 'madly in love'. The company was billeted in Sandymount, the posh part of Dublin, in a very nice house belonging to one Mr Pussy, a well-known drag act of the day and Dublin's answer to the Cork-born defector Danny La Rue. Ken was distraught at the break-up, and Sylveste remembers looking out of the window one night and seeing him eating the grass in the garden. Ken couldn't cope so he ran away to Canada; partly on impulse, partly on a suggestion of friends there. It seemed suitably far away to make a fresh start. But in the back of his mind he knew he still owed the Royal Court another show; he was booked in to the Theatre Upstairs in December. How he fulfilled that commitment marked an important transitional phase in his career. Meanwhile, the Road Show went on with a friend of Sylveste's, Eugene Geasley, filling in for Ken as the barker. Geasley had never been an actor before and just happened to be hanging around in Dublin. Well, he lived there and, what's more, Eugene Geasley was his real name. He was five feet two inches tall and he liked a drink (he died of alcohol poisoning in Camden Town in 1998). He was instantly brilliant and became one of the inner circle and Road Show regulars. For Ken, breaking up with Susan Littler was hard to do, but this didn't mean they couldn't, eventually, remain friends – the usual pattern in Campbell's love life. A vivacious comic actress, Littler had a great career for ten years, culminating in seasons at both the National Theatre and the Royal Shakespeare Company (where crucially, as far as Ken was concerned, she was in the first cast of *Nicholas Nickleby*), before she was cruelly struck down with cancer and died, aged just thirty-four, in 1982.

In Toronto, Ken fell in with the actors at the Theatre Passe Muraille, a leading fringe venue in the city that had been founded in 1968 inside a church hall in the shadow of a big department-store complex. The Artistic Director of the day, Paul Thompson, has no recollection of how Ken found them, or why, but Campbell liked the set-up and immediately offered to mount a new version of the Road Show; which is what he did, although he first had to conform to the house policy of brand-new work only. So he invented an alter ego: Henry Pilk, an unknown, entirely fictional, heavy-drinking Canadian playwright and political activist of Irish immigrant parents given to extreme bouts of insanity that manifested themselves in a series of dark surreal sketches and painfully depressing monodramas.

Thompson reports that Ken turned up as bright as a button with this miserable and often disturbing material written on the back of Player's cigarette packets. He'd found a way of transforming his personal unhappiness into creative energy and told the Royal Court that he would come back to the theatre with a Canadian Road Show immediately after the world premiere in Toronto in November. One or two old Road Show sketches, such as 'The Man Who Tossed Himself Off' (the suicide item), the elastic-panging-rebound playlet, and the one about the suburban householder who disappears up his own fundament, were smuggled in. But they were given a macabre, depressing gloss by the intensified savagery of the performance and the obbligato accompaniment of a tatty violinist. 'Who is real in this hall of mirrors?' asked the plumpest, most heavily bearded Canadian, Andy Jones, heralding the arrival of the distraught creative artist Henry Pilk. In one hilarious episode, an intellectual admirer of Pilk tries to get to grips with his art while the artist sits on his head, suffocating the life, and his brains, out of him, in a satirical echo of the trepanning scene in Heathcote Williams's *AC/DC*. And Campbell took a backward swipe at the Abbey in Dublin in Pilk's filthy Irish contribution to the national drama, 'The Playboy of the Sorrows'. Here's Father McWhirter (the McWhirter brothers, incidentally, were the editors of the *Guinness Book of Records*): 'When the bang went off, wasn't the Widow Quim woman that frighted she hugs tight hold of me, burying my weary ecclesiastical head in her two handsome diddies? Widow Quim, today's bang is after bringing me to my senses, it's me cloth and collar I'm after turning, and with a quick flash of me mickey, it's will you marry me Widow Quim, and you with your marbles peeping up above your frock like the two boiled eggs I'm after having had for me breakfast. Is it tapping them with me spoon you'll be permitting me, Widow Quim?'

Andy Jones and his sister Cathy were among several Canadian actors whose lives were transformed by Ken's irruption in their midst. Moreover, they came from the town of St John's in Newfoundland, on the easternmost tip of the North American continent, the very place Campbell came in later life to regard as his spiritual home. 'He gave us basic acting lessons,' says Jones, 'because he insisted on us doing it all straight. In Canada, actors tended to say, "Look here, I'm funny," and he never let us do that. He had a baseball bat, and he'd run around the stage screaming at us, brandishing the bat, yelling obscenities. We'd never known or worked with anyone like him before. He could see a kind of wonder in everything. And I've always thought of what he might have said or done in everything I've ever done since.' As a result of the Campbell intervention, Jones and his colleagues formed an important company, CODCO, that prospers to this day in Toronto, and Cathy went on to star in the Canadian television series *This Hour Has 22 Minutes*, a sketch comedy show about the current news, like *The Frost Report*, that has been running for eleven years. 'His attitude to doing things changed me,' says Jones: 'Just try it, just do it.'

The little breakaway sketch show had come a long way from its origins in Bolton, and was renowned in the unlikeliest of places. One of the last performers to join the Road Show in Britain was the actor and writer Chris Langham, who had seen the company with Sylveste, Terence Frisby and Marcel Steiner in it at the Open Space Theatre on Tottenham Court Road. As for so many, it changed his life: 'What I liked about it was how serious it was, while completely mad. Stupid things were done with a rather fierce, responsible resolve – it was men's theatre, like an army exercise. I was absolutely captivated by it and went up to Marcel Steiner afterwards and said, 'How do you join the Road Show?" and he said, "Fuck off." '

Soon afterwards, Langham – son of the eminent theatre director Michael Langham – who had written and appeared in student revues at Bristol University and was now writing articles in *Time Out* magazine on London below street level (sewers, bomb shelters, the Post Office railway), spotted a classified ad: the Ken Campbell Road Show was seeking a new member. He phoned up and went round to see Campbell in North London. Ken made a pot of tea on a tray and, before Langham could launch into one of his two prepared audition speeches, suddenly said, 'Of course, there's no reason really for doing plays, is there? I mean, there's no reason at all for doing *Hamlet*. So with the Road Show we've had to create a reason, and our reason is that we've got stories that SIMPLY MUST BE TOLD.' Ken picked up a tea towel and handed it to Langham: 'So if I was to ask you to play an old lady, and asked you to put that tea towel on your head and BE that old lady, could you do it?' And Langham said, 'Well, yeah...' and Campbell said, 'You're in!' A dazed Langham left the house: 'And it was only on my way home that I realise he'd done my audition for me and had thought quite highly of it.'

This was the start of one of Campbell's key creative relationships. Langham was the most brilliant of all Ken's collaborators in the coming decade. The Road Show continued fitfully through the great enterprises that followed, and Langham was noted in the *Guardian* by Michael Billington as 'a lanky, po-faced joker' playing alongside Andy Andrews, Jane Wood, Sylveste and Ken at Joan Littlewood's old theatre in Stratford East in October 1975. This show combined some new material with bits and pieces from all the former Road Shows: the ferret down the trousers, the 'William Tell Overture' played on a nose flute, the domestic shouting matches, the uproarious pratfalls, the bitter and twisted folk songs of Andy Andrews and another musician called Bob Flag, the rude ushering of the audience into the square outside by Campbell so that Langham could demonstrate the arts of fire-eating and fire-breathing, and Sylveste could explode a bomb on his chest...

Being directed by Ken was, for Langham, the first time he had been really shaken up by a director. 'There was a lot of bellowing. He would direct from the upper circle at Stratford East because, he said, that was where all the most important people sat. There were no quiet "asides", with little suggestions of just trying this or that... While rehearsing the "grandmother on the roof rack" bit, he told me to be angry, and got really cross, ran all the way down from the circle, and on to the stage, and yelled, "No, you're doing it LIKE a man who's angry... BE angry..." It had never occurred to me before that doing "like" anything was just bad acting. So what you do is forget about monitoring, just be in it. Let the creature engulf you and let go and do the scene on a visceral, intuitive level. Don't be clever. That was a huge breakthrough for me.'

'All the old tatty gear and costumes, mostly from Oxfam shops and jumble sales, reek of ridiculous times on the road,' said Campbell in the programme (cost: 1p). 'The first Road Show had a budget of £10... Sylveste McCoy used to be a quiet, unassuming little geezer called Kent Smith. As we toured the human-bomb show round Britain, then abroad, the quiet, unassuming Kent Smith realised that he had now become in private and public the noisy, assuming madman Sylveste McCoy. The matter was clinched when a beautiful Dutch girl called Agnes fell in love with him as Sylveste. He changed his name to fit her fantasy. Apparently, we are shortly to hear the patter of real McCoy little feet...' (The couple never married but did indeed have children: two boys, now adults.) This mythologising of his work was all part of the process. Campbell was wont to demand things be 'legendary' at the very moment of their instigation. With Pilk, he'd unleashed an alter ego over whom he did not always exert anything like control. Langham would reappear in *The Awesome Worlds of Henry Pilk* at the Young Vic in 1977, a show that incorporated some sketches from intervening

Campbell plays as well as vintage Pilk items on the great cheese-sandwich phobia, hallucinations and paranoia, and the reliable Synge-song standby.

When Langham went to spend a summer with his father in Minneapolis (where Michael was running the the-atre), he was invited to mount a version of *Pilk* in the studio with students while performing his own one-man show. Hear-ing that Campbell was coming out, one of the *Pilk* actors was looking forward to complaining about the philosophy of the show; he told Ken that he was worried about the places he was being asked (by Langham) to go within himself, whereas he'd always regarded 'the director' as a sort of filter. ' "No, no," said Ken,' according to Langham, 'and he got behind the actor with his fist in his back and propelled him viciously across the floor and said, "This is what a director does, he gets behind you and says, go on, get in there, you old bugger!" And the actor was suddenly really glad after all that I was the director, because he was instantly terrified of Ken.'

Langham took the joke of Pilk's creativity one stage fur-ther when he arranged for a genuine professor, George Faber of the University of Minnesota, to disrupt a performance of Pilk's psychodramas with a declaration and a request: 'I have been a serious student of Mr Pilk for some years, and while these dramatic pieces are all very interesting, I am more drawn to his poetry. Are you going to be introducing any of his poetic works this evening or, if not, could I supply some examples?' This man exuded too much gravitas to be mis-taken for a plant. A stage manager appeared to inform the actors there was no time for any impromptu divagation, then one of the company piped up with news of a vacant venue on the other side of town. So they would transfer the whole audi-ence – losing about a third on the way – to the (prearranged and prepared) Dudley Riggs restaurant theatre where George Faber would recite Pilk poems and the company would con-clude the evening with two or three of the best sketches. Then Langham started receiving letters from various academic institutions asking if Henry Pilk was available to give lectures, was he still in a lunatic asylum, could he travel anywhere?

One night, two CBS journalists from Toronto came to the show, went on to the Dudley Riggs and then wanted something more to eat, so Langham took them across the river to an old streetcar in St Paul that had been converted into a twenty-four-hour diner. 'An old black guy came up to their table,' recalls Langham, 'and started dropping jukebox titles on the table and singing them, then moving on to another table. He was a real mad person. And the CBS guys loved it, thought it was all part of the show. I felt triumphant because the whole thing had worked, and warped their minds. The point being that when you walk out of something of Ken's, the whole world looks different. When *Monty Python* first came on the television, the continuity announcer would say, when it finished, "And next, the nine o'clock news," and you'd go, ha-bloody-ha, and you'd laugh at stuff that was real. So you start looking at the world as an artistic phenomenon. That's fantastic. And that's exactly what Ken did.'

Ken was also searching, as usual, for the Perfect Woman. He returned to Toronto in late 1973 with an actress friend, Emma Williams, with whom he was newly smitten, and for whom he wrote a play called *The Toronto Pixie Capers, or The Strange Case of the Society of Elvereans*. It was to be about the two of them, he records in his notebooks, a Celtic pixie and an Ottawa gnome: 'I have been looking for someone ever since I can remember – I've not known who it was – I've looked in Dublin and in Tel Aviv and Jerusalem and Munich and Berlin and New York and twice already in Toronto and many other places – and I've had the good fortune to know well some wonderful women – but I always knew that I had something else to do – I know this is the beginning of whatever it is.' The play itself was a dotty love-struck mad picaresque adventure, an outline for the proper play he would write soon. Emma Williams (who is married today to the writer and comedian Graeme Garden) was the latest in what would become a long line of unconsummated love affairs, but she adored Ken, probably didn't know how to cope with him: 'Oh, amazing person!' she replied to one of his effusions, 'What do you ask of me? I am not frightened by you, only by your intensity.' The search went on.

5

Capers Galore

Ken Campbell was a dedicated reader of the *FT* – not the *Financial Times*, the pink 'un, but the *Fortean Times*, the weird 'un – from the minute it was launched in 1973 as a repository of 'the world's weirdest news stories', a glorious monthly compendium of strange phenomena, curiosities, prodigies and all portents in the natural and unnatural worlds. In a way, this was a ratified extension in print of the Road Show's investigation into bizarre stories and unlikely physical feats and manifestations. It was one of the great coincidences in Campbell's career that the magazine was founded – to continue the work of the American alternative philosopher Charles Fort (1874–1932) – just as the director's interest in this kind of stuff intensified; it was surely no accident that Campbell's psychic drama *The Great Caper* was premiered at the Royal Court in the very year of Fort's centenary – a *fortu-itous* congruence indeed.

Fort, who coined the term 'teleportation' and was probably the first person to suggest that mysterious lights seen in the sky might be craft from outer space, was an unscientific intellectual committed to the task of the Ancient Greeks and Chinese, that of dispassionate weird-watching, exploring the wild frontiers between the known and the unknown. Where these worlds might collide was of special interest to Campbell as a source of theatrical combustion. Of course the 'wow' factor interested him, too, but Campbell was a purveyor of wonderful weirdness, without being a dedicated believer himself. He shared Fort's fascinated scepticism and sought ways of translating the transient nature of apparent phenomena into the paradoxically ephemeral solidity of his theatrical art. His watchword was not belief, but supposition. Something might not be true, but how magical it might be to suppose that it was.

If there's anything that defines and underpins Campbell's entire output of capers, wheezes, stories, spectaculars and full-blown hare-brained excessiveness, it's this fascination with the life beyond the norm. Things could be amazing and remain beyond our understanding; the fun would be had in conveying that amazement in supercharged words and extreme action. A quality you keep rediscovering in Campbell is this capacity for relishing; for relishing the difference between people, their reality and impossible dreams. He read everything written by Fort and everything ever written about him, and committed vast chunks of Fort's books – *The Book of the Damned* (1923), *New Lands* (1923), *Lo!* (1931) and *Wild Talents* (1932) – to memory. He once declared that he never went onstage without reciting, several times under his breath, the opening page of *Lo!*: 'A naked man in a city street... the track of a horse in volcanic mud... the mystery of reindeer's ears... a huge black form, like a whale in the sky, and it drips red drops as if attacked by celestial swordfishes... an appalling cherub appears in the sea... Confusions...' The next few years saw Campbell wrestle this moonstruck obsession with the cosmic beauty of the world into the language of what Peter Brook called 'Rough Theatre', a theatre of minimal means in informal circumstances with immediate impact. Ken had adopted and developed these principles in a natural theatrical evolution from his days in rep to his daze of hippy happiness; he now embraced the social upheavals and habits of the day as a creative spur to prick the sides of his intent.

In 1972 he had moved to the same address on Haverstock Hill as Jane Wood and Dave Hill. They occupied the larger front part of the house while Ken settled into the studio flat. And in October 1974, he returned to the Royal Court as 'a proper playwright' with *The Great Caper*, just a few months after his 'entirely new and spectacular musical', *Bendigo (The*

Little Known Facts), written in collaboration with Dave Hill and Andy Andrews, was premiered at the Nottingham Playhouse. The first was about the search for a Perfect Woman through the realms and byways of psychic phenomena, while the second celebrated the feats of a legendary nineteenth-century Nottingham prizefighter who was reliably alleged to have lobbed half a brick with his left hand over the River Trent at a point where it is seventy feet wide; he could also charm worms, and was said to have done more for badgers than any man known. These two plays were related not just in their characteristic subject matter, but by the circumstances of the theatre at the time.

Although the Royal Court continued to present the work of its discovered, and now established, writers, like John Osborne and Edward Bond, a change of artistic directorship in 1972 marked an important shift of emphasis away from the emergent British fringe writers to the no-less-interesting plays of the South African Athol Fugard, the American Sam Shepard, the Afro-Caribbean Mustapha Matura and (in revival) the outrageous Joe Orton. The new Artistic Director, the impresario Oscar Lewenstein, was an old-school paternalist producer of the Left who regarded the world as his oyster and was less interested than his predecessors in the local political battles being fought in their plays by the likes of Howard Brenton, David Hare and Trevor Griffiths. This vein of new British large-scale work was promptly mined by Richard Eyre, who, after making a name for himself running regional theatres in Leicester and Edinburgh, assumed the Artistic Director's reins at the Nottingham Playhouse in September 1973 and mixed his lively classical repertoire with new work from Brenton, Hare, Griffiths – and Ken Campbell.

The artistic directorate at the Court also 'loved' Campbell – in a way, perhaps, they did not love Brenton and Hare – so *The Great Caper* survived the change of heart and was enthusiastically promoted by both Lewenstein and director Nicholas Wright. It went on to become the record-breaking loss-maker of the period, selling just twenty per cent of its seats at the box office for its twenty-five performances.

Lewenstein was unrepentant: 'It is difficult to see how the English Stage Company could refuse to do a play of such interest and originality without abandoning its purpose.' Campbell had originally submitted a synopsis of a script called *The Rough Corner* to the grants committee of the British Film Institute production board. Japanese Zen gardeners leave one corner of an otherwise intricately planned garden completely rough and uncultivated. This is so they can't be accused of hubris, proving they are aware that their idea of perfection is not necessarily that of the universe. The idea had come to him, in the form of a perfect plot-line, one summer day in 1972, when on tour with the Road Show in Israel, and it concerned Eugene Geasley, who was in the company, and how he instigated a search for the Perfect Woman: 'He went in for a Computer Dateline service,' Campbell told me at the time, 'and when things started to go well with these girls he started to get fussy; he only wanted the perfect one. So he went to see the man who ran the Dateline service, a total expert in Worldwide Crumpet Movements, and was advised that he would find Miss Perfect on the Diezengoff, the chief crumpet-strasse of Tel Aviv. He was to sit there, just looking, for twenty-one days. On the eighteenth day he found her but as soon as he realised that she was perfect, she fell under a bus.'

At the very moment when Campbell realised that his film script was turning into a play – Eugene had been punished by the gods for not leaving a rough corner in his garden, but Campbell now felt that the woman had *not* fallen under a bus – he bumped into his old school friend, Ion Alexis Will, credited in the Court production as 'spiritual adviser'. He said his thoughts had already turned to Will as someone who would know about the worldwide crumpet movement, but he'd lost touch. 'I had a few clues in my address book and started to get on with that. Craving a cup of milky coffee, I delayed preliminary enquiries in order to go and get a carton of milk from across the road. I went out the front door and at my gate was... Ion Will.' Having studied philosophy and psychology while Ken went to RADA, Will had worked as a financial confidence trickster before dropping out and going to India. 'As soon as I saw him that day and saw his face,' says Will, 'I knew something was up, and the devil in me forced me to say, quite casually, something like, "Oh, *there* you are."' Will had lately moved, unknown to Campbell, into the nearby area and was working in Compendium, the now-deceased alternative bookshop at Camden Lock. He was almost one step ahead of Ken on the ideas of coincidence and synchronicity that stemmed from their mutual interest, as it turned out, in Fort and stories of teleportation and disappearance, such as that of the British diplomat, Benjamin Bathurst, who, in 1809, stopped in a small town in Germany and went to examine the horses which were to pull his coach on the last leg of the journey – and vanished; or closer to home, the report from a couple of actors rehearsing a Campbell show in Camden that Andy Jones, Canadian member of the *Pilk* cast, had descended the lavatory stairs of the public convenience at Parkway – and had not been seen again. Actually, he did turn up later that evening – *but could give no account of his absence* (the italics are Campbell's).

The Great Caper is full of such evidence of strange occurrences. It proceeds as a series of exemplary philosophical dissertations as Ion Alexis Will (the character first played by Warren Mitchell) and his trusty Boswell, Stu Lyons (played by Campbell), adopt the cause of 'Eugene Grimley' (Richard O'Callaghan) in pursuit of his idealised sexual goal – from the London Tube system to Tel Aviv and the frozen tundra in Lapland, where they encounter Diana, queen of air, darkness and Barkingside (although it was hard to think of Lisa Harrow, wrapped in furs, and sensuously beautiful, as a quondam denizen of the Ilford Palais). No less than in the Road Show, Nicholas Wright's production reduced theatre to its basic ingredients – actors, language and the telling of tall stories. The play was an accumulation of fantastic monologues, apparently random and inconsequent, but in fact compiled with deadly seriousness, covering the same waterfronts of unreason as Heathcote Williams's *AC/DC*: 'Due to the high spirits and general sport engendered by that lively piece,' Stu says, recalling a performance of the Williams play at Warwick

University, 'the brain surgeon felt prevailed upon to show me his several bottles of cranial spine fluid in the boot of his Morris, and encouraged me to use it as a stimulating additive to gin...'

The critics were bewildered. Most felt alienated by the play, save for the reliably perceptive Ronald Bryden, who, finding himself in a minority of one, like the only character who finds merit in Konstantin's mystical play in *The Seagull*, pointed out (in a review in *Plays and Players*) that in many ways *The Great Caper* was in fact a counterculture *Around the World in Eighty Days*, with Ion Alexis Will as its Phileas Fogg and Stu as his Passepartout: 'Their passion for their alternative to science has the same energy, comic but impressive, as Jules Verne's manic conquistadors of the future imagined by Darwin's century... The difference is that the counterculture's world is internal, so that instead of proceeding by liner, elephant and balloon, Campbell's picaresque adventure proceeds by monologue, rather as if Cervantes had pared down *Don Quixote* to the chapters where his characters halt for the night, bundle around a campfire and proceed to tell rambling exemplary stories.'

The action was all in the words. Even today Warren Mitchell will launch, at the slightest provocation, into Ion's speech of sudden awareness in the London Zoo: 'Saw a baboon playing with his dick – wonderful telescopic affair – pinging at his erecting and retracting dong – eyes close together – forced to squint by the pencil-thinness of his stem – and it came to me what a sorry thing I was – deserved not my tool an equal interest by me?' Although mostly static, there were a few explosions in *The Great Caper* at the end: Diana is tracked down in a centre for disturbed Lapps and, arranged naked on a bed like a sculpture, is ravished by Eugene before rousing herself to bite him savagely in the neck by the light of the moon; and the farce accelerates as the howls of a nun, whose skirts are pulled up over her head to form an improvised sack, accompany a wizened little disturbed Lapp capering around the ward, while taking much delight in Ion's tail (the end result of his Harley Street treatment by the top bottom man there for his athlete's foot of the arse).

There was very little writing of this kind in the theatre of the day – outside of the similarly under-appreciated efforts of Snoo Wilson, probably the cleverest of all fringe dramatists of the 1970s (Bryden was a big fan of his, too) – and the script still rewards perusal. Mitchell as Ion also had a great speech about ferrets, whose praises the Road Show had had no time to sing while exploring their potential as theatrical properties: 'Amazingly instructive creatures – curiously alchemical in instinct – ferrets don't take today to have any bearing on tomorrow, and they are the embodiment of that concept of the infinity of walls – they always ask the question: "How big's this cage?" – they're always rattling hutches – nose into every crevice – always pushing and scrabbling at the walls.' And they have no concept of human affection: 'They can't see a finger as the finger of a friend; it is always an incautious, lively sausage.' Indeed, it was often said that a trouser leg is no more than a meat-filled tunnel for a ferret.

The rather baggy storyline was something Campbell would find a way of distilling and refining in his later solo shows without losing the *Tristram Shandy*-like effects of diversions and red herrings, but there is still a strong sense of quest and buttonholing obsessiveness that gives the writing real colour, and in Campbell's performance as Stu, Bryden saw a Dickensian quality – that of Pickwick as played by George Robey, the 'prime minister' of mirth himself. This was no idle comparison. Robey was the biggest pantomime star of his day and appeared mostly in the provinces. Although *The Great Caper* was a commercial failure, Bryden saw nothing haphazard or ill-considered about it, finding common ground with Campbell's Road Shows, his Jack Sheppard play and *Events of an Average Bath Night*: 'He writes like that because he means to, deliberately and with con-siderable care. You may not like the result, but you can't call it slapdash or unpremeditated. There's nothing primitive about his craft except his beliefs about theatre, which he shares with Joan Littlewood, Brecht, Shakespeare and (obviously) me: that it should be entertainment, storytelling and for everybody.'

✧

Meanwhile, at the Nottingham Playhouse, Richard Eyre had launched his regime in September 1973 with *Brassneck,* a brilliant collaboration between David Hare and Howard Brenton; a panoramic, spectacularly staged indictment of political chicanery and intrigue as seen in the activities of an influential family in a fictitious Midlands town. The Playhouse had been a landmark regional theatre when first opened in 1964 under the directing triumvirate of Peter Ustinov, Frank Dunlop and John Neville, a charismatic leading classical actor of the day. Neville soon assumed sole charge and was succeeded in 1968 by Stuart Burge. Eyre, who had worked as an assistant director to Neville, and much admired him, before going to the Edinburgh Lyceum as an associate in 1966, changed everything. He brought the place right up to date with a company of actors – including Jonathan Pryce, Zoë Wanamaker, Tom Wilkinson, Alison Steadman and Roger Sloman – who had made their names on the fringe and at the Liverpool Everyman, another seedbed of talent at the time. And the Campbell connection was to be reinforced not only with his plays and in Eyre's welcome to Dave Hill, Andy Andrews and Sylveste McCoy, but in the artistic link Campbell also forged with Eyre's wife, Sue Birtwistle, who was already at Nottingham running the Roundabout Theatre-in-Education group, one of the best of its kind in the country, before Eyre himself had been appointed Artistic Director.

While working on *The Great Caper*, Campbell had written an unproduced film script, *The Humming Top*, in which two characters, Emma and Diana, discussed childhood fears and memories, stories of odd disappearances and a general feeling of hopelessness, before bonding again; he retold a few vivid accounts of seeing animals in the flames of a fire and patterns in the linoleum. At this time, too, and very much in the spirit of *The Great Caper*, he was in touch with his RADA contemporary Diana Barrington, whose father, a multilingual Arabist called George Barrington, had died having upped sticks and gone off to another life; she knew nothing about his later life and asked Ken to investigate. The investigation became an obsession at a time when, as he later admitted in

● (*from top, anti-clockwise*) Ken, second left, aged two, with his cousins at his grandmother's house in Eastham, in the Wirral, in 1943, where he was briefly evacuated in war-time
● Getting his hands dirty in an early production
● Another early photoshoot
● Campbell as a quack psychiatrist (right) in *This Happy Marriage* by John Clements at the Renegades in Ilford, with JC, en route to RADA, in 1958
● On holiday with Elsie and Colin Campbell shortly before his mother died in 1954

● (*this page*) The budding young actor's photograph in *Spotlight*, directory of the profession, 1961
● (*opposite page*) Campbell wrote his children's classic, *Old King Cole*, for Christmas 1967 at the Victoria Theatre, Stoke-on-Trent. (*top*) A poster for the December 1973 revival at the Shaw Theatre, London, reflects the comic-book style of the production, which featured (*bottom, left to right*) Hazel Clyne, the late Susan Littler (Ken's quondam girlfriend), Bunny Reed (later in *The Warp*) and Jeffrey Taylor

● (*above*) Bob Hoskins climbs aboard (with Bernard Wrigley below) in the first ever sketch, 'The Hitchhiker', in the first ever Road Show at The Wheatsheaf pub in central Bolton, 1969

● (*below*) Posters for two festival shows, written by Campbell with Road Show colleagues Dave Hill and Andy Andrews, which Richard Eyre directed at the Nottingham Playhouse: *Bendigo* in June 1974 and *Walking Like Geoffrey* in June 1975

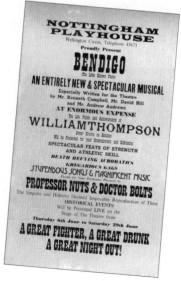

● (*right*) Sylvester McCoy as Weasel and
Campbell as Professor Molereasons ('I was
unable to continue in these conditions') in
School for Clowns at the Arts Theatre, London,
in December 1975
● (*below*) The poster for *The Great Caper* – in
search of the Perfect Woman – at the Royal
Court, London, in October 1974
● (*bottom*) Warren Mitchell and Campbell in
a scene from *The Great Caper*, directed by
Nicholas Wright

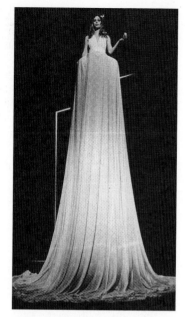

● (*above left*) A special programme, designed by Richard Adams and published by Heathcote Williams, for the London transfer of *Illuminatus!* from the National Theatre (where it opened in March 1977) to the Roundhouse

● (*above right*) Prunella Gee as Eris, Greek goddess of chaos and confusion, in the five-play, nine-hour *Illuminatus!* which first opened in Liverpool in November 1976

● (*below*) Co-conspirators Campbell and Chris Langham, who adapted the *Illuminatus!* trilogy by Robert Shea and Robert Anton Wilson

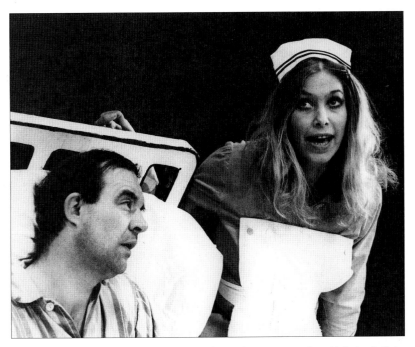

● (*above*) Gee also played Mavis the Guerrilla, here disguised as a nurse messing with the head of John Joyce as Saul Goodman – this scene was played in the vertical plane, turned through 90°
● (*below left*) Gee as Mavis hits the beach and lays down a line in *Illuminatus!* while (*below right*) David Rappaport as Markoff Chaney declares civil war on everyone – the midget against the digits – in his twenty-minute paranoid monologue

● (*above*) Bill Nighy (*second right*) helped Campbell set up *Illuminatus!* in Liverpool, but a car accident prevented his participation in the premiere; he joined the cast in London
● (*below*) Jim Broadbent as Big Jim Baron delivers his talking song ('Situation normal, all fucked up') at the Ingolstadt rock concert

his notebooks, he was undergoing something of a nervous breakdown. In February 1974, Ken wrote Diana a letter which rippled with a sense of *Great Caper*-ish adventure, as it described Ken's search for this Arabian dialect specialist, a Captain Pickering of the Far East, who apparently discovered, like Lawrence of Arabia, that his real home and real people were in the desert, and created another framework for his life. George Barrington had lately travelled by boat to Oman where he was taken ill and lost consciousness after dinner in Muscat. 'He was clearly a great adventurer, a caperer!' Ken wrote, having traced Barrington's new companion and the details of his last days working on an archaeological dig in Qatar in the Persian Gulf. In Ken's letters, which are written in capitals, and are slightly deranged, he seems to be grabbing at straws to make sense of things; the correspondence betrays a sort of emotional volatility that would not have placed him in a very good frame of mind for working on the *Bendigo* play that Richard Eyre had commissioned for Nottingham.

And within a month, Ken has become obsessed with a designer, Mavis Taylor, whom he meets on an outing to Oval House to see his old friend John Roche's Rock Electric Circus: 'Still in the throes of my mental breakdown; how splendid to have had one of these – now I can be a major poet!' he writes to Diana. He becomes aware of Mavis in her sequinned woolly jumper ('lovely face') and filthy jeans ('lovely bum') and is told by Dave Hill, who's also with him, that Mavis makes huge inflatables and designs labyrinths. Mavis and Ken ended up in bed after falafels on Haverstock Hill that same night, and she explains why she was at Oval House: 'To meet you!' Apparently, as Ken tells Diana, when Mavis was 'rapping on about colour magic and infinite mirror domes and geodesical thinking and shells as mandalas and cosmic harmony, folk have said, "You should meet Ken Campbell"'!' The Perfect Woman, Ken remembers, comes from Ilford and sounds exactly like Mavis, who talks of Glastonbury, and travels with the wind, and has had psychiatric treatment for catatonia, and fucks like a ferret. 'It's like having William Burroughs in your kitchen,' says Campbell. 'She leaves me standing. She doesn't just know about ley lines, she goes along them. She doesn't just read Wilhelm Reich and know about orgone accumulators (bright wide eyes, did I mention that?), she and her mate have built one, a huge one for forty people!'

After a Road Show gig that Ken and Dave Hill are persuaded to remount for a large fee (compared to fees in the early pub-circuit days) in Peterborough – together with both John Roche, whose Rock Electric Circus has by this time gone belly-up and folded, and Mavis, who builds an inflatable labyrinth as a forecourt novelty – the company arrives back in London and goes for a meal in Mick's all-night café in Fleet Street. Later that night, Mavis explains how she's really looking for a hermaphrodite and that her best sex experience to date was a three-up do at a drag ball. Ken then says that the only really satisfying sex he has these days is 'comedy sex' with an old actress friend: 'I explain whole theory of comedy sex, its intricate Spike Jones techniques, its final spoof-serious moments before its climactic shriek of laughter. Mavis interested in this – a novelty definitely – she explains how for sex between mere two contestants she only gets a biggish bang out of sex reversal – where the man imagines himself a woman and the woman a man (not just "positions" she's talking about here) – we merge the styles.'

Campbell had taken the precaution of enlisting Dave Hill and Andy Andrews to write the songs and, as it turned out, a lot more than that, for the nuts-and-bolts work on *Bendigo*. He was engaged on important Diana Barrington-related business in Toronto, where he admits embarking on that nervous breakdown; and in Amsterdam, where he took a more than passing interest in the pornography of the sexual revolution ('What the hell does that mean?' asks Campbell, referring, not without sarcasm, to Heathcote Williams's apothegm, 'The sexual revolution *is* the Third World War'). All the same, Eyre insists the best scenes of *Bendigo* were written by Campbell, even though Hill and Andrews wrote a fair amount of them and even Eyre chipped in, too. *Bendigo*, and its companion piece, *Walking Like Geoffrey*, were part of Eyre's opening purple patch of fifteen months which also included *Brassneck*;

Adrian Mitchell's relocation of Gogol's *The Government Inspector* to a Yorkshire backwater obsessed with Hollywood stars and showbiz paraphernalia; Howard Brenton's *The Churchill Play*, a satirical backlash to the Churchillian mythology encased in a dystopic vision of England in a detention centre; and Trevor Griffiths's *Comedians*, which starred Jonathan Pryce as a disaffected punk skinhead using comedy as a weapon of class war. It's impossible to imagine any situation in the regional theatre today in which such a programme could be presented, even if there were the talent available to do so. Eyre guaranteed a production for these plays before a word had been written. BBC television drama (where Eyre also worked as the producer and director of *Play for Today* for two years after he left Nottingham in 1978) operated on a similar principle of trust in the artist before the suits increasingly took over control of all creative areas.

Bendigo opened in Nottingham on 6 June 1974. The design was gaudily mock-classical, like a Pollock's toy theatre, with fairground lights twinkling above a wonderfully idiosyncratic bunch of musicians who had a tune or rude noise for every occasion. Nottingham's legendary prizefighter, 'William a-Bednigo-Bendigo-Bendy-Bindy-Bin-Day' (1811–1880), was played with rough-house, comical vigour by the stentorian Roger Sloman. His chief adversary, the giant-like Ben Caunt – played in the show by Tom Wilkinson – used to try and break his back by lifting him by the neck and falling over him on the ropes. Eyre once recalled how fascinated Campbell was by Bendigo's training methods: he would go into pubs and spit into people's beer to annoy them and thus provoke an impromptu bout. He once did this to a dancer, who jigged about so much that Bendigo couldn't hit him, thus giving him the key to his distinctive, prancing style. In the show, Bendigo's professional inspiration came from his mother, played as an Irish pantomime dame, who, taunted beyond endurance by her son's indolence, flattened him with a rolling pin. He thumped her right back with a powerful straight left. 'Ah son,' she said, ''Tis a metaphor surely of your life to be.'

The crucial championship match in the second act was stunningly staged, with Caunt appearing in the bar at the interval shouting abuse at the Nottingham 'Herberts', who replied in kind. The actual pugilism was a series of cheats, with fingers up nostrils, fists pummelling way below the belt and heads bashed against corner posts. But Bendigo, who also ran dwarf-baiting evenings and died attempting somersaults, proved more than a match for the great big Caunt (who got called just that, among other things). Although he directed it himself, Eyre thought *Bendigo* one of the most enjoyable things he had ever seen in the theatre and so did many of the audience – though not, presumably, the man whom Ken overheard one night saying, 'I can't imagine the sort of person who would enjoy this stuff.' So he probably didn't return the following year when Campbell, Hill and Andrews animated another episode of little-known local history based on the folk myth of the Nottinghamshire village of Gotham, where the villagers discovered, in the Middle Ages, that if they were declared insane they were exempt from paying their taxes.

Walking Like Geoffrey, subtitled 'A Tale of Old Gotham', opened in the same June spot in 1975, a time of festival and the old Goose Fair in the city. The anthropologist character, Adrian Creamwell (who removed his wet trousers before they attracted chaps), like Eugene in *The Great Caper*, was engaged on a quest, in his case into the origins of the Druidic curse that had played havoc with the aristocratic family tree of Joderell; Adrian therefore invoked the fates of various Joderells down the ages in a narrative thread that slipped nimbly among the company outbursts of village idiocy. The first act ended with Sir Eustace Joderell (played by the redoubtable Roger Sloman), a Jacobean grandee, attempting to dodge the curse by 'pranging' his soul to another universe, and then by deducing his existence as another person's dream and attempting to destroy the fabric of that dream with excessive behaviour. The curtain fell on a scene of domestic carnage and Sir Eustace stabbing himself thirty times.

Ronald Bryden was once more on hand to applaud the event in *Plays and Players*, and rated this idea, of escaping one's doom by fleeing through the time warp, worthy of Webster or Tourneur, even though it was played as a traditional piece of pantomime audience-participation. Sylveste McCoy was recruited to play Geoffrey and did so with a ferocious display of silly walking that smacked of Harpo Marx and Max Wall in equal measure. He presented a youth so retarded, said Bryden, that he could scarcely walk without tripping over his own ankles. When the bowler-hatted taxman arrives, the villagers interrupt their festival pleasures – which included a 'Dunk a Vicar's Dickie in the Custard' contest, wearing blazers and grass skirts – to go into their loony-tunes dance and drive the jobsworth official out of the village and into insanity. I thought at the time that *Walking Like Geoffrey* was weaker and less coherent than *The Great Caper*, but now I'm not so sure. It was a lot more fun, that's indisputable, but the way in which Campbell mixed up the elements of surreal nightmare and quintessentially British lowbrow humour, as typified in Donald McGill postcards, or Bill Tidy's comic strips, was unique, and justified more emphatically than ever Ronald Bryden's plea for a criticism that could tell the difference between good and bad popular art. I don't think that plea has been fully heard or heeded even today.

The cast of characters was full of scatological names such as Gillian Pubepoker, Muffplunger, Professor Niptwirler and Nicholas Knob, with 'almost everyone' appearing as villagers and the choir and 'other parts' played by members of the Gotham Rate Defaulters Association. The quartet of musicians led by Nick Bicât played banjo, swanee whistle, harmonica, pipa, saucepan, duck, violin, drum, cuckoo, nightingale, floor, recorder, jew's harp, and other assorted instruments. And Mavis Taylor made a huge inflatable elephant out of PVC plastic which broke free of the stage and trampled lightly through the stalls. It was a madhouse, and Richard Eyre is the first to admit that in these two productions, *Bendigo* and *Walking Like Geoffrey*, he unleashed something he was unable to recapture in his subsequent, highly distinguished career in the mainstream. 'A Campbell evening,' Bryden surmised, 'isn't art or even theatre, exactly, but something older: the sort of thing, perhaps, the Aristophanes family got up to among itself and a few congenial Athenian neighbours, which led some friend to suggest to young Ari that he really ought to try his hand at a floor show for the next Dionysia.'

It was the right time for Campbell to return to his writing for young people. While at Nottingham, Sue Birtwistle commissioned him to write for her Roundabout Company, and the result was *Skungpoomery*, which opened on the Playhouse stage for morning and matinee performances to audiences of seven- to thirteen-year-olds just three weeks after *Walking Like Geoffrey*. The show marked the re-emergence of Faz and Twoo from *Old King Cole* (and indeed *Events of an Average Bath Night*) as two inspired verbal delinquents going word-nurdling potty on the streets in their damp pyjamas while a hapless policeman, PC Wibble, tracks down bad behaviour and chewing-gum nasties, and enquires about a minced cat kidnap in a grocery store owned by the Humbottoms. Campbell directed what must have been the most seriously silly play ever seen on a grown-up stage. First of all, the kids in the audience were reduced to howling delirium at the sight of a grown man, Wibble, being told to take his trousers off, and get dressed properly, by his own mother. And at later points in the play, the silly cop is told not to quibble, Wibble (as in Noël Coward's 'Don't quibble, Sybil' in *Private Lives*), and not to dribble, Wibble.

Faz and Twoo invent the game of skungpoomery – which consists of thinking up a word for an unlikely action and then doing it, such as 'shankfinerbling' (going up to someone's legs and brushing and bruising, or 'finerbling' them with your nose), or 'bunkjamjamering' (smearing strawberry jam on your pyjamas and doing a bunk into the streets). The wonderful idea behind all this is that words have become boring and need new recruits. Characters are encouraged, as a matter of course in conversation that is already pretty far gone, to come up with new words first and new meanings afterwards. Faz, very much the voice of Campbell, who hits on the wheeze and is quite pernickety about how it works, is a bit like a voice teacher at drama school, only crazy. Toast, or tomato, are no good, because they don't use the mouth properly, don't use the back gums, 'which is where it matters'.

> FAZ. See, skrongleflambunkle, that's something of a word. Shnanglekrungfnippzers, that gets into the back gums. Now they *are* words.
>
> TWOO. Tee-hee.
>
> FAZ. Now, since an egg doesn't know it's an egg, it won't be insulted, it won't be bothered if we call it something else. Will it?
>
> TWOO. You mean like Horace?
>
> FAZ. No, I don't mean like Horace. I mean, like groogreazyankler. Maybe I could even work up the interest to eat this stuff – (*Picking up the toast.*) if it was called scrancruncherunk – (*Takes a test bite, chewing on the word and the toast together.*) Clangfillperwo. (*Savouring the tea now he has christened it.*) Sninkerslop. (*With satisfaction.*) Ha! Ha! (*Leaps out of bed.*) That's it, you see, Twoo.
>
> TWOO. Yes. (*Pause.*) What is?
>
> FAZ. It's time for the renaming of Things. Everything has got to be re-injected with its original zoom and jizz. (*Holding the table.*) Shankplanker. (*Goes to the tatty curtains.*) Zninglabber. (*Returns to the toast, really getting the word into his back gums.*) S-K-R-A-N-C-R-U-N-C-H-E-R-C-H-I-N-K.
>
> TWOO (*who has gone sort of silly*). Floom. Floom. Buzninker.
>
> FAZ. Yes. Ha-ha. We're on to it.

This sort of licensed anarchy is at the heart of all Campbell's work and the source of its delight for adults and children alike. And Faz's quest to make things different, make life sing, go beyond the everyday, is the fundamental purpose of Campbell's art, and quite a good principle, I would have thought, for all artists to adopt.

When Campbell's second play for children that year, *School for Clowns*, opened in London six months later, he was able to point out to Richard Eyre that it was essentially a kids' version of Trevor Griffiths's *Comedians*. Commissioned and staged at the Unicorn Theatre, in those days based at the Arts, and translated from a play by the German cartoonist F. K. Waechter that had been premiered in Frankfurt in June, the piece revealed four apprentice clowns in a classroom supervised by a tyrannous Professor Molereasons, a grotesque demagogue whose job is to instill techniques of clowning in his charges. The situation becomes riotously out of control, but only gradually – it's a classic of inventive anarchy, but it's also a rich dramatic metaphor of the relationship between pupil and teacher.

Campbell had come across the play when the Nottingham Playhouse Roundabout company had taken *Skungpoomery* on tour to Frankfurt. But Campbell's version was unrecognisable from the original play and inimitably his own. Waechter had written specifically for his five actors at the Schauspiel, Frankfurt am Main, but was more than happy for Ken to accommodate the talents of his own cast in their own way. He surrounded himself with old friends: Sylveste McCoy as Weasel, Chris Langham as Puff, Andy Andrews as Drippen, with Matyelok Gibbs, the Unicorn's founding director, as Pimple, and he himself gave what was probably his greatest stage performance as Professor Molereasons, a remorseless advocate of discipline who is undermined by the very artistry he inculcates in his pupils, driven to explode in frustration and anger: 'SILENCE, CLOWNS! I AM UNABLE TO CONTINUE IN THESE CONDITIONS!!' Ken so approved of what he achieved as Molereasons that he claimed to play every subsequent part in his career in exactly the same way. 'It's funny,' says Chris Langham, 'I can never quite put my finger on Ken's style because he abhorred naturalism because it was just boring but, on the other hand, he also abhorred untruthfulness. So the path became quite narrow when you had to perform in an extreme style. And *School for Clowns* was a big exercise in that; they were people who were born clowns, they were a different species from us.'

The play was a Christmas hit and was lau
all over the country. More than any other playwri
include Alan Ayckbourn, who has always written seriou
children, Campbell had created a body of work in *Old King Co.
Skungpoomery* and now *School for Clowns* that not only
enriched the repertoire but formed a central part of his own
creative output, not an add-on, or a subsidiary division. The
novelist Jane Ellison, then writing for the *Evening Standard*,
claimed that *Skungpoomery* demonstrated Campbell's talent
for 'capturing a comic moment and blowing it up into a great
balloon of idiotic fantasy', while both Irving Wardle in *The
Times* and Michael Billington in the *Guardian* raved about
School for Clowns, the latter registering his pleasure in the battle between anarchic individualism and repressive discipline,
and in the class's inventive use of a cupboardful of old props:
'At last, a children's show that is both inventive and original.' At
the end of the play, Molereasons is evicted from his own classroom and steps down from the stage into the auditorium of
baying schoolchildren, like a Christian thrown to the lions.
Richard Eyre recalled one particular performance: 'With great
dignity, the Professor would process through the rioting
schoolchildren, through the foyer, past the box office and into
the street, shuffling, broken, but still proud, towards the stage
door. I interrupted his journey one day, after a morning performance. "How did it go, Ken?" I asked. Professor Molereasons
stared back at me with eyes misted by tears. "I was unable to
continue in these conditions..."'

There were other adventures at Nottingham on Eyre's watch,
some of them involving Campbell's first and much-loved dog,
Werner, so named in honour of Werner Erhard, the 'mind
dynamics' guru who ran workshops called EST – Erhard Seminar Training – in the 1970s and made a big impression on Ken
at the Mind and Body Festival at Olympia in May 1975. He took
the two-week course, then used it as a model for his own
humour workshops, just as he'd moulded Waechter's play into
his own. Only Ken would change 'EST' into 'Jest', the purpose

of which was to transform everyone's ability to sense the ludi-
crous in everything, 'so that every situation you find yourself
in is seen to be the jape of the century'.

There was an application form for the Jest Humour
Workshops, which promised education in the art of capering,
mercurial humour and the opportunity to discover the trigger
word that fires off personal, instant and debilitating mirth.

Q: Will I be made to look ridiculous?

A: No. You will discover how ridiculous you already look.

Q: Will I need wellingtons?

A: Yes.

Q: Will we have to wear name tags?

A: Yes. But not your own.

Q: Will I be able to go to the toilet?

A: If we can get it unblocked.

And in his flyers to advertise these training sessions in the
Haverstock Hill flat, he announced: 'Sometimes people get the
notion that the purpose of Jest is to make you a comedian. It's
not. I happen to think that you are hysterically funny the way
you are... the problem is that people get stuck seeing how
tragic they were, instead of how comic they are.' In the middle
of one of these sessions, some small boys who had rescued a
batch of puppies from being drowned in the ponds on nearby
Hampstead Heath knocked on the door. One of the workshop-
pers said that to take a puppy would be entirely irresponsible,
but Ken – who had just been saying how it was important to
grab the moment in life, *carpe diem* – said he would take a
puppy and call him Werner. Which he did.

Thus Werner made his stage debut in Eyre's and
designer Pamela Howard's rumbustious Victorian setting of
Ben Jonson's *Bartholomew Fair*, filling the Nottingham Playhouse festival June spot in 1976 with true Campbellian
vulgarity and high spirits. Ken himself played Knockem the
horse-courser (exclaiming 'true Bartholomew vapours' whenever a jape was up), while a pair of Road Show regulars
bolstered the lowlife: Sylveste McCoy as the innocent-seeming

cutpurse Edgworth in a performance described by *Times* critic Ned Chaillet as 'Brilliant... borrowing gestures and grimaces from silent films, McCoy evoked Stan Laurel, Harold Lloyd and Chaplin with a mimetic skill so rare that the slightest of his gestures was enough to steal attention'; and Eugene Geasley as Captain Whit the pimp. Eyre cast all his pukka actors as gentry and Puritans, who descend on the fair to enjoy themselves and close it down, but he made an exception for one of Ken's 'rabble', Chris Langham, who was cast as Winwife, a young romantic lead in a red cavalry tunic. Langham remembers: 'I had to have a fight with Ken, and I always ended up rolling around in Werner's poo, and it used to upset me, because I'd joined the team of proper actors and I had a nice costume which was covered in poo every night. And he said, "Well, if it's there, use it!" Then I realised he was actually doing it on purpose. And then I noticed that as we rolled around the stage, the audience would go "Oooooohhhhh..." and when we actually rolled in it, "Weeheeeeyyy!!!" and that of course is exactly what Ken is about: what is happening in the moment, and the noisier and the ruder the better.'

By this time Ken was setting up one of the great projects of his career, the Science Fiction Theatre of Liverpool, but he would return in Eyre's last Nottingham season in early 1978 to play a definitive Subtle in Ben Jonson's masterpiece *The Alchemist*; he was described as 'a confidence trickster' rather than the titular artisan, and ruled more by a sense of fun than by avarice. When celebrating the departure of a crestfallen Sir Epicure Mammon, he and Nicholas Le Prevost's Face did indeed become, as Jonson specified in his text, 'as light as balls, and bound and hit their heads against the roof for joy', as if on demented pogo sticks. And in March 1978 he would join Howard Brenton, Trevor Griffiths and David Hare in co-writing *Deeds*, an extraordinary farewell to the departing director Eyre, in which a Manchester labourer turns his private grief at his baby's cot death – possibly caused by severe dehydration as a result of an incorrect preparation of powdered milk – into a public revenge mission. One scene contained a long speech written by Ken for a soapbox orator in Hyde Park (who really existed); this character was Billy McGuinness, the foul-mouthed Irish gypsy who would feature in both Heathcote Williams's *The Speakers*, directed by William Gaskill and Max Stafford-Clark for the new Out of Joint touring company, and Neil Oram's *The Warp*, the second of Campbell's two major epics. The long, hilarious speech diagnosed the world's ills as a result of the triumph of plastic ('You're not wearing that plastic mac, it's wearing you').

There was so much ahead of him still at the end of 1975, and his impatient mood of 'getting on with it' was contained in a love letter he wrote to Mavis on Christmas Eve. Their affair was over, but not their friendship, and he used the letter to take stock of the great success he felt he'd had with *The Great Caper* (it was a subject of study in Bordeaux University) and *School for Clowns* – 'the crits have been amazing, although let's not get to relying on these berks' interpretations of things' – as well as celebrating his close friendship with Werner Erhard and his admiration for Chris Langham. Once Langham was back from Minneapolis after *Pilk's Madhouse*, Ken told Mavis in the letter, he was off with him to found the Science Fiction Theatre of Liverpool – 'Haha! – (at last) – Chris has got a lovely mind – full of humour and offbeatness – he makes me think of how I was many (many) years ago – it was ALL fun once – then something happened – (Have you read *Something Happened* by Joseph Heller?) – anyway if you want to work with us on that – you HAVE to work with us on THAT don't you?' He then recounts an encounter with a drunk Scot on Euston Station – someone once said that if there was a madman on a packed train who picked out one person to talk to, that person would be Ken Campbell – who had told him about 'Shloko', which means you are up against life AND KNOW IT.

'I seem to be in a new phase of writing – *The Great Caper* was the fumbling beginning – of really trying to report back from the Shloko country. It's good that Chris Langham is around because he makes sure that I adhere to the discipline of expressing everything in humour. My dad didn't object to me going into the theatre as long as I promised to be as funny as possible and not sing... Theatre is always twenty years behind the times – someone of note said that – but surely the drama NOW (page four already, how splendid, Happy Christmas, Hello!) – NOW – peculiarly in this our own age (Shloko) requires us dramatists and impresarios to get our finger out and make it no more than a year (month) behind the other arts? I am sorry for (difficult this bit) all the times that my love-making didn't make you feel my love – (but then sometimes you were difficult to show love to) (no you weren't) – I WANT YOU TO KNOW MAVIS THAT SAYING I LOVE YOU (and having to go back and retype the "L" of love because I'd mishit and knocked the colon which is just below) FILLS ME WITH A "GOOD!" that is good whatever you do – I love you, Mavis, and if all I can do is say LOVE YOU MAVIS and Skyward Ho! I'm going to make this the last page (Shloko)...'

6

Pool of Lights

The background to *Illuminatus!*, and how that five-play, eight-hour epic came about, is no less extraordinary than the show itself, which opened on Sunday 28 November 1976, in a converted warehouse in Mathew Street, Liverpool 8, next door to the site of The Beatles' original Cavern Club, marked with a plaque proclaiming 'Four Lads who Shook the World'.

As an itinerant, conscientious drama critic covering the show for the *Financial Times*, I reported for duty at 9.30 a.m. that morning in Mathew Street with very little idea of what to expect. But there was a sense abroad that Campbell was coming into his kingdom. On the previous Friday, *Skungpoomery* had been given its London premiere in a production by the late Clare Venables at the Orange Tree in Richmond (Keira Knightley's future mum, Sharman Macdonald, played Special PC Bunkett from the psychiatric unit). And on the previous Tuesday, 23 November – a sacred Discordian holy day, both because of the number 23 and because it was Harpo Marx's birthday – the first of the five *Illuminatus!* plays – each play constructed in five segments of scenes intended to play for a duration of twenty-three minutes each – had opened, followed by the next four on successive nights, leading to the grand 'gala' Sunday opening. The Corkscrew wine bar next door was open all day for those wearing a badge proclaiming membership of the League of Dynamic Discord, whose leader, Hagbard Celine, describes himself in the show as 'a political non-Euclidian', and 'the Leonardo of the twentieth century: except that I'm not gay (I've tried it, of course)'. Hagbard patrolled the waters of Atlantis in his yellow submarine long before The Beatles dredged it from the seabed. His motto? *'Non serviam*; I fight the Illuminati every chance I get.'

Ken Campbell's search for ever more unlikely theatrical adventures had taken him from a convention of science-fiction writers in Newcastle-upon-Tyne to the upstairs café of Aunt Twacky's indoor second-hand market in Liverpool, run by a poet and dream-merchant called Peter O'Halligan. O'Halligan's headquarters, the old Mathew Street warehouse, had been christened the Liverpool School of Language, Music, Dream and Pun. Why? Because Carl Jung, who never visited Liverpool, described the city eerily and intuitively in *Memories, Dreams, Reflections* (on page 223, as it happens, in my Fontana edition) in a vision: 'I found myself in a dirty, sooty city. It was night, and winter, and dark, and raining. I was in Liverpool... This dream represented my situation at the time... Everything was extremely unpleasant, black and opaque – just as I felt then. But I had had a vision of unearthly beauty, and that was why I was able to live at all. Liverpool is the "pool of life". The "liver", according to an old view, is the seat of life – that which "makes to live".' This passage sounded like a clarion call to O'Halligan and his friends. They promptly held a Jung Festival in the summer of 1976 and convinced the city authorities to install a bust of the Swiss psychiatrist on the wall outside 18 Mathew Street – it's there to this day – feeling doubly validated in their discussions and explorations. Ken, attending the Newcastle sci-fi conference with Mavis Taylor, fell in with the novelist Brian Aldiss, who impressed him with his explanation of the bifurcation of literature, after H. G. Wells, into 'literature' and 'science fiction'; Ken tended towards the Aldiss view that if you were to abide by such a distinction, then the latter was superior to the former and better deserving of the pre-Wellsian catch-all description of just plain 'literature'. He realised, he later told James Nye, that 'all theatre had followed the mainstream, apart from a couple of years with the absurd. So I thought, I'll invent a science-fiction theatre!'

Back in Camden Town, thumbing through the new arrivals in Ion Will's hang-out, the Compendium Bookshop,

Campbell noted the first volume of *The Illuminatus! Trilogy* by two unknown writers, Robert Anton Wilson and Robert Shea, who were editors of the Forum section in Hugh Hefner's *Playboy* magazine. It bore a yellow cover with a picture of a yellow submarine. At once, he suspected this might be exactly the sort of material he had half-promised to O'Halligan to launch the Science Fiction Theatre of Liverpool in the Mathew Street premises. When he delved further and discovered that the Illuminati were every secret society that had ever existed, responsible for all political assassinations and international conspiracies, he knew he was on to something. He rapidly acquired the other volumes, fired up by the genre-busting mix of thriller, science fiction, and labyrinthine international – nay, intergalactic – conspiracy. As the authors' own organ, *Playboy*, pronounced in a puff, Shea and Wilson had managed to 'cram in' echoes of H. P. Lovecraft, Mickey Spillane, Wilhelm Reich, Hermann Hesse, Robert A. Heinlein, Carl Jung, William Burroughs and Terry Southern. They ticked just about every literary-counterculture box going, and then some. In the rag-bag of a narrative, a New York cop starts on the conspiracy trail, while a radical journalist is sprung from a jail in Mad Dog, Texas, where he is masturbating, by a beautiful seductive guerrilla girl (called Mavis) – and finds himself making out with a golden apple, copulating with the cosmos, before linking up with superman Hagbard as his impressionable sidekick.

The miracle of Campbell's *Illuminatus!* was to convert all this stuff – and much, much more – into an extravaganza on a shoestring. They had a pittance of a few thousand pounds from the Arts Council. Chris Langham was already on board as co-adaptor and co-director (he also played the self-abusing journalist, George Dorn). He describes Ken's theory of adaptation as 'writing down the bits in inverted commas' until they ended up with a script. There was a bit more to it than that. Just as Shea and Wilson set up a parodied type of literature, so Campbell matched that with a project designed to parody theatre methods and genres while aiming for the sky; it was an incredibly ambitious conceit. The philosophy behind *Illuminatus!*, and one which ran deep with Campbell, was that something was only really worth doing if it was impossible. 'If it's possible,' Langham explains, 'it will end up as some mediocre, grant-subsidised bit of well-intentioned bourgeois bollocks, but if it's impossible, then it will assume an energy of its own, despite everything we do, or don't do.'

Campbell's notebook for *Illuminatus!* is a typically rich A4 manuscript in hard covers, peppered with lists, telephone numbers, drawings and sudden thoughts: 'If you're not cynical about yourself, you won't be cynical about anything'; 'Life is like a cucumber. One day it's there in your hand to be eaten. Another day someone's rammed it up your arse.' In it, you get a strong sense of something about to happen because Campbell keeps saying it will: a change is imminent; action is necessary. He quotes from a letter he's written to Peter O'Halligan: 'I've felt for two years or more that there should be a Science Fiction Theatre, dispensing notions and ideas at a manic rate (since *Journey into Space*, drama has gone downhill at breakneck speed).' Other letters outline his proposals to the Arts Council and the mystic significance of the number 23 as expounded in the first play of the cycle, *The Eye of the Pyramid* – 'two plus three equals five, the pentad within which the Devil can be invoked as for example in a pentacle or at the Pentagon building in Washington... All the great anarchists died on the twenty-third day of some month or other – Sacco and Vanzetti on 23 August, Bonnie Parker and Clyde Barrow on 23 May, Dutch Schultz on 23 October – and Vince Coll was twenty-three years old when he was shot on 23rd Street – and even though John Dillinger died on 22 July, twenty-three other people died that night in Chicago too, all from heat prostration – "Nova heat moving in, dig?"' And, setting the scene even more ominously, Campbell and Langham discharged a memo to the Discordian Cabals in Liverpool and London, urging several options: minimum participation in sending a top theatre critic a darkly paranoid letter ('NB. Bernard Levin will have succeeded Harold Hobson by this time'); medium participation in sending a Xeroxed speech from *Illuminatus!* to another critic with a commentary and some logical deduction suggesting interstellar conspiracies from Sirius; and maximum participation in 'writing to the critic of your choice once a week through October and November and explaining whatever you consider important, with incidental references to the Illuminati, Discordians, Sirius, Immortality, or whatever.'

Who was going to participate in his crazy venture? It all happened in such a peculiar way, almost as an act of stupendous will on Ken's part. It had to be amazing because he said so. Charlton Heston could play Hagbard Celine (or if not, Marlon Brando could). He telephoned Sean Connery. He wrote to Vanessa Redgrave enclosing the collection of memos and letters he published in *Plays and Players* magazine, suggesting the role of Atlanta Hope. He didn't hear back from Connery (or Heston, or Brando), but an actor called Jim Broadbent said he would 'do' Sean Connery. Broadbent had been advised to go along and see Campbell by a director friend, Tina Packer. He was understudying in a Ben Travers play in the West End, *The Bed Before Yesterday* (directed by Lindsay Anderson), and opted out of that show the minute he met Campbell and got a whiff of the extraordinary project in hand. Broadbent recalls that working on *Illuminatus!* was the only time he ever worked with someone on 'a genius level... it wasn't that Ken was being a genius... it was the whole creation of doing the greatest show yet done on Planet World, promoting it, sending out letters to all the directors in all the reps; his creative imagination was just stunning, it was a real treat just to be there.' Broadbent had done four years in rep, but had never, he says, come across anyone who'd enjoyed theatre so much: 'His relish for it, his shallow-end acting bits, his stories of bad rep shows, end-of-the-pier shows... he loved it all. He'd say things like, "If you're reading a paper onstage, it's no good just reading it; you have to show the audience that you're reading it." He went completely against the grain of subtle, naturalistic theatre. But he was also endlessly flexible and contradictory. On *Illluminatus!* he was really flying in rehearsals. It was really exciting every day.'

As word got round, the project became a magnet for people who weren't quite fitting in elsewhere and whose lives were then changed for ever. Bill Nighy had been working at the Liverpool Everyman with the director John Roche (from

Bolton), and had followed him to Aberystwyth for the summer season, along with other Everyman regulars Pete Postleth-waite, Julie Walters and Matthew Kelly. But the gig turned out to be 'problematic', and Nighy returned to London to report to Roche in Belsize Park. The director was leaving on a family holiday and allowed Nighy to flat-sit for him, but not before giving him a copy of *Illuminatus!* Nighy spent the first day in London on his own, reading. He was hooked, and, after a few hours, knew that the book was about many things, including the killing (or not) of John Dillinger by a policeman outside the Biograph Cinema in Chicago in 1934, and the fact that the pic-ture of George Washington on the American dollar bill was in fact a picture of a high-ranking Illuminatus doppelgänger.

'Now, I am not a seeker, or indeed a supposer, of any kind,' says Nighy, exuding his trademark cool in a dry, even tone of delivery, 'nor am I a believer, or a cynic. But I turned on the television after I'd made a cup of tea and the first thing I saw was ancient footage of John Dillinger being led backwards into a prison cell flanked by FBI agents having their picture taken with him. I changed channels in a nervous way and the whole screen was filled with an American dollar bill. These are facts. So I get slightly uneasy and I haven't had a drink yet, so I figure I'll go to the pub. I don't know the area, but I walk into The Belsize Tavern and order a pint of Guinness, and I've got these three books under my arm – I'm used to reading in pubs at this stage in my life – and a bloke with bushy eyebrows wearing extraordinary braces comes up and says, "Ah, I see you're reading *Illuminatus!*..." and I say, "Yes, I am," and he says, "Well, I'm mounting an enthusiast's production of that in the Liverpool School of Language, Music, Dream and Pun." I told him I was an actor. "Ah," he says, "then you could be in it." And I carried on drinking and that was that.

'I still used to weekend with friends in Liverpool occa-sionally, and several months later I went there and then missed my train home at Lime Street, so I went down to Mathew Street to get a cup of coffee. I went to something I thought was the Armadillo Café. I had no idea it was about to be transformed into something else. And standing at the café counter, with a suitcase – he'd just arrived – was this bloke from the pub, and he went, "Oh, you made it then." I walked in and stayed there for six or seven weeks. I never stopped laughing.' Nighy had never seen the Road Show and had failed to recognise Ken Campbell, but he was instantly installed as his gofer. The two must have made a strange double act. 'Ken told me to go and buy a big black book and a pen. "I will be Fellini," he said, "and you will be Fellini's assistant." And we'd go to bars in search of pretty girls – we needed submariners in Atlantis who would be attractively costumed – and, as Fellini's assistant, I would go up to these girls and say, "Excuse me, my colleague and I are representatives of the Science Fiction Theatre of Liverpool and we are mounting an enthusiast's production of *The Illuminatus! Trilogy* by Robert Anton Wilson and Robert Shea and we wondered if you'd done any acting, or indeed were interested in doing any..." And they would say, "Yeah, well, y'know, yeah," and I would say, "If you come to the Armadillo Café on the evening of November the (whatever it was), you can be in it." And we did that all over town. I used to wake up every morning with sore ribs because I'd been laughing so much.

'We had a tiny office at the back of the café with a wall chart, which I think I made, a stage that was the size of a dining table, and we had no money. At first, it was just me and him. The next person in was George Harvey Webb, who was our scholar, with many boxes of research and references. Ken called me "Niffy" because he couldn't quite grasp my name. He liked everyone to have a title. Mine was something like the Amazing Memory Man. George was the Man Whose Subject Was War. John Joyce would become The Greatest Bit-Part Player in the World. One day, Ken went off to a *Star Trek* convention and left me holding the fort, with George poring over his card index. A woman from the RSC came in to ask about the project and opined that Ken had obviously gone completely mad this time. I told her we were doing the show over there, pointing to a space the size of a rabbit hutch, and that there were 450 speaking parts. She said this was ridiculous. At which point George, who never really said all that much, looked up and said, "Why don't you go back to Stratford and continue to finger-fuck with sixteenth-century poets?"'

Campbell and 'Niffy' gave up on Charlton Heston and continued their casting in a corner burger bar. They wired John Huston in Mexico: 'Come and play Hagbard Celine in *Illuminatus!* STOP No money but great wheeze STOP.' Ken then told his assistant to call Cornel Wilde with the same offer, but the agent told Nighy that Cornel was dead and therefore couldn't come along. Most of the £4,000 from the Arts Council went on such communications. The Labour MP and actor Andrew Faulds – who was in the original *Journey into Space* on radio, and thus a great hero of Ken's – was also approached; Ken wanted him to come and launch the whole affair in a spacesuit he was going to get from someone he knew at NASA.

On the appointed day, everyone who'd been contacted either turned up at Aunt Twacky's, or didn't. The doors opened, and in they tumbled, for a meet-and-greet and for Ken to start allotting the roles. Nighy had been told to bring some wine from the off-licence: Niffy in a jiffy to the offy. Name tags had been written out. Chris Langham – 'I was credited as co-director but of course I wasn't' – brought along his friend from Bristol University, David Rappaport, who was a dwarf and was teaching in Yorkshire. Jim Broadbent came along with Prunella Gee, his best friend at LAMDA, now a shooting star of film and television, and earmarked as Mavis the beautiful guerrilla; she'd had a fling with Chris Langham (who had been going out with her best friend) and imagined that Chris had a reunion in mind...

Fairly typical, too, was the recruitment of Chris Fairbank to the cause. Fairbank had left RADA in 1974 and been sent on probation to a hostel in Liverpool by the Saffron Walden magistrates' court (he'd been thrown out of two schools for drugs possession). He later joined the Merseyside Unity Theatre. After RADA, he drifted through weekly rep, but, following a production of *London Assurance* at Swansea Rep, he had decided anything would be preferable to any more work with French's acting editions in his hand. So he squatted, busked, went to sea as a deckhand, picked fruit in Avignon and did a few Friday-morning workshops with Steven Berkoff.

Then, while working in the bar at the Roundhouse, he plucked up courage to introduce himself to Campbell and asked if he was doing a production. 'Indeed I am,' said Ken, 'it's an adaptation of these three fattish volumes, and what you've got to do is read them and phone me up and tell me what part you want to play.' When Fairbank phoned him, and said he'd like to play George Dorn, he was told, 'No, Langham's bagged him.' 'Okay, then the dwarf...' 'No, we've got a real live dwarf for that.' 'What about the homosexual assassin who claims to have shot JFK, Harry Cohen?' 'Oh yeah, you can play him.'

Another actor, Chris Taynton, had done glorious work in the first seasons of Giles Havergal and Philip Prowse's revolutionary tenure at the Glasgow Citizens, and he was cast as Robert Putney Drake, Head of the Mafia and the Man who Murdered God. But one absentee at the first gathering was the man they'd marked down as playing a sheriff who had a limp. On their perambulations around the city, Ken and Nighy had found a Welsh tramp with a proper limp, and it was one of Nighy's jobs to go down to the docks at night – the tramp occupied a bench by the pier head – to give him a couple of bob and run a rehearsal. Nighy insists he would have been very good – they'd even arranged to have him deloused by the council before the Everyman Theatre would loan them a sheriff's outfit – but the tramp had limped away before the day of reckoning.

'Several of the submariner ladies we'd accosted in bars arrived,' says Nighy, 'including one who was very beautiful, wearing a sort of diaphanous shirt and nothing else, and she came over to me and said, "Well, I'm here," and I said, "Well, good," and she did look absolutely marvellous and then at one point she said, "Is there anywhere you and I can go and get a drink together?" and I said, "Well, yes, but I'm on sort of duty, it's the big night." Ken announced that we were all going back to his place with Chris to have a brainstorming session and company meeting and I said that I really couldn't join them. I said I had to go out, and pointed at this vision of a girl. "Oh, I see... but be here first thing in the morning." I took this young lady to what was then my spiritual home, the Somali social club, where I basically lived – you could eat meat and rice with pak choi sauce for 50p, drink Special Brew or neat liquor, and listen to the jukebox which was mostly playing James Brown, or George McCrae's "Rock Your Baby". Soon after getting there, and halfway down her pint of cider, this girl said, "Is there anywhere we can go and screw." I muttered something about "my place" and we got into her mother's Fiat – and she wrapped me round a tree on the central reservation in Princess Avenue. I spent a couple of months in hospital, as indeed did she. She was a charming woman. I don't remember her name. And I couldn't be in the show.'

The dreaded penta-curse, two plus three, would not be denied. After Nighy and the gorgeous unknown submariner were immobilised on the first day of the five-week rehearsal period, four more accidents came along in quick succession: Sean ('Ocean') O'Halligan, Peter's cousin, a notable installation artist, got hit over the head with a bottle of Pils in a bar fight; John Joyce drunkenly drove his motor scooter down a hole in the road and broke his collarbone; Chris Taynton got into another bar brawl and had his nose broken; and Neil Cunningham, the wonderfully well-spoken actor of the cut-glass accent and laser glare, a member of Laurence Olivier's National Theatre company at the Old Vic, who had generously agreed to assume the mantle of Hagbard Celine in the continuing absence of Charlton Heston, Marlon Brando, Sean Connery and John Huston, was bitten on the wrist by a dog – and the bite was in the shape of a 'V'. Joyce, Taynton and Cunningham were all fit enough to open on 23 November. Richard Eyre had been drafted in to help with the set-up; he had declined to participate even though offered a role. 'Peter Hall's turned it down,' Ken had told him. 'It's the part of the man who wants to run the world. It's not bad, and you're only on for three minutes.' John Joyce was Saul Goodman, the New York cop who talks faster than he thinks, George Harvey Webb the Aleister Crowley-influenced satanist Padre Pederasti, and Prunella Gee, a too-late contender for the Perfect Woman title in *The Great Caper*, doubled as an unbelievably sexy Mavis and Eris, Greek goddess of confusion, known to the Romans as Discordia and thus patron saint of the Discordian Society.

John Joyce, when invited to participate, had been asked if he would need any money. He wanted to keep his London flat going, so he said he needed £50 a week. When he arrived in Liverpool, he discovered that he was the only person being paid, so he bought all the rounds in the pub, and thus became poorer than any of them. As he had a Bachelor of Commerce degree from Melbourne University, he offered to act as administrator now 'Niffy' was out of contention, confined to hospital. Through friends at the BBC, he arranged for a short documentary on the rehearsal period to be made for a local news programme, and that raised a few bob in expenses for beer and sandwiches. He then asked around the company as to who needed money for food, transport and accommodation, and paid out accordingly. But most people lived off what they received in dole money. You could just about still do this in the mid- to late 1970s, but it was becoming harder.

'At a company meeting,' remembers Bill Nighy, 'Ken said that in terms of tone, or policy, if you like, we should ask ourselves the question, "Is it heroic?" And the designer Bill Drummond went directly to his workshop, which was basically a table out the back, and wrote on the wall above it in big white letters, "Is It Heroic?" I always remember that as one of the first "acts" of the whole enterprise... and, fuck me, did Bill deliver!' Miracles, and wonders too marvellous to relate, were wrought by Drummond, an art-school graduate, a regular at Aunt Twacky's, and a stagehand at the Everyman, who would take his *Illuminatus!* experience of subversive Discordianism into the music business when he and Jim Cauty formed bands in the 1980s called The JAMs (The Justified Ancients of Mu Mu), The Timelords and the globally successful KLF. His design was one of the most incredible demonstrations of the art of the impossible I've ever seen. 'I initially came up with far more abstract ideas than we went with,' says Drummond, 'and Ken rubbished them as not being "heroic" enough. He was immensely inspiring. And getting stuff for scenery for no money was really very easy; Liverpool was just a pile of broken-down buildings. Half the city was derelict in those days, and you could pick up almost anything.' Drummond's interiors for the show were scaled down, furniture and walls were at odd angles, and the use of false perspective was both witty and disorienting. A brainwashing scene was played simply with just two chairs and a bed; the death of Dutch Schultz (played by Jim Broadbent), who expired in a frenzy on another foreshortened bed, was the best onstage onset of paranoia I've ever seen, weird and devastating. One fortune-telling scene was played in the vertical plane on the back wall, allowing us to see the tarot cards. It was as if you were watching the scene from above: there was Velcro on the table so, for instance, a hat placed on it would stay there, defying gravity. In the second play, *Swift Kick Inc*, there was a brilliant puppet play-within-a-play and in the fourth, *Walpurgisnacht Rock*, there was a full-blown rock concert.

Brian Aldiss, writing a column in the *Guardian*, hailed the show as a long strip-cartoon version of every possible twentieth-century phobia, while describing the experience of that first marathon in Mathew Street (although the time flew past) as something Bertrand Russell and Genghis Khan might have cooked up between them while sitting down to rewrite *Monty Python*. What I most enjoyed was the seeming spontaneity of it all, the sense of both lunacy and extravagance on a mighty adventure, with Ken Campbell cackling and goading on the sidelines as if conjuring the whole madcap project into existence. If he'd left the room perhaps it would have all subsided like a deflated soufflé. Of course, some people, including one or two of the actors, took the actual content a lot more seriously than the ingenuity of their own performances. The sex, drugs and black magic came straight out of the underground cult literature of the day, filtered through the hallucinated oratory of Timothy Leary, who believed that he was receiving extraterrestrial communications from the Dog Star Sirius, which had only been successfully photographed in 1970.

'On 23 July 1973, the Sirius thing began,' Robert Anton Wilson told James Nye. 'I started getting these Sirius flashes before I knew about the Egyptian priests and their rituals to Sirius. It was all so weird and Jungian that I began to think it was more than synchronicity, and that there was real communication going on and that I had tuned in to it – into an interstellar ESP channel. As a result of the mental transformations I went through, I started developing precognition and a heavy level of ESP. I found myself projecting to other parts of the country. All these things confirmed that it wasn't just my imagination. I had objective evidence that I was seeing the future. I began to think through my experiments with certain kinds of cabbalistic magic. I had hooked into some occult tradition that's been going on since Ancient Egypt that involved contact with extraterrestrials.' Wilson's daughter, Luna, had been killed a few months before this interview in a bungled robbery, and yet Wilson found the most overwhelmingly powerful moment in the production to be the sudden frisson of guilt Saul Goodman feels about having sent people to the electric chair.

The actors played this scene twice, once without emotion, once with – the Xerox machine had mistakenly made two copies of one page, so when the actors found themselves going through the scene twice, Campbell had been quick to spot the potential bonus, a brilliant piece of direction. Campbell himself was only interested in this drug-fuelled quagmire of conspiracy and counter-conspiracy, synchronicity and sex-ploitation, world domination and rampant paranoia, as a means to an end; and that end was an astonishing theatre creation that also slotted obviously into Peter Brook's Rough Theatre category. While every word spoken was taken from the books, the choice of material was remarkable for its stage-worthiness. The most hilarious episodes included the initiation of Saul Goodman into a secret society at a black mass supervised by Padre Pederasti; an underwater battle with *Doctor Who*-like effects and a singing dolphin called Howard; George's encounter with a naked belly dancer who specialises in bringing all men to orgasm quickly and often (her efforts culminate in her disappearance through George's tiny bed); and the sudden appearance at the rock concert of a clean-cut quartet in white judo outfits calling themselves the American Medical Association.

Bill Nighy discharged himself from hospital on crutches because his father had died, and carried on supporting the enterprise, drinking with Bill Drummond and enjoying the buzz the show generated. 'We'd been accused of being elitist somewhere. Ken was irritated by that and decided that if we were indeed an elitist company then we ought to have an elitist audience, so he made it a requirement that if you wanted to buy a ticket you had to fill in a questionnaire to see if you were suitable as a member of the League of Discordia. When Peter Hall came up, I think we made a sort of gallery for him, with a sofa raised on a rostrum of boxes in the corner.' The welcome must have worked, because Peter Hall booked *Illuminatus!* to open the National Theatre's third auditorium, the Cottesloe, and waxed lyrical in his *Diaries*: 'It's mad, and deliberately kitsch, and it shows Ken Campbell's acute intelligence at work. Some wonderful things: Chris Langham's extremely impressive performance – energetic, naive, goofy, true, very funny; and Dave Rappaport's twenty-minute turn on his own in which he discusses how he's taken on the world and tried to screw it up in all sorts of minor and major ways, each springing from his various phobias. The sight of his final phobia – self-phobia – is amazing. He hurls himself round the stage trying to get away from his own diminutive body, his own tiny unwanted limbs.' The role of the midget Markoff Chaney, who declares his own war on Law and Order and predictability, and who dedicates his life to being the random factor in every equation ('From this day forward, unto death, it will be civil war: the Midget against the Digits'), catapulted Rappaport into a glorious fifteen-year career that ended in Los Angeles in May 1990 when he shot himself through the heart in a dog park, aged thirty-eight. The manner of his suicide proves, says Chris Langham, that he was never happy in his body, and the Chaney speech was a premonition of that wish-fulfilment. 'When he killed himself, it was his body he wanted to kill. David had a kind of default setting with the world and with nature.'

Illuminatus! toured to the Mickery Theatre in Amsterdam for a month before arriving in London. The Mickery, under the direction of Ritsaert ten Cate, was a crucible of the fringe and avant-garde theatre, especially from Britain, throughout the 1970s. A Mickery gig guaranteed bookings and fame and/or notoriety throughout the rest of Europe; and a very good time while you were there. Chris Fairbank reports that 'after every show, all the heads in Amsterdam would be queuing up, chopping up lines, and we snorted it up, and back we went – to a pinball machine, as I recall, in my case. One night, Langham came through with this typed-out sheet of philosophy based on the drug PCP... and there were free samples to be had. It was a synthetic chemical on grass, part of which was used to process film. The bloke had said it was like an acid trip in thirty seconds, so of course we had to do this. It sucked all your energy out and all you wanted to do was sleep for three days. We tried some before a show and it was a disaster. So I decided there and then not to start messing about with anything before the show... after the show, completely different story. But that didn't mean you didn't have a beer, or some grass or something... we were in a bubble that all seemed perfectly appropriate to the work.'

But this precautionary discipline wasn't always observed, not even at the National Theatre. Bill Nighy was recovering well, but not well enough for Amsterdam. He was up and almost running, however, for the Cottesloe opening on 4 March 1977, with John Gielgud as the voice of the speaking computer. The show started that chill Friday morning at 10 a.m. Nighy had been up all night – 'You know how it is, or at least, was' – and was walking around the grey concrete theatre on the South Bank waiting for the canteen to open at 8 a.m. 'I went in on the stroke of eight and got some eggs. There was no one else in there, then in walks this guy in a safari jacket and golfing hat with a camera round his neck. He introduced himself as Robert Anton Wilson. He asked if I was nervous and I said, "No, but I'll get nervous later," and he said, "I was so nervous this morning I had to take a tab of acid," and he offered me one and I said thanks but that I was okay for the minute with my eggs. Later, he came into the boys' dressing room with a big pad of blotting paper and twenty-four trips dropped out on it and he offered them round. He'd brought them all in from Frisco or somewhere. Everyone went very quiet and then... "Yeah, why not, thanks," and we all dived in.

So we were all tripping. It's a terrible idea if you want to act, but there you are... Neil Cunningham, whom I adored, and I were tripping, and at one point in the play we had to "act" tripping, alone on the stage together, while the building, so to speak, was "thrown" at us in lights and sound. And I said, out of the corner of my mouth, "How do we act tripping as we already are anyway?" And he said, "Well, I think you just hold my hand." And we did just stand there holding hands. It was very witty on Neil's part and also very lovely, and also very true. You can't act tripping. You just hold hands, which is as good as anything.'

There were other altered states in the play, too. There was far more definition, surprisingly in the far-out circumstances, to the *Flash Gordon* manner in which the plays jump-cut and recapitulated events, and stopped for a big hippy lecture on the magical properties of the number 23. The structure was tightened up, and a long speech about the Kennedy assassinations removed, possibly for legal reasons. The show now ended, more or less, with the rock festival at Ingolstadt in Bavaria – and a brilliant restructuring of the narrative, on grounds of clarity, contained a riveting new pseudo-Platonic dialogue between Hagbard Celine and George Dorn. There have been some wonderful 'event' shows in the Cottesloe down the years since it opened – notably the Bill Bryden epics *Lark Rise to Candleford* and *The Mysteries* – but the place has never loosened its stays as totally as it did in that opening production. Nighy recalls folk bringing in hampers and decanting their wine around the back of the seating. Alan Ayckbourn was in conversation with Peter Hall one day in the corridor when the caretaker interrupted them: 'Mr 'All, Mr Campbell's dog has been crapping in the Cottesloe again.' 'Oh, and what does Mr Campbell say?' 'He says no one ever complained about it before...'

A month before *Illuminatus!* opened in London, Peter Hall's subject in his farewell show as presenter of the television arts programme *Aquarius* was Ken Campbell, whom he dubbed 'the Firework Man'. The interview was all the more effective because it was preceded by snapshot résumés of

Hall's encounters with three illustrious 'greats': the opera singer Dame Janet Baker, who spoke decorously of the tension between fun and creativity; the painter Francis Bacon, who found most people boring; and the concert pianist Arthur Rubinstein, who summarised his job as not upsetting the dead composers. Ken Campbell set out to lower the tone, perched on a stool in a polo-necked sweater and a black leather jacket, eyes gleaming, hair frizzed like Mr Pickwick's, and Werner the dog running loose around the white cyclorama of Hall's chic and antiseptic studio. Hall is not, never was, a stuffed shirt, but an air of hallowed sanctity hung over the programme, partly emanating from Hall's seriousness and natural gravitas. But there were some spirited exchanges, as Hall accused Campbell of flippancy for the sake of it:

> 'My whole approach is based on misbehaviour, that's true, and on the assumption that everyone who tells us things is wrong.'
> 'What do you give the actor: confidence, enthusiasm?'
> 'A kick!'
> 'How do you direct a play?'
> 'I keep clear of it as much as possible.'
> 'What makes you angry about an actor?'
> 'When they're not happy enough, so I throw them against walls. I throw small, miserable people against walls. I'm a coward.'

Hall summarised the interview in his *Diaries*: 'An exhausting two hours allowing Ken Campbell to talk at me, playing straight man to his comic. He is a total anarchist and impossible to pin down. He more or less said it was a crime to be serious.' It's a bit of a cover cloud, but Campbell always maintained the pretence of not working at the craft too seriously, with a sort of self-deprecatory nonchalance that could be catching. Nighy recalls Ken being cornered by another interviewer at a later date and forgetting his own spiel. So he turned to Nighy for verification: '"Niffy, why don't we rehearse?" And I said – as I was keeper of the spiel – "We don't rehearse because it's a civil-service conspiracy to rehearse out of any material any of the danger and spontaneity that might have recommended it to us in the first place." This idea was, of course, a godsend to me as a young actor because I was so terrified and self-conscious. My least favourite bit of being an actor is rehearsal. So, when Ken didn't rehearse, it did me a power of good. My nightmare was doing stuff while the other actors watched. I didn't mind the audience so much...'

Although he was less keen on acting himself in shows he directed, Campbell often joined in – as a director – and Chris Fairbank cites the case of one Nigel Gray, who was playing a small part in Liverpool but making too much of a meal of it, and outstaying his welcome onstage. 'I was waiting to go on, and I could sense that the audience had gone, and Ken said to me, "Is he always this slow?" Nigel wittered on and suddenly Ken couldn't stand it any longer and he stuck his head round and said, "Speed it up, Nigel, for fuck's sake!" And the audience stamped and cheered... it didn't faze Nigel at all. He didn't speed it up. Nor did he miss a beat. He just carried on.'

After the sold-out run at the Cottesloe, the National wanted to capitalise on success and arranged a season, with an independent producing management, at the Roundhouse, in the small cellar theatre, where it opened on 19 April, trimmed from twelve hours (including intervals) to just four. This was a bad idea because, as Chris Langham said, 'it went from being a fantastic day in your life to being a dreadfully long play. It just seemed longer when it was shorter.' But there was a poetic justice in *Illuminatus!* ending up in the Chalk Farm fastness of the hippy alternative culture. Drugs were even more freely available than they had been in Amsterdam. 'In one of the intervals,' says Langham, who's completely clean these days, 'a guy came backstage into the dressing rooms and emptied two grams of cocaine onto the table. He said, "You've made me so happy, this is my gift..." Neil Cunningham and I looked at each other. We couldn't leave it there, obviously. So we divided it up and went onstage with lumps of coke hanging out of our noses. I sat there going "Whoooooaaaggghh!" and then Neil starts his big Hagbard Celine speech on the submarine, which is not one hundred per cent terribly interesting and could go on a bit. This night it was just incredibly gripping and, at the end, the audience rose as a man and gave this rather tedious speech a standing ovation, as though he'd just sung the most amazing operatic aria; which, that night, he had. And, as he sat down on the set next to me, he stage-whispered to me in that extravagant manner so typical of him, "I feel absolutely incandescent." '

John Joyce, too, attested to the view that the best way to fight the idea some of them had – that the Illuminati themselves had grabbed hold of this production – was to fight them with vegetables, and it was decided to take strength from vegetation. So Joyce tried cocaine for two or three nights before settling on some Thai grass, which was very strong and slowed him down a lot, something he found very interesting in performance (even if the audience did not). 'The trouble was that this dope played strange tricks, such as taking the scene we played vertically back, in my mind, into the horizontal plane, and my peripheral vision was going all over the place.'

Someone even more affected by the power of the Illuminati was Chris Taynton, who forsook the life of a successful rep and West End actor in favour of a rooted belief that he was in touch with the Dog Star Sirius. He was living with his mother in Mill Hill when he woke up one morning, he says, with a triangle of white light in the middle of the bedroom: the eye of the pyramid, the Holy Trinity. When the play was over at the NT, he started doing research on it and, while admitting he was green and gullible, got mentally enmeshed in paranormal paranoia. And he was obsessed with unicorns. In 1982, several years after *Illuminatus!*, his mind was, he says, 'a spaghetti junction' of conspiracy theories and paranormal sightings. He went completely mad and assaulted a lady neighbour in Mill Hill. He was on a mission to release her dogs, which were never allowed out. In her house, she rebuffed his attack with the leg of a coffee table, which he saw as the horn of a unicorn; he turned it on the woman and gouged out one of her eyes. He now says, ruefully, and without irony or self-pity, that he really did get hold of the wrong end of the stick. Ken got a call from Camden police station – 'Mr Campbell, we've got a man here who says you will know all about the Illuminations.' Eventually, when the case came to trial, Ken had to go to the Old Bailey and give evidence. Diagnosed as a paranoid schizophrenic, Taynton was sent to Broadmoor for three years where 'I managed to keep what was left of my sanity by working in the gardens; the first thing they did was hand me a machete!' He then spent another three years in a hospital in Ealing, then three years in an aftercare home before settling, more or less normally, into his own place in 1995.

A much happier consequence of the show was the change in Ken's personal life. Early in rehearsals in Liverpool, Prunella Gee started appearing with Werner's dog chain slung around her neck. She and Ken had fallen in love, to the surprise of everyone, including themselves. She was the new 'Mavis' – guerrilla woman – in his life and also the Perfect Woman. Robert Anton Wilson said she was the sexiest actress he'd seen since Marilyn Monroe.

The Illuminati went underground again after their exposure by the Science Fiction Theatre of Liverpool, though of course they live on in the novels. *Illuminatus!*, the play, has never been revived since. In 2008, Hollywood director Ron Howard filmed Dan Brown's blockbuster novel *Angels and Demons*, about the interference of the Illuminati in a modern-day papal election in Rome. Tom Hanks played a Harvard professor, a symbologist, who tries to track down the evil order before they execute the cardinals they've taken hostage, with an ultimate threat to blow up the Vatican. It's an entertaining enough movie in its way, restricting the definition of the Illuminati to a bunch of weirdos who've inherited the medieval grudge of their precursors against the Catholic Church because of its persecution of scientists and non-believers. So these Illuminati are baddies who've infiltrated the Establishment – even in the upper echelons of the Church itself – dabbling in the ancient arts of pentagrams, branding and Latin inscriptions; while in a parallel scientific world, Hanks's fellow goodies in the modern enlightenment are isolating the God particle in their researches. Missing from the movie are all the elements that made *Illuminatus!* such fun and so original in the theatre: genuine paranoia, conspiracy delirium, a grown-up sense of absurdity about a phenomenon which, if true, becomes a dramatic metaphor of adventurous, heroic behaviour in the drama, and a lack of moral decision-making about the business. It was always Ken Campbell's supposition that our everyday lives would be much improved by knowing a bit more about what took us beyond them and might be bigger than us and beyond our comprehension. He wouldn't have wanted to see it all stamped out in an Oscar-serious performance by Tom Hanks in an overblown Hollywood movie: the Science Fiction Theatre of Liverpool's *Illuminatus!*, as Jim Broadbent kept reminding Chris Taynton, to no avail, was 'only a play'.

7

True Prue

Chris Langham had taken Prunella Gee along to meet Ken before he went to Liverpool. He told her about *Illuminatus!* and, before she knew where she was, she was travelling northwards with Jim Broadbent to join the company, whereupon she seemed to have moved in with Ken 'terribly quickly'. Nothing in her career to date, nor her background, prepared her for this. She was posh, blonde, sexy and terribly well brought up, the fourth of sixth children in a Leicestershire family who lived in Rutland and owned Stead and Simpson Shoes. They also once owned the fledgling Midland Bank, then just a small county business. There was some small connection with the world of Ken Campbell, who spent his last years living in a Swiss chalet in Loughton on the edge of Epping Forest: Prue's mother had met her father when she was living in Woodford, Essex, working in Regent's Park Zoo; the couple had married in High Beech Church – about a mile away from Ken's chalet...

Prue had been packed off to Duncombe Park School on the North Yorkshire Moors and then Benenden School in Cranbrook, Kent, where she was one year ahead of Princess Anne. She graduated from the London Academy of Music and Drama (LAMDA) in 1972 and was immediately cast in the leading role of the free-spirited Anna Fitzgerald in Howard Spring's *Shabby Tiger*, a seven-part television mini-series in 1973, in which she achieved overnight notoriety as the first full-frontal nude on British television. She had a top agent, Peter Crouch, and her career took off.

In September 1973, a few months after the Road Show had returned to the Royal Court's Upstairs studio, she appeared as one of three home-bound siblings on the Court's main stage in David Storey's *The Farm*, a sort of feminist counterpart to his own *In Celebration*. The director was Ken's idol Lindsay Anderson, and as the youngest daughter, Brenda – her parents were played by Bernard Lee and Doreen Mantle, her brother by Frank Grimes – Prue gave a really fine performance, waging little battles round the hearth on behalf of 'the revolution'. The play transferred to the Mayfair Theatre. This led to work on *The Sweeney*, a highly popular police action series starring John Thaw and Dennis Waterman, and to fourth billing behind Sidney Poitier, Michael Caine and Nicol Williamson in Ralph Nelson's political thriller *The Wilby Conspiracy* (1975). 'So, at the time, I was quite hot,' says Prue, 'and going to Liverpool to join Ken's company was considered to be quite an eccentric move.' Her public profile – which was titivated on an almost daily basis in the gossip columns, notably the *Evening Standard* diary – placed her several show-business leagues away from the sort of work Campbell was up to. But drugs and drink are great social and cultural levellers, and the maelstrom into which Prue plunged in Mathew Street was clearly in some sort of tune with the hedonist side of her own showbiz lifestyle.

After Liverpool, she returned to London with Ken, sold up her flat in Mortlake, and learned to live with ferrets and falafels on Haverstock Hill. As a genuinely adorable and 'nicely brought-up' person, she fitted in well, too, with Dave and Jane; they were all now a fairly happy household which gravitated mostly around Dave and Jane's dining table. The Load of Hay next door was a welcoming rough-house venue and the pub of choice (now transformed beyond recognition into a gastro-bistro-theque called The Hill). And to the right, in the large villas going up the hill to Hampstead, were two or three of the longest-standing squats in the capital.

While the *Illuminatus!* cast dispersed in all directions, Campbell fretted about where his next big project might come from. *Illuminatus!* had buoyed him up and redoubled his energy. He was determined to keep the Science Fiction The-atre of Liverpool afloat and produced two remarkable but smaller-scale shows in this period. The first, *Psychosis Unclas-sified*, came about at the specific request of Chris Fairbank and John Joyce, who comprised the entire cast of two. The piece was just eighty minutes long (after the eight-hour-plus *Illumi-natus!*), thus effectively pulling out the rug from under the expectations of most critics and audiences. The play – which transferred to the Bush Theatre in London in September 1977, after a Liverpool premiere in Mathew Street, and went on to Amsterdam and New York – was adapted by Campbell and Fairbank from Theodore Sturgeon's psychological novel *Some of Your Blood*. Fairbank played George, a soldier who is under investigation by an army psychiatrist (Joyce) after an incident of unprovoked violence against a fellow soldier. The psychia-trist, in a sense, was the Campbellian 'goader', urging George to draw everything in his life that was important to him; these drawings were simultaneously projected on a screen in the theatre, lending a curious atmosphere of simultaneous con-fession and revelation. We are taken backwards through George's childhood, his first encounter with his girlfriend, Anna, while milking cows, the recreation of the knife murder of an old man who was harming his mother, the blood he con-sumed when his mother fed him – turns out he's some kind of wolf-boy and his last message to Anna was, 'Dear Anna, I Miss You, I Wish I Had Some of Your Blood.' An extreme view of maternal deprivation, perhaps, but you can see where it might have fitted into Campbell's own experience...

Joyce recalls Ken 'leaving us to get on with it and mak-ing lunch when necessary'. But Campbell wasn't happy with the performance at the Bush and summoned the actors for a rehearsal after the opening there. It wasn't bad, he told John Joyce, but there was no actual 'theatre' in the piece. He said that Chris was too busy not telling the story and that John was too busy being a psychiatrist. He introduced some actions that loosened up the interrogation, so that Joyce now brought Fair-bank some chocolate cake when he curled up in a foetal position, and relieved the tension of the inquiry by changing his (Joyce's) socks and spraying his feet. 'What Ken did was hook us properly into these human beings with bodily functions.' In doing so he created a prophetic little gem of Dostoevskyan theatre, a type of psychological chamber play that would become increasingly current in fringe theatres over the next ten years, climaxing, perhaps, in the commercial success of Joe Penhall's *Blue/Orange* (2000) – in which Bill Nighy played the psychiatrist.

Others left 'to get on with it' were Camilla Saunders and Mavis Taylor, who wanted somehow to continue their collaboration, having been Musical Director and Assistant Designer, respectively, on *Illuminatus!* (Mavis had taken over the care of the design from Bill Drummond at the Roundhouse and had provided the six-foot-high inflatable cosmic apple which was fertilised by Chris Langham's priapic George Dorn.) Ken threw them a copy of *The Case of Charles Dexter Ward*, H. P. Lovecraft's brilliant horror novella, and the result was one of the best new operas of the day – it was also an extension of *Illuminatus!* in its spirit and technical adventurousness, as was clear when the production arrived from Liverpool at the ICA Theatre in April 1978. It was also a significant stepping stone towards the mother of all Ken Campbell projects, *The Warp*, at the end of the decade. Lovecraft's story charts a necromantic collision in time between an eighteenth-century New England alchemist and his bookish descendent, Charles Dexter Ward, whose genealogical studies lead him to engage in Transylvanian pursuits beyond the comprehension both of his parents and of an inquisitive doctor. Campbell's production, aided by Mavis, traded in Drummond-style tricks of perspective and, thanks to Saunders, a concatenation of Gothic effects, linked to random sounds coming from outside through a system of cylinders. Saunders's score, written over the winter of 1977, was the most musically 'worked-out' in all of Campbell's shows, with long passages of recitative, all crafted with Neil Cunningham in mind, though Jonathan Hyde was a more than able substitute when Cunningham was unavailable (Neil later played the role during Ken's brief tenure at the Liverpool Everyman). Hyde, a superb classical actor with a long association in that decade with the Glasgow Citizens – he had most recently played possibly the grandest Lady Bracknell since Martita Hunt's – was sensational as Dexter Ward, with a waxen face of weird translucence exactly as described by Lovecraft himself.

There was no dialogue in the book, nor in this version, which was performed entirely in the third person. Camilla Saunders – who had studied folk music in Romania after taking her degree at Oxford, and had turned up in Liverpool for *Illuminatus!* when tipped off about 'an interesting bunch of people' there – says that Ken was worried for a time about the complete absence of sex or romance in the piece, but in the end they stayed entirely faithful not only to Lovecraft's carefully described landscapes but also to the heart of his magical world and its threat to the norms of social existence as exemplified in the Puritanism of Providence, Rhode Island. Mavis Taylor assembled the set from discarded bits and pieces at the National Theatre and built it in the house at Bow in the East End of London in which she was squatting with her then boyfriend, the actor and comedian Keith Allen, then right at the start of his career. He played a butler in the show. Allen borrowed a van to drive the set up to Liverpool, where Mavis literally stood it up around the actors while Camilla Saunders streamed in the music.

Two factors contributed to Ken's slightly 'inbetween state' during this year: his father died in August 1977 and Prue was pregnant with, as she turned out, Daisy Eris Campbell, born in September 1978. Ken never talked much about his father, except to invoke his injunction for him to concentrate on the comedy side of things in his work. But he was utterly devoted to him and often said how pleased he would have been had he known that he, Ken, would end up living on the end of the 167 bus route from Ilford to Epping Forest. Colin Campbell had married Betty in June 1961, just as Ken was graduating from RADA. She was a widow he had met, like Elsie, at the tennis club. She had a son, Richard, a few years younger than Ken, who played hockey for Essex and married one of *his* club's leading young players. Colin retired from the cable company in November 1968, having suffered a mild heart attack the previous September. He was in hospital for two or three weeks – he had only taken about twenty days off in forty-nine years of employment but, as he wrote in *M-I-M*, 'the whole record went for a burton a mere eight weeks from the deadline!'

He and Betty had rented a cottage in Helston, Cornwall, for a holiday one year and found they loved the West Country so much that they moved permanently to Croyde, a seaside village in North Devon, in 1972. The large residence came with an acre of land and faced the Atlantic, with a distant prospect of Lundy Island. Ten bedrooms had already been converted into three self-contained flats, so Colin and Betty were joined in the move by his newly retired brother-in-law (Elsie's brother), a bank manager in East Ham, and his (the brother-in-law's) widowed sister. Three Ilford properties thus went on the market simultaneously: three households moved to Croyde, where Ken went cavorting starkers over the dunes in the first of his great monologues, *Furtive Nudist*. Colin records that they were happy beyond measure, each family with its own front door yet always ready for 'one gigantic family party' – very different social occasions they must have been from what the *Illuminatus!* tribe got up to.

Ken's dad got stuck into his memoirs in these years, sitting out on the lawn, typing away, describing species of birds, as well as the moles and, especially, the plants in the garden and his plans for bringing more stones up the steps from the beach to extend the rockery. He diffidently explored the possibility of publication, though he never once invoked the theatrical eminence of his son when submitting his manuscript. In January 1974 he received a brusque rejection letter from J. F. Gibson's literary agency in Holborn, pleading the double excuse of the general crisis (this was the time of Conservative Prime Minister Edward Heath's three-day weeks and endless trade unions' strikes) and the paper shortage. In the summer of 1977, Chris Fairbank drove down to Cornwall with Ken – he was embarked on an ill-fated scheme to drum up a show about Doc Shiels, the self-styled wizard and psychic who had allegedly raised the Loch Ness Monster by telepathy – and stopped off with him in Croyde. (Ken's car, Chris recalls, was a light-blue Austin Cambridge with a defective radiator that required topping up at every garage between London and Cornwall.) Fairbank remembers a 'nice, quiet little man, incredibly unassuming', who impressed him with a mantra often used by Ken. Colin had once told his son, in his old-fashioned way, that the sentence you utter is so much more interesting when it does not begin with an 'I'. Fairbank reckoned that one of the main themes of *Illuminatus!* was the ego-less ego trip, which is, anyway, the ultimate trip; that ideal summed up Colin's modesty in his life and memoirs.

During Prue's pregnancy, Ken took part in two of the major BBC television series of the decade, G. F. Newman's four-part *Law and Order* series, produced by Tony Garnett and directed by Les Blair – his performance as the bent lawyer Alex Gladwell is one of the best things he ever did – and John Cleese and Connie Booth's *Fawlty Towers.* His acting agent since leaving Stoke had been Maureen Vincent of Peters Fraser and Dunlop, who kept in close touch from that time right through to the Friday before he died, when he popped into her Soho office, unannounced as usual, with a whole bunch of puppets: 'He was fantastic in *Law and Order* and probably better on-screen than onstage as an actor because he could just focus on the one take, and not worry about what everyone else was doing, which you do as a director. In some ways he was a nightmare to represent, because he never did anything for the money. He'd get obsessed about a series on television – *Lovejoy*, *Judge John Deed*, *The Bill* – then insist that I found him a part in it; he always wanted to do something for the work, not so much the money. I have never represented anyone else like him, that's for sure.'

Law and Order came out of a time in television drama, inconceivable now, when producers were left to get on with producing drama that was challenging and politically provocative. In the history of cops and robbers on television, it was both unique and groundbreaking, shot in a bleached naturalism, on location in prison cells and housing estates, pubs, backstreet garages and warehouses, with no musical sound-track and a cast of unknown actors, non-actors, and even the odd real-life villain. And it spoke of a widespread, systemic corruption operating between the police, the criminals and the legal profession. G. F. Newman had published a novel about police corruption, *Sir, You Bastard*, in 1969, in which the demarcation lines between police and villains became blurred. It was Tony Garnett's idea to write the same story, as it were, from four points of view, so they came up with the Chaucerian quartet of *A Detective's Tale*, *A Villain's Tale*, *A Brief's Tale* and *A Prisoner's Tale*. Ken was the brief, a high-street solicitor who moved stealthily between cafés, courtrooms and pubs, fixing up paybacks to guarantee immunity, support perjury and basi-cally facilitate a corrupt status quo. The main story concerns a dyed-in-the-wool criminal, Jack Lynn (Peter Dean), planning a supermarket armed robbery in Putney that misfires owing to his being 'grassed up' by a police contact in the underworld. There's also a smash and grab at the Romford gas board in which he's not involved but for which he's 'fitted up' by the fly-ing squad inspector, Fred Pyle (Derek Martin), who needs a conviction at all costs. Newman says that the series was not based on any particular incident but related to 'an assembly of things that really did happen'. And Garnett wanted to shock an audience that didn't want to believe any of what they were being told.

Almost as shocking as the content was the acting or, rather, the non-acting. The lack of style was the ultimate state-ment of one. As Ken gleefully noted, 'Everyone looks a third to half dead in it!' Ken's Alex Gladwell is quietly spoken, con-trolled, slippery, and there's hardly a muscle twitch in the whole performance. It's absolutely riveting. 'I had to take instructions in not acting – we had to retake a couple of scenes because of involuntary eyebrow movement,' he said later. He had no idea of himself as a solicitor, but he was assured that, if he wore a suit, a pair of good shoes and had a haircut, he would convincingly become one. And he did. Alex is a man who's forgotten what a conscience is and meets every situa-tion with a sort of glazed, ferocious lack of concern. There was uproar. The telephone lines to the BBC were jammed with people complaining. Sir Eldon Griffiths MP, parliamentary spokesman for the Police Federation, said that G. F. Newman should be prosecuted for crimes against the state. Ian Trethowan, Director-General of the BBC, was told by the Government that the BBC should be ashamed of itself and that the series should not be seen abroad. But the BBC stood firm, and the series led to changes in the law and a tightening-up of police procedures. Derek Martin, poor fellow, was resoundingly booed at a football match when he went along to support his team, Chelsea, because of the character he played. And Ken, too, was a marked man: 'For some years afterwards, whenever they had a story of corruption in the law, they'd print my picture – in my suit!' As Les Blair remarked, there was a legacy of Ken's great hero, Joan Littlewood, which he exploited, in the crossover between the glamour of show business and crime.

'He was a unique soul, Ken,' says Maureen Vincent, 'and unusual in that he always enjoyed *everything* he did. And he never grumbled about anything. I think he was one of those lucky people who can live entirely in the present moment, so he was always, really, quite happy.' And, according to John Cleese, who was delighted to have him in an episode of *Fawlty Towers*, he was 'such a marvellous, strange, funny man'. Cleese's famous television comedy comprises just twelve episodes, six of them made in 1975 and a second batch of six, including Ken's episode, in 1979. It was created and co-written by Cleese and his then wife, Connie Booth, who played the pert housemaid Polly Sherman, the one figure of seeming sanity in the small hotel in Torquay, Devon, where the series was set. This hotel was run by Basil Fawlty (Cleese) and his wife Sybil (Prunella Scales) with about as much sensitivity and kindness as the Macbeths might have mustered when they asked the neighbours round for dinner in the castle at Dunsinane. Cleese thought of the episode which Ken joined, 'The Anniversary', as moving into Alan Ayckbourn territory, and one of the best in the whole series. There had been a longer rehearsal period than usual following a technicians' strike. Because of this shuffling of dates, the actor Julian Holloway, who had been originally cast as Roger, was unable to complete the job before going on to another commitment, so he withdrew; and Cleese cast Ken.

As a variation on their permanent state of seething married warfare, Basil arranges a surprise party, with friends and paella, to 'celebrate' the couple's fifteenth wedding anniversary – then pretends that he's forgotten it. The ruse backfires when Sybil takes umbrage and drives off in a gigantic huff. As the guests arrive, Basil bundles Polly upstairs to occupy the marital bed, forcing her to pretend to be Sybil, suddenly struck down with illness. Because of the delay in shooting, which gave extra rehearsal time, Cleese says they could do much more than usual in the way of bits of business and visual gags. Ken's Roger, married to Una Stubbs's simpering Alice, was an extreme parody of a bar-room bore, kitted out in a blazer, cravat and white shoes, with a comb-over hairstyle modelled on that of the famous footballer Bobby Charlton – the strands drastically arranged to defy the incontrovertible evidence of near total baldness – and more than a suspicion of ill-fitting teeth. Calling up a gin and tonic when drinks are offered, Roger toasts the host with 'Up yours, Baz!' and proceeds to goad Fawlty with a stream of back-slapping compliments, culminating in a dreadful, punning pronouncement: 'Syb-ill, Bas-well!' The entire cast is caught up in an organic household farce as a rumpus in the kitchen, with spilt drinks and scattered nuts, develops into violence and physical injury in the enforced darkness of 'Syb's' bedroom.

Twenty years after the broadcast, Ken told the comedian John Bird, in a BBC Radio 2 interview, how much he'd enjoyed working with Cleese (he worked with him again, in a tiny role, in the 1988 movie *A Fish Called Wanda*, famously tagged as 'a tale of murder, lust, greed, revenge and seafood'): 'In rehearsal he shows you about a third of it. But when we came to do it, he was looking at me with a different look back from the one he'd given me; so I'd give him another one back!' In comedy, generally, he told Bird, jokes are not often the route to hysteria, noting that with a comedian like Max Wall, who was 'lurkier and murkier', hysteria came about in other ways.

And his comedy idol Ken Dodd 'plays the audience as though it's some kind of instrument. It's a bit like the upturning of a religious experience, and it's aiming towards some kind of catharsis.' *Fawlty Towers* at its best has this kind of quality, and 'The Anniversary' is a good example of comedy evolving out of the cruelty and unhappiness in the stalemate of a tragic marriage; very much as in Ayckbourn, but with, perhaps, an additional element of existential extremism.

Even though he's capable of being very funny, Campbell often doesn't seem to fit into other people's scenarios. In Derek Jarman's fresh and magical low-budget (£150,000) film of *The Tempest* (1979), shot on location in the ruined remains of Stoneleigh Abbey on the Suffolk coast, he's an unlikely Gonzago, the honest counsellor in the shipwrecked party, and there's something disconnected between his appearance and his utterance, as if he's landed from outer space and been programmed by a Shakespearean computer. His friend Heathcote Williams, on the other hand, is an unexpectedly good, very young, hushed Prospero – Jarman cast him, he said, because he *was* Prospero – while Neil Cunningham plays a well-spoken (of course) Sebastian, with Toyah Willcox as Miranda, Christopher Biggins as the drunkard Stephano and Lindsay Kemp's partner, blind Jack Birkett ('The Incredible Orlando'), as a creepily carnal and expressive, raw-egg-sucking Caliban.

The image of a wild-haired Prospero raising the storm by the powers of will and necromancy is not a bad metaphor for a Ken Campbell production, and he was about to embark on the greatest complot of his entire career. He had kept his hand in with a surreal apocalyptic comedy at the New End in Hampstead, *The End is Nigh*, by a novice Liverpool writer, a former Catholic priest, in which Jim Broadbent appeared alongside Neil Cunningham, Dave Hill and two live pigs. The piece was set in a monastery which had been infected by a leak from a neighbouring nuclear plant. The pigs were loaned by Mike Hirst, the *Charivari* impresario who ended up very rich from his hippy circus for festivals and rock concerts. His pigs were kept in a pen at the Roundhouse, and Broadbent, being as he puts it 'reliable', was given the job of pig-wrangler (assisted by John Joyce), loading the porkers into a van every day and driving them up to the little theatre, a converted morgue, just off Hampstead High Street.

John Cleese probably hadn't bargained on the pigs turning up when he invited Ken to be in the first Secret Policeman's Ball (the charity show in aid of Amnesty International) at the Theatre Royal, Drury Lane, in September 1979. But with Joyce back on pig-wrangling duty, and Richard Eyre directing the 'prang to another universe' scene from *Walking Like Geoffrey*, Mike Hirst duly delivered his porkers to the stage door. At the first house, Joyce recalls, the pigs got very upset, jumped off the stage and started mingling with the audience. They were not invited back for the second house. 'A shame, really,' says Joyce. 'Everything else was head-to-head stuff with the Pythons, and Mel Smith and Griff Rhys Jones, all very good, but especially good for television; Ken, with or without pigs, was the only one providing real theatre.' Alan Bennett told James Nye that the Campbell sketch was his favourite in the whole evening. Perhaps it was no coincidence that a film Bennett wrote a few years later, *A Private Function* (1984), featured a big fat pig alongside Maggie Smith and Michael Palin.

No one who worked with Campbell escaped one of his notorious rants; indeed, to be on the end of one was the equivalent of receiving a war decoration. Broadbent got his when he launched one day into an impersonation of Hirst, described by Broadbent as 'a huge, thatched man in wellingtons and a huge coat, and probably the smelliest person you've ever met'. When he'd finished, Ken took off into such a torrent of a rant that people standing around had to try and restrain him: 'What you just did was a maggot's view of the mighty,' he roared at Broadbent. He rang up Broadbent the next day to apologise – 'but I was very glad to have experienced it,' says the actor, 'it was a rite of passage... such beautiful language... "a maggot's view of the mighty"!' Broadbent had remained in the Campbell loop by appearing as Eugene Grimley in a revival of *The Great Caper* directed by Mike Bradwell for his touring company Hull Truck. 'Ken came up to see us,' Broadbent recalls, 'when we were staying in university digs in Newcastle,

and we played a game of table tennis; he was furiously com-
petitive, but no better than me, so we had a good game.' And,
like several other *Illuminatus!* veterans, he would soon be
booking his place on the ultimate trip.

In early 1978, Ken met Simon Callow at a party and was
intrigued by his plans to write a play about Wilhelm Reich, the
sexual psychoanalyst who claimed to have discovered God in
primordial cosmic energy called the orgone; he'd become a
hero of the libertarian left and was notably championed by
Norman Mailer and Kenneth Tynan. Callow recounts in his
book *Being an Actor* how he shyly boasted of the non-existent
play and was instantly given a date – 4 April – for its first performance at the Science Fiction Theatre headquarters in
Liverpool. The only snag, Campbell told Callow, was a lack of
money. Callow, not unreasonably, wanted to know how he
would he live. 'Oh, we don't let our people starve. It's one of
our rules.' Callow confessed that the play was unwritten. 'You
don't want to worry about that. I always think it's very stimulating for the actors if they haven't got a script on the first day.
Something always happens.' On this basis – that he wouldn't
starve and wouldn't really have to write the play at all – Callow was enthused enough to check out the premises and
concede that, yes, the venue could indeed be changed into one
huge orgone box. Back in London, the impossibility of it all
overwhelmed him and the project faded into nothing.

Further evidence that Ken was on the lookout to trump
Illuminatus! comes in a letter he wrote to Camilla Saunders in
June 1978, posted in Gwynedd, Wales, but signed from an
address called 'Uncontactable'. (The envelope was marked
'Expedite! Not crank mail' and 'Most urgent'.) The plan therein
was that he would be reviving *Charles Dexter Ward* and
expanding *Illuminatus!* – the *Walpurgisnacht Rock* play would
become a complete musical – in Mike Hirst's tent on Eel Brook
Common, near Fulham Broadway, in October and November.
He had been playing the *Dexter Ward* tape a lot, he told
Camilla. 'I think the one weak spot is Willett's trip down into
the depths. I recommend this: 1) An "oo-er" number for Willett (the inquisitive doctor in the story) and chorus as he

descends the ladder into the caverns. 2) Once in the cavern it should be like a journey through a fairground haunted house. Slime dripping. Bodies falling out. Flippers up from hatch but all set to a routine number. With breaks in it for speciality cackling and electronic twangling. The twangling should be done by the band while Willett does stage business. We don't go into Stockhausen time (although we give hints of it in the breaks) until Willett passes out. So my thinking is fairground banal horrors rather than the current subtle attempts.' None of this came about, but it shows Campbell was still out there, seeking – just as he became a father for the first and only time.

Ken and Prue's daughter was born in September 1978 in the Royal Free Hospital, Hampstead. 'It was Bob Hoskins who thought up my daughter's name, Daisy,' Ken told Sarah Lam. 'Prue was bringing me out in running sores, pressing for Tracy but also contemplating Abigail, when Bob came by and said: "Call her Daisy, then she'll get to go to all the parties. People'll like saying, 'Have you met Daisy?' and 'Is Daisy coming?'" Prue was quite taken with the advice but worried as to what her mum would think.' But her mother loved the name because it struck her as one of the lovely old-fashioned ones. Prue had been thrilled to be pregnant, said Ken at the time, but they weren't exactly the archetypal married couple. 'But there wasn't too much "archetypal" activity on Haverstock Hill in 1978,' he told *Sunday Times* interviewer Ann McFerran (wife of 'unpredictable' but brilliant playwright Snoo Wilson), 'although we were actually paying rent while everyone else was squatting. We got married, which was seen as something of a scandal. When Daisy was born I hummed a lot at certain bits. But when I looked at her I felt "Blimey!" It was all most pleasing. I liked the way it would take half an hour to walk up the road because she was pointing at things. I'm tone deaf, but, privately, during that very young stage, I attempted a musical noise to match whatever mood she was in: if she looked a bit "wham!" I'd sing her some whammy-hums; if she looked chirpy, I'd do chirp-hums. It seemed to make her happy.'

✧

Earlier that year, Ken had heard of a book, *Alternative 3* by Leslie Watkin, based on a hoax television science programme, intended as a successor to Orson Welles's *The War of the Worlds* on radio on 1938 (in which listeners freaked out, believing they were hearing a report of a real Martian invasion). *Alternative 3* was about a British brain-drain and the colonisation of outer space by a joint effort between the Americans and the Russians, prompted by the imminent demise of the planet Earth owing to catastrophic climate change. Ken then met a man called Brian outside the greengrocer's over the road on Haverstock Hill, who said that he had been round to the house bearing that very same book, newly published by Sphere, but not readily available. Campbell had been out. Then up popped Ion Alexis Will once more, outside the very same greengrocer's. 'Have you heard all this about *Alternative 3*?' he asked, innocently. Ion Will knew some bloke in a garage round the back of Holloway Gaol who was in possession of a hundred copies of the book which was, he said, 'so full of shit and weird stuff' that Sphere were now denying that they had ever published it.

Arriving at the garage, Campbell said that he was interested in something they might know about and that he had come from the *Fortean Times*. The garage hands, to a man, dropped their drills and wrenches and, also to a man, revealed themselves to be well-read experts on UFO invasions, conspiracies, disappearing scientists and interplanetary travel. One of them was Neil Oram, a poet and hippy who had lately returned from staying at the Rajneesh ashram in Poona, India... And – almost, surely, incredibly? – Oram was the man with whom Brian had called round with the book in the first place. A few days later, coincidence piling on coincidence, Campbell received in the post details of a Neil Oram storytelling session at the ICA in the Mall. He went along and afterwards told Oram that he should dramatise the material, which existed at that point in the form of about a dozen long raps which Oram had initially envisaged as a film script and score. Oram went round to Haverstock Hill in late July and rattled out a dozen more raps, which Campbell, light-fingered as ever at the typewriter, took down. Oram says he then went down to Fishponds, Butleigh, near Glastonbury, in late August and wrote the entire one-thousand-page script of *The Warp*, incorporating the raps Campbell had typed out for him.

The work was completed by the end of November, and rehearsals began a few days later at the headquarters of the Bubble Theatre in Kentish Town, North London. As it happens, I was commissioned by *Time Out* magazine to write a cover feature on Campbell to coincide with the opening of *The Warp*, so I reported to the Bubble HQ in Kingsford Street on Monday 27 November 1978. Huge, bulging files were scattered around the light-filled room on tatty furniture. I picked up one, inspecting the spine: '*The Warp*, Act One Scene One – Act Eighteen Scene Seven.' It was going to be a long day. Two long days, as it turned out. But I concluded, in an appropriately very long review of the show published in the *Financial Times* on Monday 22 January 1979, following the all-day Thursday-into-Friday epic premiere, that you should pack your bags, sell up your house, abandon your family and hurry along to see it: 'The world may soon divide into those who have been through *The Warp* and those who have not.'

8

Warp Time

The *Warp* is one of the most astounding theatrical events of the last thirty-odd years, and Campbell himself was proud of the fact that it could have happened at all: 'I mean,' he said at the time, 'if we bring this off, or even do it quite well with an allowable amount of failure, it's going to make everything else in the theatre just look like bollocks.' *The Warp* turned out to be a riot of rough theatrics that did indeed make you feel that Campbell might have a point about the bollocks quotient of most of the other stuff that goes on inside theatres. Mike Bradwell, hired as 'dialogue coach', said, with slight exaggeration, that 'at least seven hours of *The Warp* weren't very interesting', and many may have found the first five plays unmatched by the second five, but, at the time, Campbell's production made most of what passed for 'experimental theatre' look wan and pretentious. It joyously melded elements of music hall, science fiction, storytelling, sex and adventure into an unforgettable low-budget extravaganza-cum-soap opera that could be best described as 'the acid *Archers* with weird bits'. Later in life, Campbell acknowledged that Neil Oram's shaggy saga of a personal *Bildungsroman* was his 'runaway favourite thing... no play has given me so much pleasure'. We had the characters in our alternative society, Campbell always contended, but we hadn't had a Jack Kerouac or a Neal Cassady to bring them to fictive life until we had Neil Oram. Although he and Oram squabbled a fair bit both during and long after the production, Campbell never once underestimated what Oram had done.

There had been separate previews, starting on 2 January, of each of the ten plays, during which scenes were still being written and learned, small parts cast and costumes patched together. On that momentous first full-cycle day, Thursday 18 January 1979 – a day of national strikes by lorry drivers and railway men as a knackered Labour Government prepared for the worst (which turned out to be Margaret Thatcher's anointment as Prime Minister in May) – the first play began at 10.45 a.m. After eighteen-and-a-half hours of theatre, two one-hour meal breaks and a half-hour beer and coffee interval at 2.35 a.m. on Friday, we dispersed into the Mall at 8 a.m. on a – what a surprise! – crisp, bright and snowy morning. I remember feeling exhausted but elated as I made my way to my bus stop north of Trafalgar Square.

This was an achievement to set beside the RSC's first Wars of the Roses sequence in 1963/4, or indeed *Illuminatus!* itself, which boiled down to a mere nine hours of actual theatre. And it came in advance of other 'great theatre days' such as the RSC's two-play *Nicholas Nickleby*, Peter Brook's stage version of the *Mahabharata* (fifteen years in the preparation before the 1985 premiere), the epic *Oresteias* of first Peter Stein, then Peter Hall, the all-day David Hare trilogy at the National – and the longer works of Robert Lepage. Campbell's company was not even remotely part of the recognised or politically 'approved' fringe theatre. For *Illuminatus!*, in the end, they had managed to prise £9,000 out of the Arts Council; the figure for *The Warp*, over twice as long and infinitely more ambitious, was a shamefully meagre £7,500. Some of the *Warp* company subsidised the venture by cooperating with a slimming-aids firm, paid £300 each for eating tasteless biscuits and losing weight. One actor married a Polish girl (so she could stay in the UK) so as to raise another £500.

Campbell's position was clear: he'd 'had it' with plays in 1969. Everything he'd done since was committed to the idea of a theatre beyond plays, beside plays, beneath plays: anything but plays themselves. Of course, the funding bodies never understood this, any more than they understood Joan Littlewood, who was starved of subsidy throughout her time at Stratford East and only given an Olivier Award for lifetime service long after she'd left England and retired to France; or Peter Brook, who had left London for Paris in 1971 and become the darling of the French cultural establishment. Good theatre usually happens when characterised by risk, not certainty; defined by productions, not plays; audiences, not bureaucrats; spontaneity, not policies; and talent, not systematic subsidy. In that respect, Campbell's work in the 1970s was of a piece with fringe groups like the Pip Simmons Theatre Group, or the People Show, rather than the agitprop companies or the 'new-writing' stream represented by David Hare, Howard Brenton, David Edgar and the rest. Satelliting the ICA, unaligned with other venues or the major companies, and encouraged by the theatre director there, John Ashford – who, as 'John Ford', had been the first theatre editor on *Time Out* – were an ad-hoc group of artists whose accent was on the visionary, the discursive, the different and the genuinely radical. In his handy selection of *99 Plays* ('key' works since *The Oresteia*), the director and playwright Nicholas Wright, who had staged both Campbell's *The Great Caper* and Heathcote Williams's *AC/DC* at the Royal Court, said of *The Warp*: 'If we can tackle vast themes, and give hour after hour of raw theatrical pleasure for next to nothing – Oram, Campbell and everyone else seemed to be asking – then what's stopping *rich* theatres doing even better? Lack of imagination? Fear? I sometimes wish, when I'm trapped in some perfect but meaningless evening, that I was being asked that again.'

The arrangement at the ICA was one similar to that of an arrangement of fairground booths or platforms through which the audience moved on a terrain of peat – this was Mike Hirst's idea, with fumes going up the actors' noses while the peat was drying out, only for Campbell to attack it with a water spray to keep the level down, and thus start it steaming again – and the band were fully visible, as they always were in a Campbell show. The model might have been Ariane Mnouchkine's *1789*, an ecstatic piece of sideshow theatre about the French Revolution staged for a promenade audience; or the madcap Frenchman Jérôme Savary's sensational

Le Grand Magic Circus, with its trademark sex-and-sadism cavorting, both of which had visited the Roundhouse in the early 1970s; not to mention the Living Theatre's tribal explosion of love and peace in *Paradise Now*, which had so impressed Campbell at the same address; or even, perhaps, the great Serbian director Ljubiša Ristić's *The Liberation of Skopje*, first performed in Zagreb in 1977, but internationally renowned as a 'sideshow epic', focusing on social and psychological upheavals during the Nazi occupation of Macedonia in the Second World War.

Consciously or not, Campbell's production of Neil Oram's story certainly belonged with those barnstormers rather than with the predominant studio-theatre naturalism and political do-gooding of the subsidised fringe at large. Oram's hero, Phil Masters, may indeed be set on a somewhat maudlin inner voyage of self-discovery that might have thrived in a studio theatre – early on, he is submitted to a gruelling examination in a Scientology auditing session – but the theatrical expression of a hippy's heartache is extravagant, full-spirited, vaudevillian and hilarious. In its dealing with magic and coincidence in bravura poor-theatre terms, Campbell's presentation of Oram seemed almost to reinvent those eighteenth-century picaresque novels of Henry Fielding and Tobias Smollett in twentieth-century hippy Europe: jazz sessions in Soho at Sam Widges's place, Scientology interrogations, UFOs, the tranquil Bhagwan in India, the dark sinister shadow of Aleister Crowley, and the Loch Ness healing centre where 'people can give birth to themselves'. During that first performance, in a classic example of alienation theatre, Oram suddenly, and for one scene only, materialised *as himself*, haggard and chaotic in appearance, hat on head, fag in mouth, long coat trailing to the floor, recounting how he smuggled dope through a Paris paralysed by the political demonstrations during *les événements*. This was a symbolic authentication to rival that of Hitchcock sliding into one of his own shots, or John Osborne reciting one of his own rabid rants.

Our hero's quest starts with a prologue in fifteenth-century Bavaria, and transports him from a carefree induction with a luscious, naked nymphomaniac in a woodshed in

Torquay (Oram's birthplace), to Salisbury in Rhodesia, bohemian London, Paris and Italy; from Turkey, Syria and Israel to Haworth, home of the Brontës, in West Yorkshire, and to Ireland for the flying-saucer conference of 1968. What is Phil Masters, Oram's surrogate, seeking? In part, his own female consciousness that enables him to overcome jealousy when his wife falls in love with his best friend; and, in part, the ability to 'experience on a higher plane of reality' without totally freaking out. In Soho, we meet Billy McGuinness, the orator tramp (also immortalised by Heathcote Williams as 'Maurice' in *AC/DC* and in *The Speakers*) who claims to be God returning to Earth to reclaim his long-overdue royalties; King David, a tumultuous character residing somewhere between the worlds of Gogol and Pinter, bearing messages from Orion and interrupting his mission only for cups of tea and raw onions; and a hapless acid freak who disrupts a café by snorting baked beans and excreting sausages. The cast of countless characters also includes a mystic greengrocer who serves customers in gobbledygook but holds forth on UFOs with exact lucidity; knockabout Turkish policemen and comic Chinese officials; the amazing architect and futurist, and inventor of the geodesic dome, Buckminster Fuller; a naked Dutch ex-hooker and yoga fanatic bringing herself to orgasm in the lotus position while raising the sexual energy up to the 'seventh chakra' ('masturbation through concentration is the beginning of responsibility'); clowns, fire-eaters, military-art enthusiasts, a raging landlord ('I don't have any friends; just different classes of enemy'); and an eccentric postman who pops up everywhere with bad news for old Phil.

In the first scenes, the actors progressed in clockwise fashion from one set to another, establishing the narrative propulsion before exploding all over the place. Then the audience started moving from one area of the theatre to another, drawn by lights changing and voices rising in another part of the woods. Phil struggled with his 'feeling of loss and present-time problem' and the second play opened with that brilliant half-hour Scientology auditing session; immediately, he received his first warning about Scientology from a nubile free-liver-lover.

But Phil finds a reinforced emotional centre through women, and the realisation that there is a global network of consciousness dawns on him with accelerating vigour throughout the whole extraordinary saga. The fundamental difference between Campbell and Oram was that the former found this less serious a proposition than did the latter; Campbell's priority throughout was to create theatre, a show, with laughter, whereas Oram stated that he wanted to create 'a shamanistic event capable of producing a magic carpet on which light-hearted souls could fly into a nourishing, ambient, alive *question*... and therein discover how to develop their true potential'.

Campbell's theatre is always double-edged. He operates sideways-on to the material, bending it this way and that for effect. Oram proclaimed his message with a great shout of 'Yes to the Fresh!!' – his mantra, in fact – and he wasn't always amused when Campbell and the actors insisted on finding the funny side: he preferred to see Phil's quest as a battle between life and inertia. When he published eighty-seven raps from *The Warp* – the complete text remains unpublished, as indeed, amazingly, does *Illuminatus!* – Oram explained Phil's genesis. He was, says Oram, a present-day reincarnation not so much of his own former self (though the outlines of Phil's story are the same as Oram's) as of Philip Bourke Marston (1850–87), the neglected blind Victorian poet whose father John Westland Marston wrote verse dramas and was a friend of Dickens, Macready and Charles Kean. Philip mingled with these figures as well as the poet Swinburne and the great actor Henry Irving, among others, at his father's house in Chalk Farm, very near Haverstock Hill. But that wasn't the appeal to Oram. In 1977, on his return from India, he was, he says, cast adrift on a relentless sea of uncertainty. 'The queen of my heart was incarcerated in a sanatorium and our love child was entangled in a bureaucratic legal jungle.' He was working in the Holloway garage, and as a decorator, to try and keep solvent. 'I happened upon an open book in a house I was employed to decorate. Destiny designed that I'd be realigned at that moment. The name Philip Bourke Marston leapt from that book. The curtain was lifted and I entered the trip':

> Walking down the lane alone
> Conscious of my every step
> I felt a quickening, felt you there,
> Waiting in the swirling mist.
>
> Then in the dark mist of my soul
> I felt your presence clear and bright
> But nowhere could I touch your form
> As coldness crawled into my bones.

He was possessed by Marston's voice, channelling it in this, his own poem, on a walk through Regent's Park with his lover, having lately devoured three volumes of Marston's stuff in the public library at Swiss Cottage. And he realised, bizarrely, that Marston had lived in the very mansion they were passing as he spoke... He then researched Marston's life thoroughly, and was moved beyond measure by his blindness from the age of three, the sudden loss of his mother, then his lover, then his two sisters, and by his poverty and failing health. Oram was touched, too, by the fact that Marston appears never to have become resentful or bitter, despite all his setbacks, and he saw his tale as that of an acorn determined to become an oak tree. Taking the piss out of such a figure, or indeed himself, was out of the question as far as Oram was concerned. He sometimes felt that all Campbell wanted was a 'Knees Up Mother Brown': 'So we fought all the way through. I was, and still am, on a spiritual mission. Ken was on some kind of power trip.'

Who would play this heroic paragon? Russell Denton now says that it took him ten years to get *The Warp* out of his system and overcome the trauma of playing Phil Masters. And yet he wouldn't trade the experience for anything. It happened like this. He'd not seen Campbell since their days in Bolton, but he bumped into him at the Old Bailey where a mutual friend, the actor Alan Ford, who had also appeared in *Law and Order*, was on trial for hitting a policeman (the case was dismissed). Campbell told Denton all about Neil Oram, gave him a phone number, and said there would be a part for him. Denton was living in Leeds with a girlfriend and was badly out of work. He was no good at selling himself, but the girlfriend goaded him into ringing the number. It was 9.30 a.m. on 2 December (Denton remembers the date because he'd had his appendix removed on the same date when he was nine), a Sunday, and one week in to the five-week rehearsal period. Ken picked up the phone: 'Russell, Russell, where are you, come down immediately, get on a train, it's all happening, there's loads of parts for you, it's all going on, man.' Denton rushed downstairs, packed a suitcase and got on a train: 'It was the most beautiful morning. A hoar frost had descended all over the whole country, most unusual. Everything was caked in this wonderland fairy frost. I got to somewhere I could stay with friends, jumped on a Number 24 bus and went to rehearsals.' He didn't know anyone else in the room but picked up on a spirit of competitiveness in the games-playing of vying for roles. The actress and director (now also an opera librettist) Cindy Oswin remembers turning up for the assignation of roles: 'There was dirt and grit everywhere in that Bubble rehearsal room, but Russell was very clean and wore nice clothes. Ken wanted him to come on as the hero, and be heroic, and he wasn't getting it. Over the course of one long night's rehearsal, Ken concentrated exclusively, and brutally, on this task. Because Neil Oram had sweaty shoes and socks, Ken made Russell go off and come back on with his shoes filled with water and start again – he did this many times – and then Ken said, "Fill 'em again, hold your hands like this, and come on like Clint Eastwood." And he did this, again and again, until, like a light going on, he became heroic. On that one night, he was transformed into a kind of rock star, and that gave him the confidence to do the role all those many times; he'd entered another stratum.' Denton never knew whether Ken had decided to cast him as Phil the minute he walked in the door. He'd heard that Alun Armstrong had been offered the role and had decided against doing it, merely on the grounds that it was 'impossible'.

The old *Illuminatus!* hands, Jim Broadbent and Bill Nighy, knew better than to make themselves available for the larger roles. 'We knew,' says Nighy, 'that whatever happened, you didn't want a big part. So we used to stand by the door in case any big parts came up, and when they did, we'd slip out the door and down to the pub and Ken would rant and rail, "Where's Broadbent, where's Niffy?" The trick was to end up with a series of little roles so you had time off to drink... and the other trick was never to leave the room to take a leak. Because if no one had put their hand up for a certain role, Ken would say, "Who-ever walks through the door next has to play it," regardless of whether they were a girl or boy, young or old.' At the beginning of that first week, before Denton arrived, Nighy had said to Ken at the bar, after the early skirmishes, that it all seemed to be looking good, commenting that he thought Mitch Davies – more of an artist, really, than an actor, but someone who'd been drawn into the company (he'd trained at the Chelsea Art School and Royal College) – seemed very nice. 'The thing about Ken was he fed on positivity. If anyone said anything positive, it would be seriously regarded and immediately incorporated. Ken says, "So, if you like him, he can be your friend, and what-ever parts you play, your character can have a friend, and Mitch will play it!" And so he did. Even the Chinese ambassador I played had a friend, and Mitch would come on with me.' For the Chinese scenes, Davies would conscientiously lay out the suits and yellow Leichner make-up, and the two of them would rub their hands together in the yellow, smear it on their screwed-up faces, and talk funny. 'We used to bring the house down every night.' As Nighy admits, it's not hard to do that if you are playing a Chinese ambassador. Davies says Ken liked what he did because it was grotesque with lots of face acting – 'he called it German acting' – Dr Caligari-type Expressionist stuff. There are over three hundred characters in *The Warp* and at one point Mitch had twenty-seven of them. And Nighy avers that *The Warp* – in which he played about twelve roles, including a Siber-ian border guard, a man from Yorkshire who'd seen a UFO and a man having his tongue cut out in medieval Bavaria – 'absolutely liberated me as an actor, broke down all my barri-ers; not least because Ken would stand in front of you roaring his head off and beaming. I played a gestalt therapist, too, and did something with my nose and talked down it in a certain way that Ken thought was fantastic.'

Playing the longest part in the history of world theatre took a little more out of Russell Denton. 'Ken smashed me into little pieces; he'd physically assault me, almost, then he'd build me up. But he knew what he was doing. He'd humiliate me, then I'd go away for a cup of tea and, one day when I walked back in after half an hour, all the rest applauded; and I knew Ken had arranged that. I was never without the script for that whole rehearsal period. I never looked at a newspaper or a magazine. It was a process of endless repetition. Over that Christmas, I allowed myself one treat: *The Sound of Music* on television.' Denton's Phil was word-perfect, gauche and won-drously impressionable in a superb portrait of a poor lost soul to whom things happened, not just supernaturally, but also sexually and hysterically. It was one of the most fantastic per-formances in anything I'd ever seen – it still is – quite apart from being an amazing feat of memory and physical stamina. There was no prompter at the ICA, but one of the rules was that whoever had the last word with Denton's Phil in any scene had to tell him where to go next; and, zombie-like, he went there. Did he enjoy any part of the play more than the rest? 'The bit I always looked forward to was Play Ten, not because it was the last play, but because that was the point I could allow myself to be as tired as I really felt. My voice was right down, low and husky; I'd lost my woman, lost my kid, the world was closing around me, and I could allow myself to be at last a person who'd just done twenty-four hours onstage and could just about get his voice out – this was completely real and I hope it felt like that to those watching. In fact, I know it did.'

Cindy Oswin recalls Campbell's method of directing often boiling down to savage one-liners, such as 'Drama is lines taken in turns.' 'If an actor was having difficulty with a line, he'd say: "Say it, or cut it, what's it to be?" One of my characters was a Swedish woman who thought she was from Venus, and I had a long speech I was in trouble with. What to do? "I think you should play her with big tits." So I did.' The 'bloke-ishness' of Campbell's theatre was not something Oswin thought of as misogynist, though some did. 'He was certainly a man's man, and I think that was because he'd been brought up by his dad. He put women on a pedestal, and he loved beautiful women. I don't think it was a case of him not understanding women, but he was definitely more comfortable with men. He was brilliant at coaching you to make you know more than you thought you knew as a performer. He said that everybody, even a small child, knows what it's like to be on a stage… and it's true.' Like Cindy Oswin, Claudia 'Egypt' Boulton (she'd been conceived in Egypt, born in Rome and brought up by missionaries in India, not her real parents) came to *The Warp* from a high-profile fringe-theatre background, notably with the guerrilla cartoon-theatre group Beryl and the Perils, who specialised in furious feminist fun and songs about sex and masturbation. Her family now lived in Rutland, like Prunella Gee's. Since 1974 she'd inhabited one of London's longest-running squats just two doors up from Ken and Dave Hill's place on Haverstock Hill: '"Oh Claudia," Prue had said when we first met, "you're not one of those eccentric Boultons, are you?" When the call came for *The Warp* I was ready. I had a good grounding in the invisible world. I'd been in India for eighteen months, with the Rajneesh, and also hanging out for six months on a Goan beach, where nobody wore any clothes at all. That's what you did back then: you took acid and took your clothes off. We were all comfort-able in our skins, and we all had quite nice bodies. I might be slightly more circumspect about it now! I had a profound expe-rience in India and finally freaked out so badly they locked me up in a mental hospital and I had to be rescued. I really related to the Rachel role in *The Warp* – in all that stuff about "you'd better go and have a car crash before you talk to me", Neil wrote one of the really great roles for women in the twentieth century. Unfortunately, I played Meg, the wife, but I did a lot of talking to Maria Moussaka, who played Rachel…'

The whole project was one of informality and rigour, impossible challenges and basic, practical solutions as if, as John Joyce deduced, once Ken got going, then the whole world would look after him. There were sixty-five people coming and going all the time in the build-up. Miracles happened. One day, Tim Albery, the opera director (and scion of a famous theatrical family), who was starting out on his career as a production manager, and working at the ICA, arrived with a group of people from Liverpool who got press-ganged into finding the furniture and building and painting the booths. Joyce says he had never seen them before and he never saw them again. When the run started, with each of the plays being performed separately, it was Joyce's decision, as company administrator, to start the evening shows at 9 p.m., allowing a chance for the company to meet a few hours before the performance and run through the text with 'dialogue coach' Mike Bradwell (who incidentally met his future wife, the actress and playwright Helen Cooper, on the show), while Ken sorted out the design and lights in the theatre. On the third play, the actor playing Gurdjieff's spokesman in London, whom Ken had picked up in one of his local pubs, was having a problem and muttering about his throat. Joyce was designated to tell him to go home and not come back. That morning, with the third play due to open at 9 p.m., Ken sat Bill Nighy down with a script and left him to it, assuming he'd walk through the play holding that script. 'Well,' says Joyce, 'not only did he not come on with the script, but he'd also found a bunch of flowers and he'd worked out a way in which they illustrated the points he was making. There was no inkling that this could have been done by anyone else. We had a lot of that in *The Warp*. Miracles happened because of the energy that Ken gave the whole thing.'

There was only that one complete cycle of *The Warp* at the ICA, so plans were immediately afoot to continue the phenomenon, and it seemed an obvious idea to go to that year's Edinburgh Festival Fringe. But could they find a suitable venue for no money? The search ended with the discovery of the old Regent Cinema in Abbeymount behind Calton Hill, near Holyrood Palace. The place had been a brewery before being converted into a cinema in 1927, a 1,700-seater with a thirty-foot-wide stage, an organ, and a tea room. It closed as a cinema in 1970. It was now, as one of the ICA stagehands found it, totally wrecked, with no seats, huge gaping holes in the roof and no

● (*left*) Prunella Gee marries Ken on 18 March 1978 near her family home in Oakham, Rutland. The 'proper' party, after the 'official' one, was in Liverpool on the same night

● (*below*) Daisy, borne aloft by Prue, was born in September 1978, and this photo was taken in early 1979 in the garden on Haverstock Hill, north London

● (*right*) Daisy, aged three, on Hampstead Heath with Prue and Werner the dog – so named after the American philosopher Werner Erhard, whose 'EST Training' had a big influence on Ken

● (*this page, top*) Ken as the bar-room bore, Roger, with John Cleese, in a 1979 episode of *Fawlty Towers* on BBC television, 'The Anniversary', one of Cleese's favourites. 'Up yours, Baz!' was the disloyal toast

● (*this page, left*) as Alf Garnett's neighbour, Fred Johnson, in the 1986 BBC series of *In Sickness and in Health*, with Bill Maynard and (*front row*) Warren Mitchell and Carmel McSharry

● (*opposite page*) The ten-play, twenty-two-hour cycle of *The Warp* by Neil Oram, directed by Campbell, opened at the ICA Theatre in London in January 1979.
(*top*) A sausage is excreted at the breakfast table in Sam Widges in Soho.
(*bottom*) Russell Denton as Phil Masters begins an extraordinary adventure in a Torquay tool shed with Maya Sendall as an obliging nymphomaniac

● In an outline for the unperformed *****-Knows*, Ken riffed on his fascination with his own nose as a sexual weapon and as an amalgamation with the rear view of a naked female body: 'coitus proboscidalis, cunninazus, carnal nosolidge!'

● (*from top, anti-clockwise*) The three one-man shows, performed as a trilogy at the National Theatre in 1993, that took Campbell's writing into a new, fantastical dimension: *Recollections of a Furtive Nudist* (1988) with Werner, and Ken wearing his fishing jacket; *Pigspurt* (1992) with a miniature bench serving as a moustache while contemplating yet another parallel universe; and taking the plunger in *Jamais Vu* (1993), one of six he habitually applied to his head, and sporting the Ken Dodd teeth, or 'Mellors'

● (*left*) Vietnamese 'boat person' Thieu-Hoa Vuong performs in the show Ken wrote for her, *Violin Time* (1996), first performed in Newfoundland – with an onstage wedding (not theirs) – and later, in a cascade of information and nuttiness, at the National Theatre

● (*below*) Ken explains the magical mystery of Pidgin, aided by the Ken Dodd puppet pygmy to his right, as a prologue to the Pidgin *Macbeth* ('*Makbed* blong Willum Sekspia') at LAMDA and the Piccadilly Theatre, London, in 1998

● Nina Conti, one of many whose lives Campbell changed: she was saved from a career as a Royal Shakespeare Company actress and diverted into ventriloquism after Ken sent a teach-yourself kit to the stage door, and was soon one of the country's top vent acts. Here, she parades a few of her knee pals, including her signature simian, little Monk, who's pretending she doesn't have her hand up his bottom

● Ken with Fred on the back step in the Lea Valley. He was rehearsing a 1989 children's television science show, *Erasmus Microman*, and Fred helped out as Erasmus Micromutt. Ken's last home was in Epping Forest, where he walked his dogs for hours on end, never happier

plumbing. No one quite remembers how they did this, but within three weeks the local-council regulations were met and, in another two, the show was on. About three dozen people were actually living in the place, some sleeping on the floor, some on the balcony. Claudia Boulton's then boyfriend had helped to find the Regent, and she delighted in the fact that she could go and live *The Warp*: 'That's what we did. I moved my entire room from Haverstock Hill onto stage six, my own bed: it was all that close to one's life.' An eight-foot pile of detritus grew in the middle of the auditorium and four dead pigeons floated in the flooded basement. A couple of American sailors on shore leave from a nuclear submarine in the Firth of Forth called by and offered to help. While the sailors fixed the plumbing, six of the actors managed to get a huge tarpaulin stretched over the roof then went down to the public baths for a shower; they were so filthy they had to have a second douche to rinse off the first. They ran a canteen downstairs, but where the food came from was often a mystery. Russell Denton remembers someone turning up from the Lake District one day with a huge bag of chanterelles which they all devoured for breakfast. 'They were the most amazing days, the central experience of the whole thing,' says Denton, 'with lots of booze and dope, of course. A couple of plain-clothes policemen came in one night when we were working on the place. We hid the joints, but they said, "Don't worry about that, you're doing good work around here." A lot of the local kids had come in and helped us get furniture and stuff.'

Jim Broadbent didn't go with *The Warp* to Edinburgh. Finding another actor to replace him was the usual haphazard process. The playwright and director Terry Johnson was sitting in his flat one morning when the phone rang. Ken was looking for Johnson's flatmate, Jeff, who had gone to live elsewhere. 'What do you do?' 'I write plays and do a bit of acting...' 'Whoa, stop right there; what are you doing on Saturday? Can you do voices? Can you plumb a toilet?' Johnson said he could 'do' voices and indeed was handy in the bathroom; his dad was a plumber. He was cast on the spot. 'It was strange for me,' says Johnson, 'because I was quite straight in lots of ways. I wasn't coping with the heady hippy lifestyle, and I was in unrequited love with someone from university who was appearing in another show in Edinburgh, and I was spending some of the time hanging round her and some of it being depressed. That annoyed Ken because the toilets weren't getting plumbed in. He came up to me in his cups and gave me the full nasal laser treatment: "You know what your trouble is, Johnson? Apart from your incessant desire to orchestrate misery? You've got a switch *there*..." and he poked me indelibly firmly right on the sternum – "And it's OFF!" He was absolutely right and I think that moment granted me twenty per cent of my personality; certainly the most attractive twenty per cent, possibly the most life-enhancing. It was one of the prime moments of my life, although at the time it destroyed me utterly. He was so fearless about attacking your ego. Having primed you with that extraordinary way of speaking and thinking that had formed his own world view, he would help people make breakthroughs which literally changed the way they saw the world, and the way they saw themselves in it.'

How formative an experience *The Warp* was for Johnson can be gauged by his acknowledgement that he had not, at this stage, completed work on *Insignificance* (1982), his brilliant fictional encounter between Albert Einstein and Marilyn Monroe, and that his next play was *Cries from the Mammal House* (1984) – 'without Ken, the second act, in which they go to Mauritius, wouldn't have existed' – featuring an obsessive conservationist, a failed psychotherapist and a depressed vet (and the evocative stage direction, '*He goes, deep in Western thought*'). Johnson learned from both Campbell and Neil Oram ('Though I was never around Neil all that much. I was only outer circle; inner circle was a bit scary') that it was no good 'just orchestrating things; you had to go and seek as well'. This mindset of involvement and relish can be illustrated by a simple example that is, in fact, Johnson's favourite Campbell story: 'We were rehearsing and we were in some greasy spoon, and Ken was finishing his dinner. He stood up to leave when a guy walked in holding a length of hemp rope at the end of which was a goat. He'd brought in the goat because he'd been chucked out the day before for bringing in a dog. Ken stopped in his tracks, took off his coat and said, "I'm staying for pudding if there's a goat!" It was a crystallisation of how to live a life: you get more pudding if there's a goat. There was a big set-to and the mad Italian woman who owned the café started screaming at the man and chased him and his goat out the door. It was incredibly good fun...'

The playwright also learned a lot about directing: 'An actor was faltering in one scene and Ken told him to imagine a white-hot ball bearing in the middle of his hand. "Got it?" "Yeah, I've got it..." "Well, stick it up your arse and do it again." One day we were doing a "fucking" rehearsal, the one where Phil would draw her with his prick then shag her, and the actress was feeling a bit nervous in her nudity; so Ken made us all come down to the front of the stage and watch her do it. That cleared up the problem!' This way of directing, Johnson says, is inspirational, daring, and it makes actors laugh but corners them totally. The mode of 'pure Ken' sometimes comes through Johnson's own work today, he says, like a rocket. One of the male dancers in his 2008 Menier Chocolate Factory revival of *La Cage aux Folles* was having trouble: 'It was time to have a word. And he said, "I know there's that bit in Act Two and I don't sometimes get it, so last night I ate a banana just before I went on and I said to myself, it was really rather good..." And I heard myself say, "You know what you should do: you wanna have a banana on stage-right, and one on stage-left... and one up your arse!" And it worked.'

After Edinburgh, *The Warp* played a three-month season, weekends only, downstairs at the Roundhouse, where it became something beyond theatre, a sort of post-hippy phenomenon that defied any cultural classification. The company was also invited to perform the complete cycle in Hebden Bridge in West Yorkshire – an unlikely, but thriving outpost of cultural innovation and, as it happens, same-sex mini-communities – and in Essen, Germany, where an avant-garde structuralist film-maker, Werner Nekes, threaded the story of Phil Masters into a bizarre, opaque and modernised retelling of Homer's *Odyssey*. Nekes had wanted to film the show, but could only raise money for the Homer idea. So he 'disguised' *The Warp* as a film called *Uliisses* and recast Phil Masters as Telemachus, the son of Odysseus and Penelope, wandering through some cunningly evoked analogues of Homerian episodes involving Calypso, Nestor, the lotus-eaters, Proteus and the Cyclops. The ninety-four-minute film – although hailed as a masterpiece by one or two German critics, and awarded prizes at festivals in London, Berlin and Portugal – is virtually incomprehensible, for all its experimental ingenuity and the governing idea that the brain of Ulysses (the director) is the creator of all light. Ken Campbell is a sinister Nestor, moulding Telemachus/Phil to his mission with a battery of magic lanterns.

The Essen gig was nearly undermined by bad behaviour on the train journey. John Joyce was getting seriously into character as Billy McGuinness – 'Something entered into me as Billy and I was talking deep stuff to people who probably didn't understand English, and after a while, apparently (although I have no memory of it), enough was enough and they called the guard. A whole lot of us were going to be thrown off, but Russell calmed everyone down and promised to look after me until we got to Essen.'

More significantly, Campbell directed two ingeniously creative Science Fiction Theatre of Liverpool spin-offs from *The Warp* at the ICA, either side of the Edinburgh gig. Douglas Adams's cult BBC radio series, *The Hitchhiker's Guide to the Galaxy* – in which Campbell had had a role specially written for him – opened in May 1979, and reunited Campbell with Chris Langham and Neil Cunningham, both of whom had missed out on *The Warp*. *Hitchhiker's* was another piece of rough theatre, but of only ninety minutes' duration, a delightful distillation notable for a design that floated a restricted audience of eighty people (upwards of 1,500 were turned away every night) on twelve metal air skates, each containing an inflatable diaphragm. Once the skates were pumped full of compressed air, stagehands pushed the audience around at a height of one two-thousandth of an inch off the ground (the invention by Rolair was used for moving heavy machine tools). The delicious ingenuity of all this was lost when the show was moved, disastrously, to the Rainbow Theatre at Finsbury Park in July 1980, where it was restaged on a much larger and boomingly inappropriate scale, and without the floating. But at the ICA, the mixture of Adams's sci-fi spoof and Campbell's absurd, madcap knockabout was just right, especially as Chris Langham returned to the fold – in what was to prove his last Campbell collaboration – as Arthur Dent, commissioned to bring the Guide up to date, with his old friend Ford Prefect, glowingly played by Richard Hope, another splendid *Warp* veteran. The show started in the ICA bar where Arthur's house was to be demolished to make way for the new intergalactic highway. We were then transported into space, i.e. the theatre, where the update task became a search for the ultimate question (to which the answer is, famously, forty-two). We floated around on the hovercraft as goggle-eyed as Arthur himself. Chris Langham made of Arthur a likeable goofball who came over as an adventurous second cousin to George Dorn in *Illuminatus!*, greeting each strange encounter with the same level of quizzical enjoyment. 'If this *is* Southend,' he opined, leaning back in a deckchair in his badminton shorts, 'then there's something extremely odd about it.'

Cindy Oswin had gone along to meet the drama panel of the Arts Council, then situated in 105 Piccadilly, to see if she could have some kind of modest bursary for being Ken Campbell's assistant. The very idea of such an application was laughed out of court by twelve sober-suited bores sitting round a long polished table; the idea of 'learning' anything by working with Campbell was, well, beyond their comprehension. On her way home she dropped into the ICA, where *Hitchhiker's* rehearsals were underway, to report back on the meeting; she was promptly cast as one of the two glitter-spangled space-maiden narrators. The other narrator was another *Warp* veteran, Maya Sendall, and they insisted on their sexy costumes being a joke, too: they had the corsets fitted with springs so that the property breasts wiggled and jiggled and zoomed out of their cups. The cast list also featured a slinky temptress in skin-hugging rubber played by Sue Jones-Davies, Langham's first wife; a character called Deep Thought, who created the universe; and a David Bowie-esque silver-lacquered paranoid android played by a very sleek and beautiful looking Russell Denton.

Instead of the Illuminati, it was the Vogons who constituted the dark force behind the symptoms of universal upheaval, led by a sort of green-faced Mighty Mekon, and it was Campbell's job to find the physical dimension to the fictive dissonance between the sci-fi surrealism and the suburban expectation; he succeeded in a way that Russell T. Davies only occasionally did in his overrated *Doctor Who* scripts on television. In their first trial, Arthur and Ford were subjected to a reading of the leader's ghastly poetry. They survived but were squeezed through an airlock into the galaxy where they were rescued by another planetary force assisted by an eccentric megalomaniac – played in his best Hagbard Celine vein by Neil Cunningham – who had received an award for designing Norway: 'I had endless fun doing the fiddly bits around the fjords.' A two-headed spaceman called Clive was played by Mitch Davies and Stephen Williams wearing one composite costume. Davies cites the fact that he and Williams had to struggle up a ramp, as if they were in a three-legged race, as an example of Ken making life as difficult as possible for the actors in the belief that the task would extract something extraordinary in the performance. 'And it did: one night, we fell over the back of the set, so we had to deliver our lines upside down, which was terribly entertaining for the audience but of course we couldn't see why. I was just this silly bad-tempered bloke with an upside-down doppelgänger as my other head. When Ken saw this, of course, he wanted to keep it in.' Langham concurs that Ken's type of theatre could become a form of kamikaze: 'That's exactly what it felt like. You felt you were being required to strap on some explosives, walk out in front of an audience and detonate yourself for the higher cause. We were so terrified of him that that is exactly what we did.'

Nor did Campbell make life any easier for Mitch in *The Third Policeman*, the other show that bookended *The Warp*, an inspired adaptation of Flann O'Brien's wonderfully ridiculous 1940 novel that ICA director John Ashford dragooned Campbell into producing for a 'Sense of Ireland' festival. As the feckless, nameless hero, Mitch had to go into a police station and report the theft of his father's gold watch. Ken told him to bang his head on the table: 'There was absolutely no give in the furniture. Next day, I had a terrible headache and thought I'd dislodged my brain. You did whatever he told you. It was up to you to somehow save your own life.'

Camilla Saunders is one of the few women who worked with Campbell who is prepared to admit that he sometimes demeaned them. On *The Warp* she was starting out on a feminist path that would take her to the Greenham Common peace camp (protesting against nuclear weaponry) in 1981 and a decisive 'coming out' as a lesbian. 'I didn't like the way women actors were treated in *The Warp* rehearsals, but being a woman didn't get in the way of my work with him as I was a composer, and he left me alone to sort out the music. What he's great at doing is starting people off, giving them a push.' So she came back to work on *The Third Policeman* and wrote a witty score for accordion, violin, clarinet, percussion and bicycles. The production, which Campbell co-directed with the Irish actor Oengus MacNamara, also featured a lot of 'dental' acting: everyone looked as though they were wearing false teeth, possibly because they *were* wearing false teeth. Campbell was worried about the Irish accents and thought the dentures – which he acquired from Irving Rappaport, David's elder brother, who was then working as a dental technician – would provide a uniformity of accented strangeness; and he was right. Mitch Davies looked and sounded like Bernie Winters playing a ventriloquist's dummy, with his eyebrows shooting permanently into his hairline. Mitch says he played the nameless hero – 'You can't possess a watch if you don't have a name' – as George Formby in hell, with two voices, one high-pitched and squeaky, the other gruff and authoritative for the instructional part of his role; he was supposed to have been a graduate of Dublin University. 'I see you're a BA,' beamed Richard Hope, whose glance then crossed the stage to find Mitch bending down to look in a cupboard so that the BA could be interpreted (by us) as Big Arse.

Flann O'Brien once wrote to William Saroyan suggesting his novel might provide material for 'a crazy play': he would probably have liked what Campbell and his clowns made of it. Although the text (adapted by Campbell with Richard Dunkley) omitted the hero's erotic encounter with a lady bicycle and spared us the sight, alas, of fourteen one-legged desperadoes bearing down on the country police station to rescue one of their own, the bones of it were joyously intact: Mitch's character connives in the murder of an old man and is transported to a netherworld of garrulous coppers, sympathetic unipeds, and the atomic theory of 'bicyclosis' on the road to eternity.

Both *Hitchhiker's* and *Third Policeman* wefted *Warp* threads of an alternative lifestyle, mysteries of the paranormal, a search for truth without really knowing what that is, adventurous propulsion through a dizzying and often surreal landscape of characters and changeable states of consciousness. They were, in a sense, the application of the method and approach that was the essence of *The Warp*, the big daddy of fringe theatre projects and its touchstone *magnum opus*. And in Russell Denton, we had the hippy Hamlet of the era, taking to its logical extension the David Warner Hamlet for the Royal Shakespeare Company in 1965, a prince out of sorts with himself and his society even before the drugs, the communes and all the sci-fi stuff came along. There's a scene in Notting Hill Tube station where Phil is sharing a joint with an anarchist poet when he goes into a trance and contemplates jumping the life to come (onto the live tracks) and being reborn in death: 'Does that mean if you were *me* you *could* do it, because you've already done it, and it would be easy: or does it mean that if you were me, you'd feel so *wretched* that you'd see nothing else worth doing, but jumping?!! But what if I jump on the lines and I don't get reborn? I'd be toast and you'd be laughing, wouldn't you...? You'd let me die for a laugh.'

'To be, or not to be' is definitely sometimes the question for Phil, but he's a spy for love who will fight on all fronts against the conspirators who deny the human spirit, and that's what ultimately gives *The Warp* its fantastic energy and imperishable joy: people tell Phil things all the time and he listens (he's got no choice; he's in virtually all the scenes) and he learns. In Edinburgh, Terry Johnson noted the actor had entered a new dimension: 'The thing about Russell was that he'd gone mystic. I remember vividly doing a scene with him after about twelve hours, and he started talking to me under his breath while I was doing my lines; and he was saying, "Slow down, slow down, hold on..." and if you dried he was in immediately – he knew all the lines, everybody's lines, the whole thing. He could prompt you as he carried on, so he'd really gone somewhere else. It was amazing.' Denton agrees that he hit a new level in Edinburgh. 'It was the central experience. Almost every night Ken was up there saying something, giving us some sort of Henry V-style pep talk, but more subtle than that. He said one night that we may have to start changing our names: in our former identities, or pre-*Warp* selves, we would not possibly be good enough to carry on in other, more normal circumstances; and that we had reached some sort of level of transcendence; he really believed that. The old identity had to go, and you had to create a new identity, one commensurate with this extraordinary thing that was going on.'

It was always a question for Russell: how to follow *The Warp*? The answer for him was... with great difficulty. Although the show was revived one year later in Liverpool, and he took part, there were simply no other mountains left for him to climb, no challenges to take up. Denton's post-*Warp* life has been, he admits, a sort of recovery process, but he says he's recovered now. He had a short-lived marriage to an actress in Liverpool; he had a near nervous breakdown; he did a lot of drugs: 'My brain was so mangled by playing this part... nobody, not even Ken, understood that when you're onstage for twenty-four hours, something starts happening to your brain; it's not just time, something else takes over.' In all, he played sixteen twenty-four-hour cycles of *The Warp* over two years. 'After eight hours, your body is screaming, "Okay, that's enough now, you've got to lie down," but you can't, you've got another eight hours to go; and after that eight hours your body is crying out even louder, "Lie down, stop"; and you can't, you've got another eight hours... I used to have to look for places in the show where I could do a special kind of breathing I'd learned with a voice teacher to energise the body, and I'd be doing this secretly while somebody else was delivering a speech. I didn't stop dreaming about it all for at least ten years, and I'd always wake up sweating.'

Did he ever regret making that phone call in Leeds? 'As far as I'm concerned everything turned out as it was supposed to be, right down to the moment where I'm sitting here in this café having a cup of coffee with you. I moved into a whole other area of thinking about the world and how I saw myself in it. I did a lot of drugs, lot of acid, lot of ecstasy, a lot of ketamine – it's a dancing drug, a sort of anaesthetic, and you can go into another world experience, fantastic stuff... I reached the point where there was nothing more to explore out there...' At this point in our interview in the aforesaid café in Belsize Park (and I have the tape to prove it), the sound of Edith Piaf singing 'Je ne regrette rien' comes over the background music system. 'There was no play out there I particularly wanted to do, *Hamlet* of course, perhaps, and so I had to go somewhere, and the only place I could go was inside... a lot of spiritual exploration, you could call it that.' He did some lorry-driving and took small parts on television. He played Prince Hal in a touring production of *Henry IV* with Leslie Phillips as Falstaff, and was directed by Terry Johnson in a 1987 revival of Alan Ayckbourn's *Bedroom Farce*. But the work started drying up, and in 1990 he took a job as a part-time handyman in a children's nursery near the Abbey Road recording studios and stayed there for ten years. 'I just loved it. I always got on well with kids, but this was my first experience of very small ones, from six months to four years old, and they helped me to readjust totally. I was blissed-out by the experience. I packed in my agent and stopped sending my photograph to *Spotlight* and took honorary withdrawal from Equity.'

Neil Oram had always stayed in touch, and Denton loved visiting him in Goshen, on the edge of Loch Ness, five miles from the nearest village. 'It's one of the most beautiful places I've ever seen, breathtakingly beautiful, like fairy woods. I've seen Neil stand there and whistle and the sky will fill with blue tits. I've walked through the woods in bare feet because the moss is so gentle. And on one visit, one of the young women living with Neil seduced me. And I started an affair and decided to go and live up there in 2000.' The idyll backfired badly, the drugs became a real problem, the affair turned to dust and after eighteen months he left to recover from yet another traumatic experience in a friend's cottage in Pennan, the little Scottish village where Bill Forsyth filmed *Local Hero*. Is he at peace now? 'Oh yes. I've had a relationship with a professional woman who lives six or seven yards up the road from me in East Finchley. We were good friends before I went to Scotland, and now we're consummated, as it were. I live in my flat. She lives in hers. I have sufficient money from the state to live on. Occasionally I do a bit of painting and decorating. And I cultivate my allotment.'

The Age of Aquarius gave way to the age of the blockbuster, but nothing would ever rival the shoestring majesty of *The Warp*. The Royal Shakespeare Company, an incorrigibly expansionist organisation under the artistic directorship of Trevor Nunn, announced two major projects for the first half of 1980, as if mocking *The Warp* with a boast of bigger resources and higher cultural aims. The RSC's London base was then the Aldwych Theatre, where, in February 1980, the company unveiled a ten-play, all-day cycle of mostly Euripidean ancient tragedies, *The Greeks*, recounting the full story of the House of Atreus, from the sacrifice of Iphigenia in Aulis, through the conquest of Troy, the murderous rifts in Agamemnon's palace and the confusion of Electra, to cathartic reunion on the barbaric soil of Tauris under the supervision of a rational goddess. *The Greeks* was staged by John Barton, using Kenneth Cavander's translations and John Napier's designs. It was a fantastic achievement and yet it probably got as little enthusiastic critical recognition as *The Warp*.

The show that stole everyone's critical thunder – after a slow start and then a rave from Bernard Levin on the main editorial pages in *The Times* that led to frenzy at the box office – was Trevor Nunn and John Caird's staging of *Nicholas Nickleby*, adapted from Charles Dickens into two long plays by David Edgar and, again, designed by John Napier (with Dermot Hayes). *Nicholas Nickleby* opened to the press on 21 June 1980 and closed on 26 July. Nationwide in-depth coverage of the show had been guaranteed not only by Levin's review, but also by the strange business of the Royal Dickens Company hoax, perpetrated towards the end of that run. The production returned to the Aldwych later that same year, in November, and went on to become a huge West End and Broadway success; Nunn followed up with *Cats* for Andrew Lloyd Webber and Cameron Mackintosh in 1981 and, with John Caird, *Les Misérables*, which in 1986 exploited RSC *Nickleby* values and staging techniques in a popular commercial setting. Ken Campbell had a critical part to play in all this, but his role was subversive and sarcastic, not participatory. He'd made his own statement about epic theatre. And his inimitable brand of it, in the paradoxically cheap but monumental *The Warp*, left no room for further commercial exploitation.

Dickens of a Hoax

O n 14 July 1980, halfway through the first run of *Nicholas Nickleby* at the Aldwych, a series of letters was dispatched from the London headquarters of the RSC, written on Stratford-upon-Avon notepaper, signed by one of the joint Artistic Directors, Trevor Nunn, offering the distinguished recipients important work in the next stage of the company's artistic evolution. In every detail save one, the notepaper replicated the RSC's official square letterhead, but substituted the heading 'RSC Royal Shakespeare Company' with 'RDC Royal Dickens Company', the initials bordered with the correct thin black lines and a circular emblem of the swan of the Avon. The RDC was, the heading declared, under the overall direction of Peggy Ashcroft, John Barton, Peter Brook, Terry Hands and Trevor Nunn, exactly as was the RSC; the Royal Dickens Theatre was similarly incorporated under Royal Charter, with Her Majesty the Queen as Patron, Sir Harold Wilson as President and Sir Kenneth Cork as Chairman. One of the recipients of these letters was the director Bill Bryden, well known for his National Theatre productions of *The Mysteries*, the sea plays of Eugene O'Neill and an adaptation by Keith Dewhurst of Flora Thompson's rural Oxfordshire documentary *Lark Rise to Candleford*:

> Dear Bill,
>
> As you have probably heard, there has been a major policy change in our organisation. *Nicholas Nickleby* has been such a source of real joy to cast, staff and audiences that we have decided to turn to Dickens as

our main source of inspiration. So that'll be it for the Bard as soon as our present commitments decently permit. The first production of the new RDC is hoped to be *Little Dorrit*, adapted by Snoo Wilson and directed by John Caird and myself. I feel your theatrical development has probably led you close to the field we now move into. Would *Pickwick Papers* fire your imagination, Bill? With the prospect of a Keith Dewhurst script, and music by the Albion Band, it certainly fires mine.

Looking forward to your reaction.

Love,

Trev.

In similar letters, with slight variations, but not in the basic structure and information, Peter Hall was asked about the idea of Alan Ayckbourn turning his attention to *Martin Chuzzlewit*; Howard Davies was invited 'to have a look at' *A Christmas Carol*; and Campbell's old mentor Peter Cheeseman was encouraged to let the Stoke house dramatist Peter Terson fall on *Hard Times* – 'Let me know your reactions, Peter, together with any plans you might have for altering the shape of the auditorium.' Nor was the grandiloquent, seigneurial, theatre-loving Minister for the Arts in Mrs Thatcher's Government, Norman St John-Stevas, kept in the dark on these developments. He was assured that 'Dickens will prove as big a draw as Shakespeare, if we can keep up this terrific standard... Any thoughts you have on this will, as always, be treasured. Love, Trev. PS: Perhaps we could get together for lunch sometime soon to discuss this. The Pickwick Club would seem appropriate!' Richard Eyre might have cast a beady eye over the suggestion of yoking Trevor Griffiths to *A Tale of Two Cities* and Nunn's rider that 'Jonathan Pryce would seem to me a perfect Sidney Carton'. But film-maker Mike Leigh, who had worked as a young director at the RSC and had cancelled a new RSC commission tentatively called *Ice-cream* ten weeks into rehearsal at the very start of the Trevor Nunn and Terry Hands co-artistic directorship in 1978, was only momentarily fooled by his overture: 'Let bygones be bygones, Mike, and let's really try to put your inimicable [sic] style to work on this new venture. I can offer you twenty-three actors for a seventeen-week rehearsal period in the spring of 1982 if you are prepared to take on the challenge of *Bleak House*. Looking forward to your reactions. Love, Trev.' Apart from the uncharacteristic and unlikely mishmash of 'inimical' and 'inimitable', Leigh noted that Trevor never actually signed off as 'Trev' and that, unlike on the RDC letter, the 'T' of Trevor was always a sort of crossbow signifying a fraternal, perhaps even affectionate, kiss. One wonders how John Barton must have reacted to his letter, which also implied a little less erudition than you'd expect from Nunn: 'Which is the unfinished one, John? Are you the man to finish it?'

Fooled or not, neither Leigh nor anyone else knew who was the real author of these letters. Ken had gone to see *Nicholas Nickleby* with Dave Hill, chiefly because their old Road Show colleague, and Ken's former lover, Susan Littler, was in the cast, playing Kate Nickleby and Mrs Curdle. They both loved it but there was something niggling away inside Ken about the comparative lack of acclaim for his own efforts in the epic sphere. He wanted to goad the RSC into a really major effort of risk-taking, something more concomitant with their vast funding. Susan Littler would be their 'mole'. Ken and Dave paid a visit to their friend Richard Adams, a brilliant graphic designer especially associated with *Oz* magazine and other underground press titles, who had started and run the Open Head Press publishing partnership in his office near the Portobello Road with Heathcote Williams. Adams and Williams had been 'completely knocked out' by *Illuminatus!* at the National and had produced the unofficial programme when it transferred to the Roundhouse. Having secured the RSC square-format notepaper, Adams faked-up the artwork which became the RDC letterhead, a considerably trickier task than it would be in these Photoshop days. With the letters in circulation, and speculation as to their source running wild in the newspapers, word from within the RSC suggested that an increasingly agitated Trevor Nunn had three top suspects: Snoo Wilson, Ken Campbell and Heathcote Williams – so he wasn't far off. The saboteurs now decided to produce the posters for the putative RDC 'opener' *Little Dorrit* on the penultimate night of *Nicholas Nickleby* and so get the box office humming in the hours before its last performance.

The poster was quickly and cheaply produced, though it was not all that easy in 1980 to find an A2 photocopier. Adams used the image of a sweet little bonneted girl, Amy Dorrit, in a black-and-white engraving that was an eerie premonition of the angelic waif designed by Dewynters for *Les Misérables* a few years later. Adams's Amy appeared discreetly in an otherwise classic RSC replica design, crediting Snoo Wilson as the adaptor, with the full list of RSC *Nickleby* actors listed in alphabetical order down the right-hand side: Suzanne Bertish, Christopher Benjamin, Susan Littler, Roger Rees, Timothy Spall, David Threlfall, John Woodvine... Terry Johnson, who claims to have 'cast' the hoax as he'd read more Dickens than anyone else around Ken, and was just finishing off *Little Dorrit*, says that the dummy letters were written on four typewriters in the dressing rooms at the Rainbow during the ill-fated transfer of *Hitchhiker's*. One night, Ken appeared and said, 'I've got an announcement to make on the Royal Dickens front. I've got good news and bad news. The bad news is that we can be done, each and every one of us, under the Public Mischief Act of 1923. But the good news is that the posters are ready!' About fifty posters were made up, and the trap was set. The plan was to fly-poster the whole area around the Aldwych, make a special presentation pack of the letters for Trevor Nunn, and a rolled-up copy of the poster in a cardboard tube for Roger Rees, playing the title role, to be presented in his dressing room when the curtain came down, along with a cake – 'a real masterpiece' says Adams – which had been made by a couple of neighbours of Dave and Jane, covered in blue icing with yellow piping and a quotation on the top: 'Please, sir, can we have some more?'

Late that Friday night, the chief conspirators convened on Haverstock Hill: Richard Adams, Dave, Jane, Prue and Ken. After curtain-down in the theatres, they piled into Ken's little Morris Traveller van with a small set of ladders and a made-up bucket of paste. Adams says that 'Ken also whipped out three crown toppers for the three baldies, and all this added to the hysteria. We drove down to the Aldwych at midnight. It was pretty much deserted at that time. And we hit the area, plastering the theatre, the bus stop, and all the noticeboards.' Most of Saturday was spent phoning the box office making enquiries about *Little Dorrit*. And then they all reconvened in Adams's studio to brief the man charged with making the deliveries. This pregnant messenger was a white American black-cab driver called Wally, a draft dodger who'd come to England as a fully paid-up proselytiser for the legalisation of cannabis (so much so that he had plants of the stuff growing in the back of the cab). Wally was the key, and he didn't let anyone down. With his cab lights still flashing in the Aldwych, he braved the last-night throng with his special deliveries for Nunn and Rees, made it backstage, and into the dressing rooms. Nunn's presentation pack of letters was covered with a beautifully calligraphed quotation from *The Tempest*: 'As you from crimes would pardoned be, / Let your indulgence set me free...' But by this time Nunn was very far indeed from being amused. To add insult to injury, someone (unconnected with Campbell, as far as we know) had placed an illuminated penis masquerading as a banana in Roger Rees's fruit bowl.

Nunn had to confirm, rather wearily, that no further Dickens adaptations were scheduled. A few days later he told *The Times*: 'It is now deeply embarrassing; a lot of people have written to me refusing, or, even more embarrassing, accepting the offers.' As another week rumbled by, there was a difference of opinion between Dave and Ken as to whether to own up to the hoax or not. Dave was against, Ken anxious to put an end to it all. It must have been like the dust-up between Brutus and Cassius over whether or not Mark Antony should be allowed to speak at Caesar's funeral. Ken went on the BBC 2 television programme *Newsnight* on 4 August, remaining in a mystery silhouette until he was called upon, and confessed to the interviewer Jeremy Paxman, claiming that he had been 'inspired by the excellence' of the RSC's *Nicholas Nickleby* and that he 'wanted to write a fan letter to alert the world to it'. This wasn't just a hoax. It was a serious interventionist caper for both Ken and Richard Adams, expressing important aspects of their respective creative lives in terms of engaging with the culture of the day and offering a critical perspective. As much as any thunderous jeremiad about the course the RSC was set upon, the jape queried the possible deleterious effect of abiding by the charter which demanded that they concentrate on Shakespeare, and the jokey tone of the correspondence highlighted the casual way commissioning was conducted.

As far as Adams was concerned, the project was a continuation of the satirical work he and Heathcote Williams had been up to for some time. Adams's Blenheim Crescent studio was in a house that had produced the first animal-liberation magazine, *The Beast*, and had seen Emma Tennant launch the magazine *Bananas*, and Gilbert Shelton and his Fabulous Furry Freak Brothers leap about in comic-book form. Adams and Williams used to publish what they called anarchist porn in book and poster form, even publishing Earl Russell's notable maiden speech – the pacifist, liberal, controversial peer was the son of Bertrand Russell – in the House of Lords, with a Ralph Steadman drawing. 'So Ken saw us,' says Adams, 'as a mouthpiece for views that he shared anyway.' The Notting Hill base also served as the embassy for the Free and Independent Republic of Frestonia, founded by Nicholas Albery, the social inventor, writer and activist, whose younger brother, Tim, had been production manager on *The Warp*. Albery and Heathcote Williams had been squatting in Freston Road, running the Rough Tuff Cream Puff Agency – an estate agents for squats and empty properties – when the residents, threatened with eviction to make way for a factory, voted in favour of independence from Britain. The area became a site for housing and craft workshops, with Heathcote Williams acting as Frestonian Ambassador to Great Britain, David Rappaport as the Minister of Transport and Adams as the President of the Royal College of Heralds. Albery initiated the campaign over the use of unleaded petrol in cars by pinpointing the effect of petrol fumes emanating from the nearby Westway in a gypsy encampment on the edge of the estate; ironically, he died in a car crash in 2001, although he never drove a car himself.

This was very much Campbell's social milieu around this time, and although he had applied for the directorship of the Liverpool Everyman Theatre, he would keep in touch with Adams, Williams, Albery and the rest; indeed, he collaborated on a fascinating and rather fruity social experiment with Albery just a couple of years later. But having 'hoaxed' the future policy of the RSC, it was time to test his organisational capacity for real in the one city where he felt really at home and likely to succeed.

10

At the End of Hope Street

The Liverpool Everyman was an appealingly scruffy theatre at the Catholic cathedral end of Hope Street, where it nestled nearby both the Philharmonic Concert Hall and the other Philharmonic, the famous Victorian 'Phil' pub with its decorated mirrors and polished wooden alcoves and bars. Hope Hall was a former chapel that opened for business as the Everyman in September 1964 with a production of *Henry IV, Part One* directed by Martin Jenkins and Peter James, with Terry Hands (the third of the artistic triumvirate and future director of the RSC) as Sir Walter Blunt, Susan Fleetwood as Lady Percy and John McEnery as Hotspur. The place soon acquired a reputation as a seedbed of acting talent but also, more importantly perhaps, as a theatre with a unique connection to its city's politics, football and music. It was blessed with a feisty Chairman, Harry Livermore, who fought tooth and nail for his theatre and always defended his artists when they ruffled feathers or worse.

In May 1974 I attended the first night of Willy Russell's *John, Paul, George, Ringo... and Bert* ('Bert was me and another 43,000 people in Liverpool who claim they once played with The Beatles,' said the author) – a night to treasure alongside those during the contemporary Richard Eyre period in Nottingham – and the raucous tradition of folk plays with savvy Scouse wit and a vivid local application continued through the roustabout regimes of Alan Dossor, Chris Bond and Pedr (as opposed to Peter) James. There had been a rebuild in the mid-1970s, but the place was essentially the same: gloriously informal, with a buzzing bistro and a clear identity separate from the more sedate and traditional repertory theatre, the Playhouse, in the city centre. It was to the Everyman that Campbell had first taken his *Illuminatus!* proposal, but they declined to take him up on it, though their scenic and costume departments were always helpful. So when the chance came to run the place himself, Ken jumped at it. He'd applied for various artistic director jobs around the regions with no success; he was either too dangerous or simply too unpredictable. What a breath of fresh air, though, he would have been, and might be now! Glen Walford, a successor to Ken at the Everyman, says that when he applied for the job, he rang up and asked them to send two forms, 'in case I make a bollocks of the first one'.

Glen, the founder of the touring Bubble Theatre, had circled Ken on the fringe for years – like him, she is an only child and she was the only other director client on the books of the agent Maureen Vincent – and she remembers once going for the same job at the Crewe Rep. They sat in a room together with the other applicant, Philip Anthony (who got the job), sitting correctly with a briefcase on his knees. They were guarded by a town councillor. The window gave out on a deeply unattractive prospect of Crewe Station. Ken, says Glen, got up, looked out the window, turned round and said, 'I think I've done Crewe now, I think I'll go!' A deep silence fell among them. Ken was called in for his interview, emerged forty-five minutes later, and said: 'Well, I don't know what to make of that; I turned at the door when I finished, but they didn't even give me cricket applause...'

His interview at the Everyman was no less bizarre. It was a late-spring morning in 1980 and Campbell knew that the Board would want to know his plans for the Christmas show – the cornerstone of any repertory theatre's economy – and he knew the preference was for something original, not a traditional pantomime. He reckoned he had a killer idea: *Fungus the Bogeyman* by Raymond Briggs. Years later, when he finally directed *Fungus* as a 'plop opera' at the Belgrade in Coventry, he explained what happened. 'Briggs's masterpiece had not been out long and I was an early enthusiast. I'd packed my copy in my bag. It was like having a bomb in there. Came the moment... the Board were clearly impressed by my plans for the opening of the season... "And for Christmas, Ken?" I put my bag on the table and with a theatrical flourish I unzipped it: my copy of *Fungus* wasn't in it! Had one of the other hopefuls (there were six candidates) nicked it? I don't know. What *was* in the bag was that week's *Sunday Times* colour supplement and on the front cover was a photo of a beautiful, full-of-life, dancing, teenage black Welsh girl who'd just won the world disco-dancing championship. So I whisked that out the bag: "I shall put on *Disco Dance Queen*, gentlemen, starring this lady on the front cover, Julie Brown!" The Board had all read the article. "Could you get her?" "Yes." "Have you spoken to her?" "She was out, I spoke to her mum. There's no problem." I got the girl. We put on *The Disco Queen*. It was a hit. Julie went on to be a *Crackerjack* hostess on children's television and then moved to New York to become "Downtown Julie Brown". *Fungus* had to wait in the wings, festering, for fifteen years.'

The Board had also liked his suggestion of opening up with a revival of *The Warp*, given in a weekly rep format of one play a week for ten weeks until *The Disco Queen* took off. It was a no-brainer, or seemed to be, with Russell Denton reprising Phil Masters, joined by a promising newcomer from the Everyman Youth Theatre, Mark McGann, and such other offbeat irregulars as Jim Broadbent, Helen Cooper, Lewis Cowen, Terry Johnson, John Joyce and Mitch Davies, with Neil Cunningham dispensing another master-race masterclass in deadly precision. The seats were removed and the audience either squatted on the floor or milled around the five main acting areas, with the band discreetly amplified above to represent the expanding mind of the hero; this was a big change from the scrappier interchange of dialogue and music at the ICA. And the whole show seemed meaner, leaner and tighter. It heralded a new era, perhaps, in the fortunes not only of the Everyman (which had dipped, slightly), but also in the country: if everyone did *The Warp*, our national theatre would be revolutionised overnight! At the time, the Everyman still gloried in the Liverpool school of playwrights led by Willy Russell, Alan Bleasdale, Chris Bond and Bill Morrison (though the schism wasn't far off when this Gang of Four decamped across town to the Playhouse, the start of the disastrous Arts Council-instigated blurring of the edges between the two venues). Campbell and *The Warp* seemed just the right sort of jolt everyone needed. Trouble brewed, though, when a weekly wage bill of £3,800 – for fifteen actors and four musicians – proved unsustainable even with packed houses. The theatre was soon £44,000 in the red and was closed for ten days before *The Disco Queen* even opened. This disastrous overspend resulted in half the staff being sacked at the end of May 1981, and Campbell was happy to take a back seat as 'Consultant Artistic Director' while the Board recruited Bob Eaton from the Contact Theatre in Manchester to run the theatre from day to day.

In catapulting Julie Brown onto the Everyman stage, Campbell was light years ahead of today's theatrical exploitation of television talent-show contestants, and even of their judging panels. In the show, she was belched, with her band, from a train making an unscheduled stop on a railway platform where Campbell had stirred up the station staff into a sort of Spike Jones frenzy in a spirit of mutinous good temper. One of them was the Huddersfield eccentric Wilf Lunn, who gradually took over the first half with an exhibition of his loony gadgets, including a laser contraption for preventing birds from stealing your milk-bottle tops, and a halitosis helmet with a periscope apparatus ensuring that any bad breath you might exhale would sail harmlessly over your friends' heads. This was the curtain-raiser to the disco section, but it was obviously the part of the show Ken himself most enjoyed. Julie proved a likeable personality and a graceful mover though she lacked (in my view) the killer punch of true stardom. Still, the theatre went up like a rocket as she led a company of schoolgirls and disguised railway porters in a potted history of dance before inviting the audience up onto the stage for the Everyman's own disco-dancing competition. Campbell loved audience participation probably more than anything else in the theatre. Not because of its democratic properties, but because it put the wind up the actors and created an air of 'anything could happen next'. And he liked dogs to join in, too. At the auditions for a dog in *The Disco Queen* he stood on the stage in full referee's kit, complete with whistle and ball, and blew... All hell broke loose, and he simply couldn't control it. Dogs carried on barking and fighting each other for hours, and the theatre took a whole day to recover from the mayhem. But nepotism ruled, and Ken's Werner got the role, anyway.

Bob Eaton says that his arrival in Ken's hot seat worked out okay because the obligation of running a building wasn't quite what Ken had wanted or bargained for – though what he did want wasn't all that clear, either. He'd basically spent the grant for the entire year on the first production, so he followed *The Disco Queen* with a few cheap and cheerful fillers; but of course, none of them involved Agatha Christie or Alan Ayckbourn. In that sense, he remained true to the spirit of the Everyman, and there was great local critical appreciation for a tribute show about the folk singer Hank Williams and a return to Liverpool by John Joyce and Chris Fairbank in *Psychosis Unclassified*. And in March 1981 (the production visited the Riverside Studios in London in July) he managed to sustain the great strand of sci-fi wackiness in his work with Kenny Murray's drastic adaptation (which he directed) of Karel Čapek's 1939 sci-fi satire, *War with the Newts*. He also revived his enthusiasm for the aqua shows of Bournemouth by placing half the *Newts* acting area in a vast tank, and first seriously indulged his growing taste for impressionism and improvisation in supervising a cornucopia of impersonations of politicos and television celebrities: Prince Charles, Alan Whicker, Mrs Thatcher, Esther Rantzen, Russell Harty, Malcolm Muggeridge, Bob Dylan, David Bellamy and Michael Foot all took a bow in a saga of man's inhumanity to newts. Charles and Diana even adopted two newts named collectively as Olivia Newt 'n' John.

Campbell's second season was subject to the final say-so of Bob Eaton, but Bob shared Ken's enthusiasm for the idea

of a theatrical tribute to John Lennon – who had been murdered in New York the previous December – followed by a
revival of Ken's *Old King Cole* for Christmas. This seemed a
good plan, though Campbell went further, of course, in suggesting a whole-weekend Lennon extravaganza, including
every song The Beatles ever wrote. Eaton knocked that idea
on the head and proceeded to compile a conventional bio-
musical that performed brilliantly at the box office and was
brought back into the repertoire the following February.

Ken had one last inglorious fling at the Everyman in April 1982
with an ill-advised epilogue to *The Warp*, Neil Oram's
Chameleon Blue: the Further Adventures of Phil Masters, in
which a young actor fresh from RADA, John Sessions, played
the leader of a tribe of tepee people. Nothing in the show
matched the fervour of Neil Oram's programme note in which
he advocated a popular uprising against all weapons around
the globe. Stories abound in Everyman folklore of this copper-
bottomed lulu of a flop. Glen Walford says that Russell Denton
complained to Ken on the first night that he hadn't given him
a note during the entire four weeks of rehearsal. Ken obliged
with, 'Do what you've always been doing but don't make a cunt
of yourself.' Ken had left the last rehearsal halfway through,
and Russell ordered the deputy stage manager to go and find
him. He was in the bistro drinking whisky. Why had he left, the
minion asked, Russell's going nuts... and Ken calmly replied,
'It seemed to be going well, so I didn't have to see it. And if it
was going badly, I wouldn't want to see it.' In one scene, a
stuffed goat came flying through a plate-glass window and,
like the play itself, thudded lifeless to the floor. Russell Denton
was distraught with the failure of it – the joy and juice of *The
Warp* was drained away in a weak chronicle of tiresome,
sponging hippies. Six weeks later, still distraught, he married
an actress in the show; they lasted ten months in what he
described as 'the most terrible things that went down
between two people' (though they renewed a friendship of
sorts many years later).

John Sessions, however, came out of the experience relatively unscarred, or rather, scarred in a good way, taken up by Campbell as his latest protégé. He'd written to Campbell towards the end of his time at drama school, inviting him to come and see an improvised one-man show he'd put together. Ken had a positive response when he went along to see it and said that as he was now at the Everyman he'd have to interview Sessions 'officially'. Sessions left RADA – where his friends and contemporaries included Kenneth Branagh and Douglas Hodge, who were obviously going to take care of the business end of the acting lark – unsure of his future, good at taking the mickey, perhaps seeking an oddball niche of some kind. He was working as a security officer guarding property by night when Ken's call came, so he went round to Haverstock Hill in his Securicor uniform for the interview: 'I don't know whether it was his idea or mine, but I did Mike Leigh as a Chinese-takeaway emporium and Ian McKellen as a flying-eye helicopter, and I remember Daisy's toys scattered all over the floor.' Campbell said he 'quite liked' what Sessions was doing but wanted to see if he'd run out of steam. 'So he persuaded me that I could do a whole one-man show about Ulysses, and I was naive enough to think that I could. I never did it, but he put so much wind in your sails, daring you all the time, and gave you so much ebullience... and then he said I should go to Liverpool with him and become a proper actor.' But first, because of Sessions's lack of confidence, Ken paid for him to take the Werner Erhard EST course, stripping away his emotional layers until he endured, at the end of the weekend, something akin to a nervous breakdown. 'I felt this mad elation that I'd never known since I was about three; this was powerful stuff, and it obviously sunk a little seed in me because, in the following summer, after *Chameleon Blue*, the sensation came back, unannounced, while I was doing, of all plays, *One Flew Over the Cuckoo's Nest* at the Royal Exchange in Manchester, and I had another mini-breakdown. And I wasn't happy about it, but Ken's kindness and steering of me was amazing.'

In Liverpool, before rehearsals started, Ken made Sessions perform improvisations all day, every day, in the old tea parlour in Mathew Street that had been the *Illuminatus!* theatre and was now The Beatles museum, recording the Sessions sessions, and giving detailed notes. Then, during the run of *Chameleon*, Sessions appeared in a late-night improvised revue called *Are There Camiknickers After Death, Wack?*, and if he repeated any material from the night before, Ken made him forfeit his wages. Sessions spent his days pounding the streets thinking up new material on The Beatles, the Liverpool poets and performance artists: 'Ken gave me enormous confidence and even after a bad night when the audience would just sit there numb with incomprehension, he'd simply say that it was up to them to catch up. He knew I needed toughening up; out of the blue, he'd say that he'd booked me into the Runcorn Leisure Centre, or into the roughest pub he could find in Toxteth. I remember being pelted with Coke cans.' Ken – who said that if Billy Connolly was Lenny Bruce and had an MA in literature, he'd begin to look like John Sessions – also made him go and perform for the women at Greenham Common. 'It was a grey and miserable day. We drove down there with Werner the dog, and I did twenty minutes of utter crap, which was certainly received as such, and then we got back in the car and drove all the way back to Liverpool in utter silence until, eventually, Ken said, "Well, that wasn't one of your finest hours." There was never any down time with him. It was always full-on, with lots of drinking. Some of the drinking would make him very peculiar, and he'd suddenly scream and yell. I'd been put off sword fighting at RADA when a boy was blinded and paralysed in a free-fencing episode which should never have happened. In the *Chameleon* rehearsals, I was kneeling down while this lovely big Northern comic Ted Robbins [a second cousin of Paul McCartney] was coming straight at me wielding a knife. Ted and I agreed we'd stage it carefully, with minimal chance of a mishap, and Ken went berserk, screaming and shouting that he didn't believe a fucking minute of what we were doing and it was too fucking actor-y, and when I said I was sorry but I'd seen this terrible accident... he just shouted that he'd make *me* a fucking accident. He would come to rehearsal with a crate of beer and work his way through it, just as Simon

Gray used to do with a crate of champagne, though I never saw either of them drunk, or at least visibly drunk.'

The Science Fiction Theatre of Liverpool stuttered briefly back to life in London with a Gothic opera, *Carmilla*, as Ken withdrew gracefully from the debacle of his brief tenure at the Everyman. Bob Eaton struggled on for another year before Glen Walford slid into the hot seat and presided over a good programme with ever-diminishing resources for the next five years from September 1983. Ken went to see her water-logged version of *Macbeth*, with the witches swimming under a bridge through what looked like fetid bracken. 'It was right up Ken's street, he loved it. He loves water in the theatre any-way, and he told me that he'd said to himself, "She's not going to have Macbeth and Macduff jumping off that bridge at the end, is she?" and was delighted that they did! The Everyman is an "event" theatre and is really there for exploring ways of how theatre should operate.' Years after *The Warp* was on there, hippy characters would drift through the bistro and pro-claim, 'I was in *The Warp*, man, and I never got paid.'

Whether or not *Carmilla* was a casualty of the Everyman restructuring is not clear. The script consisted of Sheridan Le Fanu's Gothic horror stories, ransacked by the American librettist Wilford Leach (whose 'rocked-up' version of *The Pirates of Penzance*, first done for Joseph Papp's Public The-ater in New York starring Kevin Kline, had just opened at the Theatre Royal, Drury Lane, with Chris Langham in the cast). With creepy music by Ben Johnston, a pupil of John Cage, it was presented for just one performance by the Almeida Festi-val at St James's Church off the Holloway Road in June 1982. Campbell's production, witty and restrained, was designed by Mavis Taylor with musical direction by Camilla Saunders and film by Mitch Davies. Neil Cunningham played a mysterious traveller falling in with two girls, one in crimson, one in white.

But you felt Ken was itching to get back to something more crude and visceral: that turned out to be a riotous pro-duction of Beckett's *Waiting for Godot* at the Young Vic in the very next month. John Sessions was cast as the gibbering Lucky, the dope on the end of a rope, whose long speech, more usually bustled through to gloss over its incomprehensibility, was a clue to the whole protean quality of the production. Beckett's tramps, Estragon and Vladimir, lived on a rubbish tip, the detritus of a consumer society, which included chamber pots, old clothes, a broken television, as well as Pozzo's stool and an old Hoover which prompted a gag on the line: 'I don't like talking into a vacuum.' The clown tramps alluded directly to other great double acts – Morecambe and Wise, Laurel and Hardy, and the 'Pete 'n' Dud' act of Peter Cook and Dudley Moore. If, as the Beckett line goes, something gave these two the impression they existed, in this instance they also existed to give us impressions, a whole range of them, some left over from *War with the Newts*, some new-minted in the style of *The Goon Show*. But all these voices were of little comfort in the second act as Andy Rashleigh's Vladimir continually pulled Jonathan Barlow's Estragon back from the brink, the gaping void. The show was clearly a poignant taster for Campbell's growing obsession with what he considered the deleterious effects of the media – in the realms of television, surveillance, political spin-doctoring – and the common background of the quartet of characters was underlined by Pozzo's appearance in pyjamas. Had he escaped from the madhouse, or was he joining them there? It's impossible to imagine how this great production ever made it past the vigilant Beckett estate – perhaps they were just not told about it – but the play was released in all its power and beauty in a way I'd never seen before, and Camilla Saunders's dangerously random piano accompaniment lent a mythic, silent-movie quality to the proceedings while underlining the waywardness of the behavioural patterns within the structure. And you wondered, too, what Campbell might have done in other areas of the modern classical repertoire had he been more interested in going there.

The dual interest in madness and television, and what must have been a slight sense of panic about where he might go next in the theatre, led Campbell to a phase of frantic ideas-touting and activity, a phase that only settled down as he stumbled towards his apotheosis in the solo-show format towards the end of the 1980s. His papers reveal scripts and first drafts for screenplays of increasing outlandishness and lunacy. But two of them found their way into responsive hands. First, *Unfair Exchanges* was produced for the BBC in 1984 by Kenith Trodd, one of the indisputably outstanding and creative television producers of the modern era (closely associated with the work of Dennis Potter). This was, in effect, Ken's first television screenplay and featured Julie Walters – in her first major screen role since *Educating Rita* – as a single mother, Mavis Potter, a magazine journalist on *Today's Lady* who is bugged by late-night phone calls with a sinister ring and develops a scary paranoia. Interestingly, the process is two-way, as the telephone system itself comes alive as a living organism, and Mavis gets sucked into a paranoid quest for the truth. She watches a television play about telephone lines, and her own begins to sing and burst into mad laughter. She meets a writer, Tim Ricketts, played by Ken himself in best beaming and 'up-for-it' mode, who is bearing a copy of the *Fortean Times*. 'Do you believe all this?' asks Mavis. 'No, I don't believe it,' beams Tim, 'I'm a Fortean. I collect the cuttings.' The piece is impeccably directed by Gavin Millar and takes on a new dimension of horror when you realise that the voice on the phone is always Ken Campbell's – as it was for so many of his friends in the small hours when he was suddenly seized by a new thought or campaign of obsession – and he's driving everyone mad! Then Mavis starts hearing her own voice, and breaks into the exchange, pulling at wires until the film freezes on her, tangled up in a Triffid-like labyrinth of brain-scrambling communications.

It's a disturbing finale; but what exactly is it saying? In an unproduced drama, *Wogan's Potatoes*, which he called 'a television play for the theatre', Campbell wrote a weird and remarkable sitcom, a sort of alternative *Royle Family* based on his ongoing research into the effects of television-watching on the mind. The phenomenon of television-watching was translated into a paranoid pile-up of domestic incidents, meetings about 'what to do', visitations from outer cathode rays and a happy ending with Terry Wogan and Bob Geldof diving for cover on screen while a real-life marriage was renewed and the offspring smashed up the television set. As with the telephone, there's a sense that the television is a destructive agent with a life and a mind of its own. Campbell remained a technophobe and Luddite all his working life – when his daughter Daisy urged him to go and buy a computer, he went instead into the pet shop next door and bought an African Grey parrot. But he was much taken by the ideas of commentators like Jerry Mander in San Francisco and Milton Shulman in London who were concerned about the effects of television on society and viewers' mental capabilities. The telephone, too, was something to be wary of, perhaps. And we still had mobiles and iPhones to come...

The second television play to make an impact in this period was *The Madness Museum*, broadcast on Channel 4 in September 1986 as part of a 'Mind's Eye' season on mental health. The season had opened with *The History of Psychiatry*, no less, a documentary narrated by John Sessions, who also appeared alongside Campbell in *The Madness Museum*, a house of derangement supervised by Campbell as Dr James Skipton, a Victorian 'psychologist' very possibly more lunatic than his patients. Campbell's not-so-good doctor inducts Sessions's astonished apprentice in the duties of a physician in this bizarre *Alice in Wonderland* chamber of horrors with its halls of mirrors, restraining chairs, and treatments such as communal vomiting designed to inculcate a sense of camaraderie. The cast included a touchingly restrained (and literally so) Simon Callow as a bath-bound booby whose visions of green beings earn him an early Victorian form of water-boarding, and David Rappaport as a scampering inquisitor asking people about the difference between things.

'By a curious oversight,' said Nancy Banks-Smith in the *Guardian*, 'Dickens forgot to invent the terrifyingly spry loony Dr Skipton... so Ken Campbell invented him instead.' But he had also written a still-pertinent film about the treatment of schizophrenia: do you go along with it, or do you stand up against it? Made with the help of the Wellcome Trust and Friern Hospital, the film still has a lot to say about medical treatment, quite apart from still looking as fresh and funny as the day it was transmitted. Campbell had written the role of Dr Skipton for Sessions, but the director/producer Nigel Evans insisted on Ken playing it himself, and he does so not only with an already-noted Dickensian relish, but also with a fierce, almost understated sense of his own plausibility, leading Sessions around the echoing vaults and corridors with his own dog, Werner, scurrying slowly behind. And he buckles the role to his own theatrical persona, giving a lesson in what he was later to term 'enantiodromic', or split-visaged, acting: he leads the inmates of the laughter room in a ten-minute laughter session – 'Now mutate the laughter upwards,' he cries gleefully, jumping on the table – so that the performance takes on the nature of a typical Ken Campbell rehearsal. And you can have fun spotting a few of the irregulars, too: Mitch Davies, Stuart Pearce, Russell Denton, John Joyce (as a man groaning about the loss of his cows), Bunny Reed, Toby Sedgwick, Tim Morand and even Marcel Steiner.

The film was shot in Friern Hospital in Hertfordshire, then still functioning as an institution, with cries of inmates clearly audible to the actors as they worked. Simon Callow recalls that Ken was much preoccupied, 'but in common with other geniuses, he carried a sort of force field of personality around with him, so that Campbellian things happened even without him being directly involved'. During a tea break, Callow met a pleasant young man, a real-life patient in the hospital, wearing pyjamas, who asked him how he felt about not having played Mozart in the film of Peter Shaffer's *Amadeus*, a role he had created on the stage. So Callow told him exactly how he felt and the young man listened intently before replying, 'Yeah, that's just how I felt when I found out that I was Jesus. I mean, I thought it was a joke at first, and then I kind of got used to it, but it has not been easy.' Callow was called back to the set at that moment and never saw the fellow again.

✧

Buried among Campbell's unmade film and television scripts, there's an outline for *The MGT*, the tale of an all-conquering midget, to be played by David Rappaport, who infiltrates Buckingham Palace, collects phobias, interferes with the EEC, inserts himself into a nuclear warhead and kicks off World War III. Another outline, co-written with Keith Allen, is a hate letter to Max Bygraves, featuring Allen's fantasy of streaking naked across the stage while working (as he did) as a stage-hand at the Victoria Palace on the ingratiating crooner's *Swingalongamax* show. Yet another outline, provisionally titled ****-*Knows*, amalgamated Campbell's fascination with his own nose (which he saw both as a sexual weapon and as representing the rear view of a naked woman's body) with his perennial interest in Oriental and Asian women. In his note-books, he ponders his various powers of proboscis: 'A snort job, giving nose, a night in the snout, coitus proboscidalis, cun-ninazus, CARNAL NOSOLIDGE [a corruption of *Carnal Knowledge*, the 1971 Mike Nichols movie that queried the emotional price of the sexual revolution].'

The residential weekend he arranged with Nicholas Albery in July 1983 is indicative of the volatile personal life he was living through in this period. In Liverpool, he'd embarked on an affair with nineteen-year-old Ayanna Myat Saw, a student at the university, one of three Burmese daughters of the head of a Buddhist Centre in Oxford, and had told Prue about it. She'd said, 'Fine, go ahead,' and that was the 'official' start of their marital split. Ayanna's merry and penetrative laugh had con-vinced Ken that he should become its protector, and he insisted that she came to all his shows 'to get the audience laughing'. Their physical relationship lasted several years, but their spiri-tual one even longer. 'He told me,' says Ayanna, 'that when he'd started to lose his hair so young, he realised the best way to cap-tivate a girl was to make her laugh, whereupon he took to perfecting the art of comedy and making himself as witty as possible. I was a spoilt, impressionable girl straight from board-ing school with highly protective parents... He was, however, one of the most genuine and considerate people I'd ever met. His honesty was disarming, and he could lay bare his soul and reduce me to tears. The strength of his emotions, along with the fact that he knew me better than I knew myself, was partly why our close friendship – against all odds – lasted so long.'

And Ayanna's younger sister, the acupuncturist Hla Myat Saw, became a significant influence, too, when, while working for a psychology degree in London, she explained to Ken – who went to see her when troubled with arthritis – the principles of the left and right hemispheres of the brain, reflected in the two sides of the face that had clear implications of personality definition. When Ken applied this theory to his own face, he saw, on one side, the demure demeanour of the obliging housewife and, on the other, the fierce frown of the spanking squire: the nice and the nasty side in his soon-to-be-developed enantiodromic approach to acting, which would later result in Janus workshops and exercises in 'phrenological performing'.

The Albery weekend, which attracted just twelve participants (nine men, three women, paying £55 each) was part psychotherapy, part games-playing, inspired by two books: Luke Rhinehart's *The Dice Man*, in which the hero embarks on a life of risk-taking by throwing dice to dictate his actions; and Keith Johnstone's *Impro*, a key text in Ken's life and a wake-up call to both self-awareness and peripheral vision: 'As I grew up,' wrote Johnstone at the very start of the book, 'and everything started getting grey and dull, I could still remember the amazing intensity of the world I'd lived in as a child, but I thought the dulling of perception was an inevitable consequence of age – just as the lens of an eye is bound gradually to dim. I didn't understand that clarity is in the mind. I've since found tricks that can make the world blaze up again in about fifteen seconds, and the effects last for hours.' Sounds psychedelic? Well, it was, in a way. Albery wrote an account of the proceedings which included exchanging personal histories, taking off clothes, swimming in Hampstead Ponds, mutual masturbation and massaging, 'rebirthing', confessing to sadomasochistic fantasies, and a group streak. There was no coercion involved, so who cares, really, but it does sound a little odd – and rather late in the day, for 1983.

In early 1985, Ken met the actress Sarah Lam at a party at the Chinese Embassy in London, and she became one of his more passionately unconsummated affairs at a time when he was hitting the drink big time and thrashing around in his private life. In the unproduced, unpublished ****-*Knows*, the character of KC, discovered in a pub, topping up his snuff with dog droppings, places a small ad in *Time Out*: 'Established playwright, 42, has nose which looks like a naked woman sitting with her legs apart and her back to you. Seeks her.' Campbell had actually placed such an ad in *Time Out* and received several appropriate replies and photographs, one of which he later incorporated in some of his publicity. In the outline, following the replies, KC dates a young woman from Singapore and goes to a dominatrix club near Foyles bookshop on the Charing Cross Road. He bursts wildly onto the club scene, goes to Los Angeles, and contemplates a goodly display of well-tanned rumps on the beach. Following a punch-up back home in Camden Town, and a pursuit by dwarves, he ends up in hospital, tended by a five-foot-tall Guyanese naked nurse with her back towards him... They marry. It didn't work out like that with Sarah Lam, but Campbell was entering a period of marked emotional instability.

The marriage with Prue had been fairly chaotic from the start, though they found a satisfactory, if unconventional, way of bringing up Daisy. The question remains about Prue's career, which was taking off like a rocket at the time of *Illuminatus!* – would she have gone on to become the English Brigitte Bardot had she not gone to Liverpool? 'I would have been a hopeless case whatever happened,' she says now. 'I couldn't organise myself; I'm much better now! All I did was go zooming off at the next thing. So there was Ken, and it felt exciting, and off I went. It was chaos, my life, I never really knew where I wanted to go, and I was being pulled a lot in different directions. If I'd got my head down and been a bit more sensible, and hadn't drunk so much and hadn't taken so many drugs, I would have made a choice. Instead, I just hopped about, and nobody knew what I was doing. My agents didn't know what do with me, and at one point, when I was at the Royal Court in *The Farm*, an Arab prince was in hot pursuit and sending Rolls Royces to the stage door every night.' In 1983, Ken and Prue, who had been married when Prue was three months pregnant – to please her parents, she says, and at Ken's insistence – started living apart, so they both said goodbye to Haverstock Hill. No one remembers when the divorce went through, but, as Prue says, 'we went on being back and forth'. For the rest of Ken's life, the couple went on holidays to Prue's cottage in Anglesey together, and with Daisy. 'We always wanted to get back together,' says Prue – who survived an extended relationship with drugs and alcohol to come through as a qualified psychotherapist, now studying for a doctorate – 'but not at the same time. We were best together when neither of us had anyone else. We would have ended up together, no question. Even when I had a nine-year relationship with someone else, that didn't realistically stand a chance because Ken and I always spent Christmas and summer together. Ken had a huge pull over me which I wasn't fully aware of at the time. He was a hard act for other men to follow.'

Prue bought the bottom half of a house on the Tufnell Park side of the Highgate Road, where she lives to this day, while Ken, who at first followed her there, struck out in a few dodgy places including flats in King's Cross and Stamford Hill (where he was burgled several times) before settling, for a time at least, in Blackstock Road in Finsbury Park. He bought this place on the day of his first date with Sarah Lam, 1 March 1985, for the cash price of £27,500, because he insisted on having a bath in it that afternoon before he went to meet Sarah at the Almeida Theatre in Islington at 9.30 p.m., presumably for a late-night cabaret following Brecht's *Man is Man* with John Sessions in the cast. She arrived 'excitingly late', Ken said in a subsequent letter, to inform him that she was too ill to come along.

By the time Daisy started going to primary school in Gospel Oak, she could oscillate fairly happily between parents. But sometimes the arrangement was chaos. 'School mornings,' she says, 'were basically hilarious. Mum would come in and say, "Oh dear, up you get, I've left it a bit late." And at Dad's, he'd yell, "I'm getting the wet sponge if you're not down here in five minutes." Then he'd come into my room and squeeze it over my head. That's the main memory of my childhood. I'd get the train back from Gospel Oak to Tottenham Hale and he'd pick me up. He'd brush my hair with a fork in the mornings, because there was no comb: "Let's get those rat tails out," he'd say! I'd ask for a packed lunch, which he hated doing, but he insisted on doing it his way. So I'd open the box each day and there would be, like, a cress nest with grape eggs and a little bird carved out of peanut butter: completely inedible but beautiful. The opening of that box every day was quite an event, and my friends would all crowd round to see what he'd come up with this time.'

Sarah Lam saw exactly how all this worked when she went round to Blackstock Road for supper and sent a postcard of thanks saying how impressed she was with the microwave oven (something of a novelty in those days), Ken's raised platform with its winching mechanisms and its views of the multiracial hubbub outside, and Daisy's little café which she assembled out of the planks and stanchions on her bunk bed as a welcome point for all visitors. She was about to go to Wales on a film location and gave her address as the Three Cocks, Brecon, Powys: 'I need a break so I'm very glad to be going there.' The letter that Ken sat down to write to her, the extraordinary document to which I've already alluded, is typical of how he wrote his life at the same time as living it. And the way he patchworks in memories of his childhood, current concerns and projects, and general philosophical commentary, is indicative (unconsciously or not) of how he was moving towards the monologue form in his final creative efflorescence. It's as though, after twenty-odd years in the practical theatre, he's returning to the room in Haigville Gardens where he wrote out his first stories and holiday experiences in school exercise books.

In this instance, having decided to cast Sarah in 'third-person' mode, he sets the scene with a flourish: 'It's 11.47 by the microwave-oven clock on Thursday 14 March 1985 and I am perched on the bar stool in the kitchen of 9 Blackstock Road N4 typing this out on my Hermes 808 (Golfball). The sun's blazing through the kitchen window. And something else occurs to me to do. To pop out and Interflora her a bunch of something. Apparently, when she began filming in Yugoslavia last year, her hotel room was bedecked, festooned, crammed, with floral tributes. Nice if she can arrive at The Three...' The sentence breaks off as he now recounts, as if in real time, and for a couple of pages, the arrival at the front door of Doros, the Greek guy who sold him the flat, to try and interest him in a scheme to save money on his television and video rental... 'at The Three Cocks, Brecon, to at least one bunch'. He then confesses to his anxiety over sending flowers at all, as this would indicate his possible view of her as a potential girlfriend, but decides that if his resolve alters from the eighty/twenty per cent for and against the idea by the time he gets to the florist's, then he'll knock the plan on the head. He sent the flowers – the figures had changed to ninety-nine/one at the point of purchase – and recounts (by now it's the next day) last night's meeting with Kenith Trodd, Rick McCallum and Derek Jarman over plans to forge ahead with a) his own ****-*Knows* film (it never happened) and b) Jarman's seven-year simmering film about Caravaggio (this happened in the following year). He describes the nose garden through which he can stick his nose so that it looks like a Renoir nude from the rear in a floral setting. Talk ensued of the special effects needed for a whole bunch of electronically controlled noses (possibly with dwarves inside) to chase Ken up the street...

A long passage subtitled 'Things we know or surmise about Sarah' develops into a hymn to her 'domestic-goddess' status, based on the evidence of what happened when she served him a spaghetti lunch in her Fulham home – 'She's neat, she's tidy and she puts things away *the minute she has washed them up*.' And this riff in turn is spliced with a backward glance to his own motherless childhood: 'She is one of the legendary ladies of whom my late dad spoke who can see the dirt which men can't see. We know it's there, and it does sort of bug us, but we just can't quite locate it. Mrs Durrant [who 'did' for Colin and Ken in Haigville Gardens] was another of these legendary ladies. Every Wednesday night we had to tidy and clean the place to the fullest extent that males can and then on Thursday morning Mrs Durrant would rid us of the "invisible" dirt.' (The only surprise here is that he doesn't include the information that his stepmother, Betty, Prue tells me, used to insist that he washed the soap as he made such a mess in the bathroom.) While Sarah pops off 'to tidy the tidy and clean the clean and freshen up the fresh as a daisy' prior to going to visit her mother, Ken helps himself to a whisky, which he'd spotted in its 'proper place' while she was about her invisible business, and launches into a conversation with his dead father. It's not Hamlet and the Ghost, exactly, but it's fairly revealing:

> DAD. Hello, son. You see what I was trying to tell you now and then?
>
> SON. Yes.
>
> DAD. You see, that's the sort of thing I was trying to steer you towards.
>
> SON. Fantastic. So why did I end up with such a slutty bunch?
>
> DAD. You were a rebel. That's all right, I suppose, but you rebelled against everything so you lost out. You know the saying, 'He slung the baby out with the bath water'?
>
> SON. Yes.
>
> DAD. You slung the baby out AND THEN NEVER EMPTIED THE BATH!
>
> SON. Blimey. What should I do now, then?
>
> DAD. Change.
>
> SON. Oh, yeah... and Sarah's got it! The film! What do I do now?
>
> DAD. She's coming. It'll be clear. But move, really move, when the time comes. Bye.
>
> SON. Bye. Hey – Susan [Littler], she wasn't slutty, was she?
>
> DAD. No, she was great. I carried on writing to her, you know, after you split up.
>
> SON. Yes, I know you did. But she's dead now. Hey, do you see her at all?
>
> DAD. Got to go now.

The letter goes on through the night to another day – taking in the visit of John Joyce that results in yet another correspondence, 'the John Joyce letters' contained within this correspondence: 'John Joyce has just belled me up from the road: get a bottle of wine, John.' 'Red?' 'Yeah.' – and the extended reminiscences of his father's working life, his early days in rep and his friendship with Warren Mitchell, with whom he's just been reunited on a filmed insert scene on *In Sickness and in Health*, then just a pilot, but soon (from September 1985) the sequel series to *Till Death Us Do Part*. As Fred Johnson, Alf Garnett's neighbour, he'd been shouting at him in the road: 'Some people you JUST love. My dad was worried when I wanted to go for a theatrical career. He'd read in the *Express*, and largely true as well at the time, that ninety per cent of males in show business were homosexual. But I wanted to do it, so he said okay. "But," he said, "only do comedy, won't you? People don't really want all that misery." Dad always liked my relationship with Warren: a) one of the ten per cent normals, b) funny.' Just think how lucky Sarah Lam was to receive this letter when you next survey your latest batch of grim, joyless text messages or minimal, functional e-mails. So, is it a letter? Ken finally asks himself, on page 23 (that number again!). 'No, I don't think it is. I don't really think it's finished, either. Pity in one way it isn't because if it was I could now write something like, "See you when you get back from The Three Cocks experience – Love, Ken XX."'

The friendship faltered slightly when, on her return, Sarah had to make it clear that she was 'involved' with somebody else, but the amazing thing about this is that the two kept in touch and spoke often on the telephone right through Ken's life and Sarah's happy marriage to the television journalist William Woollard, who used to present *Tomorrow's World*, *Horizon* and (before Jeremy Clarkson came along) the motoring programme *Top Gear*. Talking to me about her relationship with Ken, Sarah says, 'We never got round to talking about how much we meant to each other, but it ran very deep. The times we spent together were magical, treasures of the heart. It would make his day when I phoned him out of the blue, you could hear the joy down the phone. And I don't think that ever diminished, no matter who I was with. He couldn't be threatening or salacious. He was always an absolute gentleman and in that you can't separate Ken the man from Ken the performer. There was a time when I became seriously involved with my husband and a period of tension developed when we all three met – alpha male and all that – they sparred quite a bit, William and Ken, but so cleverly. That all changed when I took William to see Ken's first solo show: he adored it, and from then on he was always ringing him up, giving him notes.'

So was Susan Littler, Ken liked to think. At a nearby dilapidated church, fitted out with some weird bestial statuary, the congregation tried to get in touch with the dead in a sort of group seance. Ken was a regular, and was surprised one evening to find his former girlfriend accurately described. Susan was asking, the medium reported, why was he shouting so much these days (it wasn't getting him anywhere). And wasn't it about time he put that bathroom cabinet up? 'And this really got to me,' Ken reported on a YouTube snippet, 'because I was the only man who knew this, and I'm not a "bathroom cabinet bothered" chap at all. But in one house I had bothered to buy a cabinet, and I'd taken it down when I moved house and stuck it under the bed.' Where it still was. He also claimed to have communicated with Laurence Olivier (who died in 1989) in the same church: 'He was raised by a woman there – he'd come through talking in his Richard III voice – and I said to him, "Sir, I heard that when you were asked, who was the greatest actor of your generation, you'd replied, Charlie Chaplin. But are you able to tell us who is the greatest living actor today?" – and without any hesitation, he said – "Jackie Chan." Not many people would agree with Sir Laurence on this point – or the likelihood in the first place that he came through talking about kung fu fighting – but Ken always used the anecdote to justify his growing enthusiasm, kindled by Sarah Lam, for the martial-arts movie star. He shared that enthusiasm with anyone who'd listen or, ideally, who'd sit in front of his home-movie screen with him for hours on end watching endless reels of the sort of routine adventure escapade that makes you long for the intellectual delights of a James Bond movie.

The John Joyce letters, historically inserted within Sarah's missive, and which he composed in the spirit of the Royal Dickens hoax, but on a smaller scale, were perpetrated in order to find work for one of Ken's favourite colleagues, who was quite often out of it. They were addressed from Joyce's pad in nearby Upper Tollington Park. And they were written to friends, with no chance of too much going wrong as a result. Game-show host, quizmaster and serious librarian Jeremy Beadle, a friend of Ken's from Ilford days, was thus greeted: 'I'm Ken Campbell's partner in his SF exploits. I'm up for anything. Particularly this week. (You've done many great things, but for me I am doubtful if you will ever surpass giving Ken *The Complete Works of Fort*.) Despite flappy ears, I can pose as normal. Also "daft" I can do. Well regarded, three testimonials quickly available, own spy equipment. Do I hear from you? Capers anew, skyward ho! While it lasts, John Joyce.' Joyce, through Campbell's invention, informed G. F. Newman that he had successfully posed as an Open University employee recording interviews with central-heating salesmen, which would stand him in good stead for any available roles as a radiator- or household-fittings specialist in any documentary drama he was planning. But surely Richard Eyre would have twigged a ruse when he read: 'When I see your films I get a funny nervous feeling inside. Not all the way through, but at certain moments. And suddenly, tonight, I know exactly what it is: I think I'm just about to come on. Carry on filming. Love, while it all lasts, JJ.'

Part of Ken's impetus for wanting to help his friend – and entertain his correspondents – was his own continued success in a series of cameo screen appearances. In Peter Greenaway's *A Zed & Two Noughts* (1985) he hardly does more than ride a bicycle and ram a rotting shrimp down the throat of comedian Jim Davidson, but it's at least of interest that he's in the film at all. Campbell told Ian Shuttleworth that he never really knew what was going on: 'I was only there [on location shooting in Rotterdam] on days when I wasn't needed; the one day I really couldn't go to Rotterdam was the day they decided to do my scene, so they did it without me. I didn't have much of a part anyway, but it was a lesser one by the time I hadn't done it.' More conventionally, Campbell played a news reporter, another one-scene job, in Chris Bernard's delightful *Letter to Brezhnev* (1985), a sort of Scouse inversion of *On the Town* in which two Soviet sailors – played by Alfred Molina and Peter Firth – spend shore leave with two good-time girls – Margi Clarke and Alexandra Pigg. Pigg falls for Firth and is so determined to follow him home that she writes to the Russian President. 'Why do you want to get into Russia,' asks Campbell's not-all-that-convinced-of-his-own-nastiness reporter, sucking on a biro, 'when everyone wants to *escape*?' She is further obstructed by a smooth-talking diplomat from the Foreign Office played by Campbell's old mucker, Neil Cunningham, putting her off (or trying to) suavely from behind a big brown desk in a pinstriped suit, sipping whisky. It's a strange irony that Campbell and Cunningham should be playing the nay-sayers in such a life-affirming film, and one set in the city of their great theatrical triumph together. This was Cunningham's last film before he succumbed to AIDS and died in 1987. I last saw him onstage in Edinburgh on the 1985 fringe when he brought Thomas De Quincey to pulsating and terrifying life in Andrew Dallmeyer's adaptation of *The Confessions of an English Opium Eater*.

One other old friendship shook out in a race to the line to play Doctor Who: in 1987, the sixth doctor, Colin Baker, was due to leave the series, and the final two contenders to replace him were Ken and Sylvester McCoy. As McCoy remembers it, 'The executive producer of BBC series and serials wanted Ken, but the producer of *Doctor Who* wanted me, and his argument was that he thought that Ken would frighten the children, and I think he was right. I think Ken should have been brought in as one of the long-running baddies, the Master, or something like that. The producer in fact threatened to resign if Ken got the job. So I got it.'

There was just one last 'hangover' from the Liverpool Everyman years when Ken returned to the Young Vic in December 1987 with a production of Kenny Murray's *Outbreak of God in Area 9*, a piece that never really lived up to its title. It tells how a scientific conspiracy between inventor Clive Sinclair and international business magnate Tiny Rowland was undermined when God got into the works, and the water supply. One performer, though, gave a prophetic taster of Ken's developing passion for virtuoso improvisation: Mark Lockyer delivered dazzling, off-the-cuff impersonations of politician Tony Benn, tennis star John McEnroe and (unfazed by the example of John Sessions) Ian McKellen, who poutingly declaimed Shakespeare in flat Bolton vowels while being goosed from within by Marilyn Monroe.

It was high time for a change. On 4 October 1987, Campbell took part in a memorial evening for Jimmie Cooper in the Kenneth More Theatre in Ilford, mixing in with old Renegades, troupers from the Betty Finch Stage School and Liz Robertson, another sort of inspirational Renegade with aspirations (her dad was an Ilford policeman), who found fame as a West End musical-theatre star and seventh wife of the *My Fair Lady* lyricist Alan Jay Lerner. Campbell's friends and associates welcomed him that night as though he'd never been away. He was the star of the show, but he remained curiously subdued in the shade of the great multitasking JC, whom he idolised. 'Trevor Nunn never tore tickets, did he?' he said in the wings.

This last great shift in Campbell's career coincided with a move from Blackstock Road to an almost idyllic small housing estate on the banks of the River Lea at the edge of the Walthamstow Marshes. Immediately, he opened a brand-new notebook. Soon, he was asked if he could help out with a problem at the little Offstage Theatre on the Chalk Farm Road: a booking (with Susannah York, no less) had fallen through, and something was needed quickly to fill the gap. The owners, Alec and Buddy Dalton, had previously owned the New End Theatre, where Ken had directed the chaotic monastery play with Mike Hirst's porkers. If he could come up with a show at such short notice, would he promise them that there wouldn't be any pigs to deal with this time round?

11

Flying Solo

There was a time in his life now when Ken Campbell became the magus of the marshes, the not-too-ancient mariner 'who stoppeth one in three', the weird bloke with scripts and special effects trundled round in a trolley. He was the person you avoided speaking to on the top of a bus, not least because he'd started speaking to you first. His dilemma was that, because he played the eccentric, that's what people thought he'd become: a peripheral nutter. Nothing could be further from the truth, though he did sometimes exhaust the patience and listening power of even his oldest and closest friends. It was all probably down to his move to the Walthamstow wetlands. His rant became a byword in the locality: he merged his Ilford origins with Leytonstone ley lines and Hackney history, buried himself in a primeval landscape and emerged into the sunlight, blinking.

Essex is odd. You have to have lived there, and I'm not talking stockbroker commuter belt. For Ilford boys, Hornchurch is posh and Theydon Bois the Riviera of the Central Line. It's all East End overspill, yet strangely rural round the edges. It has London's heartbeat but exists as an experimental compromise between the town and the country, the expanding city and the defiant swamplands. Ken's childhood was split between the cinemas of Gants Hill and Barkingside, the public library and the Fairlop Fields, the old aerodrome and Valentines Park; and in some ways he never really left.

Suddenly, as he faded into Walthamstow, with his dogs and his notebooks, he discovered this new, other Essex: an urban watery inlet with old archways; towpaths that led all the way along the canal to Bishop's Stortford and Banbury; a classic one-bar pub, The Anchor and Hope, a Fuller's hostelry with a clientele of philosophers, drunks and dope-dealers; and the pullulating life of an area that had become an accidental nature reserve. Regulars in The Anchor, where Les the landlord held sway, included Buster Bloodvessel, leader of the Bad Manners ska-revival rock band, and Buster's sidekick and roadie, Timothy Fiddler, who had been a sound engineer and recalls Ken trying out his monologues in early form sitting right there on the narrow-backed chairs, ten yards from the river. Fiddler – who also recalls bonding with Ken at a Buster Bloodvessel dinner after *The Madness Museum* was broadcast, though neither of them saw it because neither owned a television – became a close friend in this period, as did Richard Kilgour, a composer who had worked on the Science Fiction Theatre of Liverpool shows and had just returned from Brazil.

The Viking invaders sailed up the River Lea in the ninth century to raid Hertford. The Anglo-Saxons you read about in *Beowulf* worked on the place to improve their trade relations. Down the centuries, there were fisheries, drainage projects, small boat industries, reservoirs and river barges carrying coal, copper, malt and timber. The shadows of this life, and those days, still hang around the place today. Springfield Park, opposite the little marina, boasts fine lawns and a top-notch café. A.V. Roe, the aviation pioneer, flew the first planes on British soil in a series of chaotic experiments on these Walthamstow marshes, a tradition celebrated in Ken Annakin's 1965 movie *Those Magnificent Men in Their Flying Machines*. No wonder Ken Campbell felt he could take flight in this environment. He was happily at home among such worthy pioneers, but he challenged this 'heritage' status with many an impromptu 'try-out' and rehearsal in the shadow of the 'Avro' Bridge before the barbed wire went up; you can't get near the place today.

He is writing voluminously in his notebooks at this point, but it's not clear whether he's being a diarist or writing a show; as always, the two functions start to overlap. He begins a marsh journal, titled *Office Accommodation: Volume One*, having laid claim to a park bench as an al-fresco centre of operations, as if setting his own scene: 'I want to get a fisherman's umbrella, then I can come to the office in all weathers. Office almost surrounded by deep puddles today. There's been a fire at some time just to the right of the table. Crows cawing. Bright train, four carriages, rumbling over the Avro Bridge. Forgotten the potatoes. Maybe George [at the café by the pedestrian bridge, not the Avro, where Ken regularly had breakfast and iced buns] knows where to get anglers' brolly. Had the thought yesterday of touring round solo with the Memoirs – No – *Recollections of a Furtive Nudist.*'

Some of the people who passed by 'the office' would eventually figure in the solo show, including members of the Hassidic community in nearby Stamford Hill: 'It is possible to get a minimal time of day from the most forbidding of Hassidics if you've got a hat on. Otherwise absolutely forget it. It's like you're a flasher, mac open, dicks away, saying "good morning" to a Mary Whitehouse outing.' In these precious pages, he's finding his new performance voice. His constant companions are Werner the bitch and Fred the terrier. He throws Fred in the river a couple of times and monitors his reactions. He buys that big umbrella at Don's fishing shop in Edmonton. He spots a fisherman's jacket with sticking-out pockets that exerts a great appeal: when worn with jacket, those pockets are like drawers – a chest of drawers! 'No one about – I'll plant another potato. Planted it three short paces from the second. I think I'll plant one here by the bench. Two small ones – put them both in at the right of the bench.' A 'breather' goes by, a regular, and Ken asks him if he lives in the bushes. 'What?' he replies, 'in this weather?' Turns out he's a manic homophobe and therefore suspect.

This new regime in the al-fresco office, coupled with an important encounter with the American screenwriting guru and script-fixer, Robert McKee, who was to have a profound effect on the way Campbell worked, formed a springboard for the monologue-writing routine Ken fell into, at first almost by chance. John Cleese had talked about McKee's course, which anyone could take, on the set of *A Fish Called Wanda*, and Ken got there as soon as he could. The appeal to Ken was similar to that of the old actor-manager Seymour Hicks on acting. McKee talked about narrative in devastatingly practical terms, breaking classic scripts down into a five-part structure: inciting incident; progressive complications; crisis; climax; and resolution. He would wind up with a scene-by-scene analytical screening of Michael Curtiz's Bogart and Bergman classic, *Casablanca*. As always with Campbell, he'd got so excited about this new guru that he made all his friends go along to the course, too. He even took along his daughter Daisy, who, in 1987, to celebrate her dad's arrival in new lodgings on the river, wrote a morbid story (she was not even nine years old) about a family (called 'Lea') of squabbling kids, a sickly brother, a bed-bound granny – 'she died before anyone could even bring her some flowers' – and a suicide: 'So one night he walked slowly and sadly to the River Thames. Eventually he gave a huge sigh and jumped. There was a huge splash and a few bubbles but Andrew was – DEAD! (THE END)' There's an ambulance and a police car written in as sound effects: 'NI-NON-NI-NOW-NI-NON-NI-NOW.' The upshot of the McKee course was a McKee group, a loosely affiliated bunch, who met every Thursday unless there was a good reason not to, and read each other's work out before inviting comments and criticism. Occasional stalwarts of this cabal, which prospered for several years, were Jeff Merrifield, John Joyce, James Richmond, Claudia Boulton, Daisy, Irving Rappaport and John Constable, the writer now known as the Bard of Southwark, on account of his riotously successful *Southwark Mysteries*, and a self-confessed 'automatic' poet who wrote loads of stuff on loads of acid; 'Ken's mission with me,' says Constable, 'was to stop me writing like David Hare'. The true beneficiary of the group was of course Ken himself, who knew that he could only make his 'stuff' work if he gave it theatrical shape and structure, so that all the characteristic elements in his writing of coincidence, synchronicity and flat-out wonderment were given a special new lease of life in a theatrical context where nothing could be too surprising to be credible (or vice versa).

The genius of Campbell's new-minting of the solo show – which found its richest expression in the trilogy of *Furtive Nudist*, *Pigspurt* and *Jamais Vu*, ultimately performed on one day at the National Theatre in late 1993 – was in telling stories which sounded as though they had been experienced, 'devised' almost, solely for that purpose. In what became known as known as 'The Bald Trilogy' (because 'The Hare Trilogy' of plays about the church, the law and the Labour Party, by David Hare, was playing simultaneously in the National's repertoire), the medium became the message, the aesthetic the argument. Like many clever schoolboys – and the monologues reflected this – Ken had always specialised in getting his teachers off the point and into the forbidden byways of irrelevant, that is, really interesting, information. In the case of his Latin master, George Harvey Webb, he found the ideal foil, the dean of digression, and an example of how best to interpret the world – by relishing its peculiarities and seeking out the evidence of the real mystery and spirituality of life. The producer and writer Michael Kustow summed it up perfectly: 'Ken is a walking human junk shop, bricolage on rubbery legs. You are led from one glittering trophy – a story, a character, a prop, a memory – to another; you can't recall how you got from one to the next, he lets the line of his mind spool out every which way, but over two-and-a-half solo hours the net tightens and, cliffhangingly, it all coheres.'

I remember finding Ken down by the River Lea one day when he opened a small tin box and showed me his next production. In smokers' parlance, these were the makings. 'The idea,' he said, 'is to look at one's life as if it was someone else's.' And then he ruminated: 'As far as the general run of theatre is concerned, they get on quite well without me.' At no stage of his career was he anything but a maverick outsider, as far as the Establishment and perhaps even the critics were concerned, and the clarity with which he saw this defined his material. Campbell's theatre was now turning inwards, repelling the spectacle but inflating the ego. Nothing was interesting unless it was filtered through your own experience of it, and this was the point about truth: nothing was true unless you supposed that it might be; nothing made sense until you made sure it did, or at least celebrated the fact that it didn't. If that was your mindset, you were up for anything. And, it therefore followed, anything might happen.

And the sudden commission at the Offstage Theatre forced his hand, so that the notebook ramblings were immediately transplanted to the stage in a more disciplined and theatrical structure. *Furtive Nudist* opened for a short run in June 1988. I went along to review the show for the *Financial Times*, in whose august arts pages I'd charted all Ken's productions since the early 1970s. But the other critics kept schtum, apart from a couple of smart-ass, condescending commentators in *Time Out* and its rival *City Limits*. This in itself was indicative of a lack of confidence in how best to deal with Campbell, generally and critically. He didn't fit into any recognised category. He was left to his own devices by the big theatres and funding authorities who should have known better, and he didn't bed down with the fringe because a) he was too old, and b) he would keep saying unpopular but true things like: 'Ken Dodd is the greatest comic in the world.' Undaunted, he bounced into the spotlight in the little basement theatre in Chalk Farm with all the vigour, relish and glee of a true Ben Jonson refugee and raconteur. He presented himself, like Fort's hero in *Lo!*, as a 'naked man on a city street' capering on a midnight streak over the sand dunes in Croyde, where he'd gone to visit his old dad, often peeping at the universe through the large telescope Colin kept in the big bay window of 'the front room'. He said something simple, but also chilling, that I've never forgotten. His life, he said, had been foreshadowed in the fiction of Charles Fort and Philip K. Dick, the science-fiction novelist Campbell most admired. So he may not have existed at all except in other people's versions, including his own, of himself. This was so strange: that a man presenting himself as a 'character' who was impelled to communicate might, in effect, be a mere chimera to start with, a genuine figment.

This first play in the trilogy that would come to be regarded as Campbell's fourth great project – following the Road Show, *Illuminatus!* and *The Warp* – was not just another example of an actor creating work for himself in a solo format as a pension fund, or stopgap: it was a full-blooded mission to test the limits and structures of a theatrical narrative in which his own life story, his own intelligence and curiosity, were factors almost predetermined for this very purpose. And the development, eventually, marked a concerted swing in critical approval towards him and his work. This was not stand-up comedy, either, more a case, as Campbell himself said, of sit-down tragedy in which he stood up a lot. He wasn't one for sitting at a table, as the American actor Spalding Gray did in his riveting (and influential) one-man show *Swimming to Cambodia*, or for reclining in a cosy chair, as Ronnie Corbett did in his television monologues. He tended to be up and at it. And, as an audience of 'seekers', we were implicated in the show for the very good reason that our host was bursting to tell us things. There was never any 'fourth wall' for Ken Campbell, no retreat to fictional memory, and he'd always find encouragement in the saws of Seymour Hicks, who recommended a golden rule of comedy as 'getting a laugh on your first appearance' and never ignoring the audience: 'The audience is the instrument on which the actor plays, the multitude on which he imposes his personality. How then can he be oblivious of its presence?'

There had always been solo shows in the modern theatre. John Gielgud's *Ages of Man* was a Shakespeare digest delivered by a top technical exponent, while Emlyn Williams and Simon Callow have, in different eras, given Dickens performances in the spirit of Dickens himself – no mean barnstormer – pressing the material against the personality of its author. But in the latter half of the twentieth century, the solo performer was more usually a comedian, and in British comedy the best of them – Jack Dee, Eddie Izzard, Ross Noble – spun worlds of mayhem, madness and melancholy in their big arena theatres rather like rock stars condemned to perform without music. And there was a parallel school of possibly less popular, but more theatre-based exponents of the genre. Spalding Gray was the chief example. Gray, who died in 2004 in what was termed an act of creative suicide, was a patient of the neurologist Oliver Sacks and a founder member of the Wooster Group, one of the most significant New York theatre collectives of the past few decades. Gray 'gave me the clue as to what I wanted to do,' Ken told John Bird in their radio chat. Apart from the sitting-down bit, he relished Gray's manner of looking at something sideways and creating something better as a result: *The Killing Fields* is a good film, but Jonathan Demme's film of its offshoot, *Swimming to Cambodia*, which charted Gray's experience on the film as an actor, is even better. Turning your life into an event is far easier said than done, but Gray was one of several American theatre figures who mastered the art form and allowed Campbell to blaze along their trail in his own inimitable fashion – others were the rock musician and poet Laurie Anderson and the brilliant, multi-vocalising Eric Bogosian, star of his own *Talk Radio*, and originator of many solo shows that visited the London fringe in the 1980s. The even-higher-art precedent was that of the fictional memoirist in Samuel Beckett's *Krapp's Last Tape*, brooding over his pre-recorded snippets of a past, lost life on a Grundig tape recorder.

The question for the solo performer, then, is: who is the person you are playing, if it's not exactly yourself? Is it an alter ego; or a slightly less recognisable version of you; or even a more recognisable one? The danger of waxing Campbellian on this topic was posed by the actor himself when, right at the top of *Furtive Nudist*, he speculated on the true meaning of his name: Kenneth in Celtic means 'the handsome one', so a translation of 'Kenneth Campbell' might be PRETTY BOY TENTRINGER. Thus launched, Pretty Boy was free to streak across the dunes like a Samurai warrior in the Kurosawa movie, knees bent, arse swinging low, so as to keep his bollocks out of the way of the arrows. There's no way of resisting such a hilarious prospect, and the point was that the harum-scarum vision of the fugitive frolicker was as amusing to Campbell himself as it was to the audience. Chalk Farm chuckles were echoing round Camden by the end of the month in that tiny basement. Campbell had not so much adopted a persona as grown into one: it was 'commercially inadvisable for me to trim my eyebrows as I sometimes pick up these little parts on the telly playing somebody who's just invented something'. *Furtive Nudist* was directed by his old friend Gillian Brown from the Stoke company. The scenery comprised merely a few blotchy, stand-alone paintings done up by Mitch Davies. Another blast from the past came when Ken reintroduced the story of Andy Jones, his Canadian chum, who had descended to a toilet in King's Cross (or Camden Town, was it?) and disappeared (or had he?). It was well known in teleportation circles that 'apparent invisibility' could be achieved in the careless adoption of bizarrely unalarming postures. It was therefore possible, Ken surmised, that the two actors waiting at the top of the gents' toilet for Jones had unwittingly adopted such postures, therefore rendering themselves invisible to Jones and perhaps even each other. It's a characteristic of all the Campbell monologues that he revisits the past in order to make it more interesting than it was or might have been. And to stitch it all together in order to create the illusion that life makes sense.

Even *The Great Caper* cropped up again as a scenographic backdrop in *Furtive Nudist*, and Ken finds that a girlfriend in Stoke has a place that reminds him of his parents' home in Ilford. The girl is Emma Way Wang, for whom the real-life model might have been an Asian film-editor girlfriend who lived briefly at Watermint Quay, Campbell's address by the river, and who was treated for a tumour on her forehead. Emma Way, a devil of the airwaves, armed with a Black and Decker power drill, believes that radio disc jockeys are pirating her compositions, and she commits suicide by trepanning herself with a wire clothes hanger at the very moment of sexual climax with Tentringer. In a stunning, charged moment of theatre, Campbell produced a lock of her hair with which, he said, he made himself decent on the dunes. The accumulative interconnections are revealed simultaneously as bizarre coincidences and intended narrative links. This was what gave the show such extraordinary potency – especially with Campbell himself, writhing like an eel and blathering like a fishwife, caught up in the middle of its re-enactment. By the time I saw the show again a few years later, I was reminded of no less a figure than Robert Lepage, the brilliant, dangling Canadian, also a dabbler in the doppelgänger syndrome, artistic soulmate of Laurie Anderson and Eric Bogosian, who also forges metatheatrical links across time and space. *Furtive Nudist* climaxed in a chase sequence from Farringdon to Paddington Station – where travellers sat, bemused, on 'those nine-seat pod arrangements' (a world is conjured!), via Chelsea and Dingwall's in Camden Town – which was a masterpiece in lunatic and detailed storytelling, a supercharged Beckettian speech in full flow, ending ecstatically on the Philip K. Dickian invocation, 'YOU'VE GOT TO GET HOLD OF THE THREAD OF MARCHING TIME AND PULL THE FUCK THING DOWN AND GET ON IT AND PANG YOURSELF TO THE INFINITUDE OF ABSOLUTE MIND.'

Campbell was aware of his progress as, back at the office, he makes another notebook entry: 'Tonight, first night of *Recollections of a Furtive Nudist* [the title was eventually curtailed to the last two words] much altered from preview. Thanks mainly to Robert McKee. A beautiful sentence was coming over the bridge.' That sentence could have been Emma Way Wang herself, or it could have been, perhaps, the voice of Philip K. Dick himself. 'I remember Robert Anton Wilson, co-author of the *Illuminatus!* trilogy,' wrote Campbell, 'who used to stay with us sometimes until my wife objected to his using the washing machine for only one shirt – anyway, late one night, in awed tones, he said: "Have you read Philip K. Dick's *Valis*?" He gave me my first copy. Literally mind-twisting, it's one of those books you end up buying loads of copies of. Because you're either going to have to find new friends who have not read it, or force old friends to get into it.' Dick suggested that the world we see around us is not necessarily the only world that exists, and is not even perhaps 'the true world'. And the really interesting thing, as with all science fiction – and Ken Campbell always seemed to be skimming off the top of H. G. Wells, J. G. Ballard, Dick and Michael Moorcock – is that we are creating metaphors of our muddled 'real' world in those of space travel, advanced technology, even mind-altering drugs or metaphysical religion. Campbell was on a mission in a parallel universe. When the great Dick – author of *Total Recall* and *Do Androids Dream of Electric Sheep?* (filmed as *Blade Runner*, and also the inspiration, clearly, for the *Alien* and *Terminator* movies) – was celebrated at the ICA on the tenth anniversary of his death in 1992, Ken said that *Furtive Nudist* was in part a tribute – a series of desert island Dicks, perhaps – to their shared love for conquering outlandish words: when he'd played Maurice in Heathcote Williams's *AC/DC*, he had spent a whole morning wrestling with the pronunciation of 'dimethoxyphenyathylamide' (which means 'the pink spot in the urine of every schizophrenic'). It was only with this first solo show that I began to think of Campbell as a true missionary figure in relation to words, the theatre and the universe. He was always at least as clever as the people in the theatre who had the reputation for being so. But he was something of a prophet in the wilderness with *Furtive Nudist*. By the time it resurfaced in 1991 at the Riverside Studios, he'd been dragging it round all over the place – to Dublin and Munich, and St John's, Newfoundland (Andy Jones territory), a place where he probably felt more at home than anywhere else on Earth – but all with little critical reward. For those three intervening years, as Daisy says, 'he didn't have anything else'.

Meantime, Prue was engaged in her own struggle that would lead her away from the theatre into rehabilitation, study and addiction counselling. She'd had a couple of clean years at the end of the 1980s, but had relapsed. Now, she gathered herself for the ultimate break. She had her last drink in 1990 and celebrated by playing an addict – to cleanliness – in a monologue Ken found tucked away in a book about the philosophy of Andy Warhol. *Warhola!*, which played for a few weeks at the very end of 1990 in the Offstage Downstairs (two years after *Furtive Nudist*), was in essence a pop-art rewrite of Jean Cocteau's *La voix humaine*. A character named B, played by Prue, dressed in red high-heeled boots and a skimpy plastic apron – advertising Campbell's Soup, naturally – poured out her obsessions in a one-way telephone conversation and flushed her collection of hypodermic needles down the toilet, while a zonked-out Andy Warhol, played hilariously by the playwright Snoo Wilson, listened impassively, spooning jam into his face. Christopher Renshaw's production was a witty statement of intent to reform on Prue's part, an intention she's adhered to for two decades.

Ken was travelling around with *Recollections of a Furtive Nudist*, partly as he had nothing else to do, partly because he was still working on it. Colin Watkeys, a producer running a late-night cabaret programme at the Finborough Theatre in Earl's Court, booked the show and offered to help Ken arrange some further bookings; in effect, he became Ken's manager, and succeeded Gillian Brown as the director of the show, too. When it opened again at Riverside Studios in January 1991, simply retitled *Furtive Nudist* (as it was generally known anyway), it was now free of hiccups and illogical inconsistencies. They'd McKeed it even more! That cake in George's café on the marshes had become Proust's madeleine, a passport to memory and a former life. Michael Billington in the *Guardian* acclaimed Ken as the Harun al-Rashid of the Lea Valley; Irving Wardle in *The Times* marvelled at how Ken's evocation of a lost civilisation in the disused Walthamstow filter beds suggested Shelley exploring the Baths of Caracalla; and Ian Shuttleworth in the *Independent* opined that 'Campbell has created a hilarious, mystifying, compelling one-man digest of all that lurks in the undercurrents when one swims out of the mainstream.'

Ken had achieved critical lift-off: but to demonstrate that life went on as relatively normal, he wrote and directed a playful skit, *Frank 'n' Stein* for the Cork-based theatre-in-education company Graffiti. And the third of his clown plays, *Peef*, based on *The Galoshes of Fortune* by Hans Christian Andersen but with the now familiar characters from *School for Clowns*, was produced by the Unicorn Theatre Company at the end of 1991, moving to the Arts in London in February 1992. Neither this, nor what had been the second play in the series, *Clowns on a*

School Outing (premiered at the Oldham Coliseum in 1986), are as good as the original but, as Richard Eyre suggests, the whole trilogy should be performed on a regular basis on a single day of clownfest.

Colin Watkeys, having convinced Ken that he'd had it with Professor Molereasons and that this solo stuff was his new route, went ahead and made many more bookings, precipitating further creativity. Having established his 'new brand', Campbell soon got on with the second solo play, *Pigspurt*, which premiered at the Riverside Studios in March 1992. It was a fantastic stew of strange and multilayered experience, prompted once more by contemplating Dick. 'The voice had spoken to me,' writes Dick in his *Valis*, 'reminding me of the place to which Horselover Fat had gone. In his search... As we had been told, originally, long ago, to do; I kept my commission.' Campbell's friend Jeff Merrifield had organised another Philip K. Dick celebration in Loughton with contributions from Brian Aldiss, John Constable, Fay Weldon and the film critic Philip Strick, and it was this event that led to one of the main strands in *Pigspurt*. Campbell claimed that, after Heraclitus, Carl Jung and Dick, he would be the fourth person ever to use the word 'enantiodromia'. This is the Jekyll and Hyde phenomenon of people switching suddenly to the opposite pole or attitude, in belief or emotions; the notion chimed with the way Campbell saw his own divided self – and chimed, too, with Hla Myat Saw's theories of the divided face.

In *Valis* (an acronym for Vast Active Living Intelligence System), Horselover Fat spends much of his time – in between his picaresque adventures, hopeless love affair and 'pink light' experience – writing his exegesis: 'Fat believed that the information fired at him and progressively crammed into his head in successive waves had a holy origin and hence should be regarded as a form of scripture.' And the book's opening aphorism is, 'One Mind there is; but under it two principles contend.' With its theological overtones, could such an exegesis suggest that the phenomenon of enantiodromia is of divine origin? Campbell wanted to go further with this enquiry in *Pigspurt*. Dick found in his own identity 'a malevolent force that had filled him with fear and a craven attitude towards governmental authority'. The Jungian definition, the sudden transformation into an opposite form or tendency, coincided exactly with a theory of acting that Campbell had in fact already developed, taking no heed at all of Stanislavsky, the Method, or 'motivation'. In the film footage of *The Warp* rehearsals in Edinburgh, you can see Campbell furious with someone for making something sentimental. Sucking on his cheap cheroot, he shouts several times, 'Stop Chekhovian-ing it!' Elsewhere in the film he says he doesn't think anything that isn't funny should be put on: 'Serious drama is a travesty of life, and the spirit of life.' 'Phrenological Pphorming' is what he also called it, and he distinguished the two distinct halves of his personality as inept housewife and spanking squire. The aim was to keep these halves in an ideal balance, even merge them, so that one could be called upon as easily as the other. Philip K. Dick coined the term 'pigspurt' to describe his sec-ond self. Ken saw his own two sides connected by his bulbous nose in a hilarious search for a woman with a bottom to match. Paul Taylor in his *Independent* review of *Pigspurt* was reminded of John Malkovich, in a stage play, *Burn This*, using an enantiodromic technique in his contrasting profiles of a brutal thug and a beautiful woman.

While contemplating the whole world, Campbell is simul-taneously inhabiting a specific part of it. I particularly love a short passage in *Pigspurt* where Ken is demonstrating the art of snuff-taking to Les, the landlord of The Anchor and Hope, when in walks the local star, Buster Bloodvessel – 'Buster's like the Laughing Buddha on one side – and like Boris Karloff in *Grip of the Strangler* on the other – Buster entered the bar enantio-dromically, and for humour he went: "AAAAHHH-*TCHOOOO!*" in my snuff tin – blasted all the snuff everywhere – "I'll have to get some more now" (posing as amused) – But not to worry – because that day, Buster had this little runaround boy who was doing everything for him – any little errand – on a BMX bike – And so I told the lad to go round to Patel's – and to be sure to get it ground up with the menthol – and I gave him the right money.' Ever on the lookout for new workshop (and money-raising) opportunities, once *Pigspurt* was up and running, Ken immediately instigated some 'Enantiodromic Approach to Drama' sessions, charging £5 a throw. His sign-up register in his notebooks includes the (then twenty-two-year-old) actress Rachel Weisz. Ken is clearly impressed by her talent and touched by the fact that, aged ten, she had attended the memorial service for his girlfriend Susan Littler.

Pigspurt is also where Campbell introduces one of the great themes of his last years: the idea that you make Shakespeare better, and funnier, by not performing him in his Elizabethan or Jacobean English. In what, then? Pidgin, of course. The linguistic fantasy world of Ken Campbell harks right back to his nonsense verses, his clown plays, his innate surrealism and his love of glossolalia, or speaking in tongues, as a source of theatrical delight. It starts with Ken Dodd, too, whom Campbell sets as a study task for an actor who needs to learn a thing or two ('This is an educational show,' says Dodd; 'You'll go home after this and say, that taught me a lesson.') In a dream, this minimalist actor ('who made the stage seem somehow fuller when he left it') is charged with seeing every Ken Dodd show for a year. One of these is slated for the Solomon Islands, which I suppose should not come as a surprise to anyone who's ever studied Dodd's hectic schedule. As recounted in *Pigspurt,* Dodd, uncharacteristically, fails to show up in the Solomons, but the actor – suitably named David DeNil, but whose real name was, improbably, David Blank – is primed to stand in for him with Dodd's stand-up routine translated into Pidgin. This Campbell demonstrates in the show with the aid of a song sheet and a cucumber in possibly the most ridiculously bacchanalian sequence ever seen on the modern stage. DeNil's routine comprises one gag, which, Ken recounts, he repeats several times, and with which, apparently, he tours to nineteen islands in the archipelago: 'Im fulugud dei. Im fulugud dei blong yumitufala pushem lifala salwata wanae insaed postofis letahol blong praeafala pasta talim – "ski aelan twinki twink plantifala ia!" Which, in the original Doddy, is: 'What a beautiful day for shoving a cucumber in the vicar's letterbox and shouting: "The Martians have landed!"'

It could have been worse. It might have been – Ken had them all in his notebooks – 'What a lovely day, chaps, for taking all your clothes off and tucking your legs behind your ears and shouting – "How's that for an oven-ready chicken?"' Dodd's special brand of humour, Ken noted, *transgresses* the language barrier. But he has brilliant jokes, too: 'I thought I was a great lover till I discovered that all my girlfriends had asthma.'

David DeNil embodied, said Ken, a legendary minus quality. And he needed to learn from the master of stage command, the great Dodd, whose jokes in translation comprised the main thrust of the campaign, which was to establish the Pidgin English they speak in Vuanatu as 'wal wantok', a one-world language. 'It's easy,' Ken said, 'it's only got about fifteen hundred words and you can learn it in twenty minutes.' DeNil became known as the Man Looking for Ken Dodd. But as he was also renowned for his knack of making you forget he'd ever been there when he'd gone, he was always doomed to failure. In the real-life story that underlay this outlandish scenario, David Blank had a version that was different from the fictional 'reality'. He remembers the Dodd assignation originating during *The Warp* at the Roundhouse (Blank, a serious, Method-minded actor who trained at Mountview School, joined *The Warp* in Edinburgh 'for something to do' and soon found himself at odds with Campbell's anti-Method method).

However, Blank says, he was young and carefree and eager to please. He agreed to Ken's commission before being told what it was. Ken thought his acting would benefit from a long spell of Dodd-watching. Blank wasn't so sure, but set off to see him anyway in Hull, and then Scarborough, where, sleeping on the beach after the show with a whole Bank Holiday congregation of Mods – it was the time of the Mods and Rockers revival in the early 1980s – he was soundly beaten around the head by a truncheon-wielding policeman and told to wake up and clear off. He visited Dodd backstage, but the comedian seemed reluctant to give him any solid information about his schedule, though he did divulge that he was playing a date in Acapulco (not the Solomon Islands). So Blank dutifully reported back to Ken for a sub of a couple of hundred pounds to make the trip. When he got to Acapulco, he discovered Dodd had given him the wrong date and he'd missed the gig. Blank, who in real life never went to the South Seas, or learned Dodd jokes in Pidgin, is memorialised in the show nonetheless. He renounced the mission after Acapulco, and never worked with Campbell again: 'I now have decidedly mixed feelings about him; but then I never wanted to be an actor in the first place, I just became one and I don't like them; and I don't like Ken Dodd, either.' Blank is nowadays perfectly happy as the editor of the *Oracle Occult Magazine*.

On the New Hebrides, which became Vanuatu in 1980, gaining independence from the joint control of Great Britain and France, Dodd nonetheless soon became as honoured in reality, almost, as their resident cult hero, Prince Philip. But no thanks to David DeNil. Tanna, which Ken visited when encouraged to do so by Michael Kustow, after the success of *Pigspurt*, and in order to instigate a modicum of Doddy cultural influence on the South Seas (and match up his own story), is the southernmost island, 1,500 miles east of Australia. In the secretive tribe of the Iounhanan, who live high on a thickly forested ridge, the women wear grass skirts and the men nambas, or penis gourds, straw codpieces which hold the sex organ in a permanently erect position. And here, the women do all the work because the men are permanently spaced out on kava, an intensely addictive brew (a single dose is the equivalent of six large Scotches) made from the root of a local plant spat into a coconut shell and mixed with water. Women are not allowed to witness the kava ceremony. If they do, they are handed the traditional punishment: a whack on the head with a single kava root.

The *Observer* journalist Alexander Frater reported that when the men are high, they sit silently staring at stones, each of which contains the spirit of some plant or object important to the tribe... and the most special stone of all is the Duke of Edinburgh stone. No one knows how Prince Philip became divine to them, but the dedicated airstrip is kept permanently ready for his landing. However, as the (now late) Chief Jack Naiva became even older than Prince Philip, so the worry grew that time was running out for the great day: 'He will be guest of honour and we'll roast pigs and bullocks for him,' the Chief told *Daily Mail* journalist Richard Shears in 1996 (Shears was writing a feature in anticipation of Prince Philip's seventy-fifth birthday). 'All the girls will dance for him. We want him to spend the last years of his life here, because we believe that when he returns here as our god, his powers will make our wrinkles disappear and we will have many wives to attend to our every need. He won't have to hunt for pigs or anything. He can just sit in the sun and have a nice time.'

When it opened at the National's Cottesloe 400-seater auditorium in October 1993, *Jamais Vu* had already been trimmed to a running time of three hours. He'd been rung up, Campbell said, by Richard Eyre's office asking if, after *Furtive Nudist* and *Pigspurt*, he was planning any more one-man shows. He said yes, though he wasn't; he'd squeezed his life dry of material already with the other two. Eyre reminded him that it was the year of the trilogy. He had no choice. 'I'm not mad,' said Ken, 'I've just read different books,' describing his new show as 'a comic-epic-sci-fi-conspiracy-weepy'. One of those books was Theodore Roszak's *Dreamwatcher* (1985), whose heroine, gifted with other people's dreams to which she alone is privy, finds herself tormented with nightmares. Ken's notebooks are full of quotations from the novel as he prepares *Jamais Vu*, and he peppers them with the thoughts, too, of Mark Twain and Truman Capote. Twain expresses the view that, of all creatures on the Earth, man is the most detestable, in that he alone possesses malice, inflicts pain and has a nasty mind. And on reading Capote's *Handcarved Coffins*, a non-fiction account of American crime, Ken makes a special note of the following: 'Anxiety, as any expensive psychiatrist will tell you, is caused by depression; but depression, as the same psychiatrist will inform you on a second visit and for an additional fee, is caused by anxiety.'

On the opening night (7 October 1993) of this psychological sideshow otherwise known as *Jamais Vu*, the critics were handed a gift pair of socks from Australia – with the promise that they, the socks, would fall up instead of down. Benedict Nightingale wrote his review wearing them. The National, Ken said in his opening salvo, was a military fortress housing the arts, with a secret tunnel system of cavernous vaults holding an array of arms, gas and water cannon. He then veered off into a discussion he'd had with Eyre about what this show might actually be. The gist of this was that Eyre had proposed several alternative plans, including that of entertaining and sustaining the status quo, including its wrongs; or *posing* as exposing the wrongs but not (this could result in an OBE or knighthood); or really exposing the wrongs and effecting change (this was not possible); or, fourthly, and this might be possible, 'To *pose* as exposing the wrongs... but in fact *deceive* but with a wilful mix of truth and lie, research and fantasy, so inscrutably compounded as to send the status quo hunting for needles that nobody's lost, in haystacks that don't exist, diverting attention from the ensuing release of hitherto imprisoned forces, which *will* bring about change, but of an unpredictable nature.'

It was an amazing riff that just about summed up the whole post-war British theatre project, and identified Campbell as an artist who was both beneath and beyond the fray, contemptuous of his National paymasters but happy to exploit their bovinity in inviting him to play their game. Richard Eyre was too clever not to see the beautiful irony of all this, and he later expatiated on the challenge of commissioning his old friend: 'He was impractical, and difficult, up to a point. But he knew what putting on a show was about. People who didn't know him, or understand him, were rather frightened of him because he seemed to be operating at random. He wasn't like someone like Simon McBurney [director of Complicite, the nearest equivalent we have to the work of Robert Lepage, and one of the few really outstanding British companies of the last two decades] who, when I first got him working at the NT, used to say, "You know, I'm not going to be a creature of the institution," while being very canny politically about what he'd been offered.' Campbell wasn't like that. He was innocent, always, and without political side in the arranging of his work.

Because of this, he represented something pure to Eyre, an idea of work in the theatre that was impossible on a daily basis if you were running the whole show. 'He was grateful I put on his shows at the NT, but in essence I increasingly thought he disapproved of me because I'd sort of deserted the cause. I was explaining this to Daisy, and she said, "Look, he thought everyone was a traitor to the cause."' Eyre had recognised that *Illuminatus!* and *The Warp* were really imaginative, epic pieces of production and directing, years ahead of their time in some ways, out of step with the general temper of the theatre culture on the fringe: 'Ken was deeply suspicious of the middle-class proletarianism and agitprop of the 1970s. So in his time, he had no bedfellows but many admirers. Lindsay Anderson I always thought of as an unlikely patron of his; I think he probably put Ken on in the Theatre Upstairs to annoy [his fellow director] Bill Gaskill!'

It was having come through all that, and having done what he'd done, that gave Ken's monologues such deep authority and flavour, quite apart from their essential brilliance. On his television tack in *Jamais Vu*, he barges into a National Film Theatre interview with John Birt, the man who, as Director-General, gave the BBC its dull-as-ditchwater 'time and motion' management overhaul. 'It was exciting how little charisma Birt had,' says Ken in the show, evincing himself the very opposite of 'uncharismatic' as he pulls on his trolley behind him, sporting a pink and green striped vest and an oatmeal overcoat, shaved bald, a living Magwitch. Birt looks like an inadequately briefed alien, he reports, suggesting that the 'real' Birt is holed up in an asylum in Hounslow; he's liberated into saying exactly what he likes, this loon, sticking plungers on his head and false teeth – his 'Mellors', so named in honour of the Tory Party minister of the day, the buck-toothed David Mellor – in his mouth, and striking attitudes of beatific serenity.

Ken was later invited by the *Independent* to reply to the mostly positive reviews, and wittily queried, with a nice edge of sarcasm, why anyone should think the South Pacific story 'impossible': 'I went [there], I saw the notice [about the cult of Prince Philip], I met the man [the Chief]. And that a disturbed schizophrenic should think he's John Birt is eminently possible. People also assumed I'm anti-Establishment, quoting the opening salvoes and assuming they're my views. But it's the *media* establishment that's anti-Royal and anti-Birt, so that's how I start; it's the old comedian's ploy of initially bolstering other people's prejudices. In fact I became a worshipper of Prince Philip *and* a Birt fan. And I'm thrilled that Benedict Nightingale mentioned the computer socks. They're like the ever-sharp razor or the car that runs on goat-shit, all those great inventions. He's right, I'm the Ancient Mariner, not Coleridge... I see these shows as like a bus tour to the Taj Mahal, where everyone on the bus decides to get pissed instead. Nightingale fought his way through the lout behaviour and had a look at the view.'

Jamais Vu won the Evening Standard Best New Comedy Award, much to the annoyance of one or two of my fellow judges that year. It was Ken's first award since the one from the *Ilford Recorder* back in 1959.

It was this open-hearted, delighted glee in the universe and all its works and quirks that made Campbell such an exceptional man and remarkable artist. In this decade of his solo shows he also became a unique television presenter of programmes about things that fascinated him: quantum mechanics, philosophy, the Big Bang, the creation of subatomic particles at CERN in Switzerland, scientific experiments that changed our view of the world, the way the brain works. But it was the transformation of all that stuff into theatrics – the television programmes themselves became more matter for a mummer's May morning – that made these stage shows so very special and endearing. And guess what – he became Doctor Who after all, an adventurer through time and landscapes of his own devising, with dogs as helpmates, in a ceaseless war against the dull. On television, he proved an unlikely comic inquisitor, a robust alternative to the great television 'educators' like Kenneth Clark (*Civilisation*), Jacob Bronowski (*The Ascent of Man*) or Jonathan Miller (*The Body in Question*). The most powerful image of Campbell in his remarkable television series *Reality on the Rocks* is of a man wanting to know where the world ends, where time starts, where the edge of the universe might be. While regarding this whole exercise as a prank, he was turning it, like an alchemist, into the gold dust of theatre, of performance speculation.

Between *Furtive Nudist* and *Pigspurt*, Campbell directed a National Theatre workshop production in February 1992 of *The Whores of Babylon*, a piece that had long festered in his notebooks. In it, he attempted to join up his acting theories with his enthusiasm for seminars and his dislike of global television networks. Television, it transpired, was not the beast: the viewer was. There was little theatrical energy, in the end, to *Whores*, which must have confirmed Ken on his new solo path. But the material itself was dynamite, and the cast included Russell Denton, Celia Imrie, the pyrotechnical impressionist Mark Lockyer, Timothy Fiddler (who helped out on research, along with James Nye) and a likeable, large American actor, Mac McDonald, who resembled a cross between Mike McShane before he lost weight and John Goodman before he gained some more. In one typical flourish, Denton talked himself into the exponential curve of the Robert Maxwell story – the disgraced businessman and media mogul had died in mysterious circumstances at sea, slipping from his yacht, in November 1991 – by revealing that the wife of Maxwell's collaborative *Daily Mirror* journalist, Nick Davies, was indeed 'the very fine actress' with whom he had enjoyed simulated sex scenes in *The Warp*.

In his 'bald' trilogy, Campbell had pursued his interest in weird sects, tribes, linguistics, comedy, acting styles, artistic schizophrenia and the cult of Prince Philip in the South Seas. But in *Whores of Babylon*, and a related National Theatre Platform performance, he organised his arguments for the elimination of television. He acknowledged some pioneering scientific work in the field, notably in a book by the San Francisco writer Jerry Mander, *Four Arguments for the Elimination of Television*, which had been usefully summarised in *The Times* by journalist Anne Karpf as early as July 1978: 1) Television helps expropriate knowledge by making us doubt our own experience until validated by experts; 2) American television is dominated by a handful of corporations and gives voice to the powerful; 3) Television produces illness, submissiveness and conditions us for a *1984*-style autocracy; and 4) Only the grossest linear information can be effectively conveyed by it.

How ironic, then, that Campbell should become such an effective boffin on the box. *Reality on the Rocks* is easily the best of his several series, not only a classic documentary of the time, but also a most original splicing of his investigations into the origins of the universe, quantum mechanics and the Big Bang, with a recorded stage performance – *Mystery Bruises*, his fourth solo show, had opened at the Almeida Theatre in Islington in June 1994 – which uses the television experience as material for theatre: 'I can't fix my own car, but I'm a quantum mechanic now!' He starts by filling the screen with his face, a bald Magwitch again, wondering how much stuff he could cram into his own skull. And then he goes to Oxford to start at the end: Stephen Hawking, author of *A Brief History of Time* (which Campbell cheerfully dismisses as unreadable), might have the ultimate answer. But first, did he, Campbell, have the ultimate question? He leaves Hawking and starts taking a brainy seminar with his dog, Fred, and Mac McDonald, the big American actor, down by the River Lea. Discussing curved space in the pub, we suddenly see him performing the spin-off show in the theatre. There's a memorable scene in the first of the three programmes, where Ken is seeking the complete theory of everything, when he discusses gravity in a bus shelter with a very bright small boy in red school uniform. Unlike, say, Stephen Fry or Griff Rhys Jones doing a travel programme because it sounds like a jolly idea, Ken goes to the edge of a cliff on the Canary Islands because *he really wants to know* if he can see where we come from before facing the melancholy fact that we are as far into our own future as we could possibly be: the furthest objects we *could* see are the quasars of twelve billion light years ago.

In the second *Reality* programme, he looks into atoms, literally, in the CERN research centre of particle physics in Switzerland, where a twenty-seven-kilometre tube generates subatomic particles whizzing around at a ridiculous speed; the top man at CERN tells Ken that he's started a new nothing and is not interested in matter. Even more alarmingly, he suggests that it was very unlikely that all this atomic whizzing around would go bang and create a new, or indeed old, universe: but he couldn't rule this out convincingly. If a face may goggle, Ken's does at this point, as he contemplates the enormity of it all with a physiognomy literally bursting with uncontainable joy and wonder. You've never seen anyone look so entranced and excited at the same time. In the third programme, he discusses the alternatives we face, our choices in life, with a fellow in Cambridge who was indeed a Fellow in Cambridge, 'the master of the multiverse', the chillingly intelligent and totally comprehensible David Deutsch. There is, we are told, a separate universe for every possible history of the universe. There is a different universe in the pub, or when you visit your auntie. And, right at the end, Ken has the long-awaited interview with Hawking, whom he pushes around in his wheelchair, the two of them unconsciously aping the interdependent figures in Beckett's *Endgame*.

Ken offered *Mystery Bruises* at the Almeida partly as a footnote to, or résumé of, the making of *Reality on the Rocks*, 'a two-hour trawl through the mysteries of the universe from Gants Hill to Camden Lock'; then, he revealed that the reason the Almeida had rung him up was because, in their words, 'the bollocks we've got on has been rumbled' and they needed a stopgap. The rumbled bollocks in question was a revival of Ben Travers's *The Bed Before Yesterday*, which was so irredeemably awful that it had to be yanked off the stage before the end of its run. The one good thing to come out of it was the definition Campbell now came up with in *Mystery Bruises* for dramatic criticism: 'grading the bollocks'. He then got going on how the furtive nudist had become a hypochondriac transsexual (there are known cases, we were reminded darkly, of men lactating), as told by an angel who had visited Ian Holm – his fellow Ilfordian – on this very Almeida stage where he was appearing in 'some bollocks with pauses' (a somewhat harsh, if not entirely inaccurate, phrase to describe Harold Pinter's

Moonlight). Holm had been urged not to become confused with The Man Who Mistook His Wife for a Bollocks (a similarly robust reference to a seminal work of the neurologist Oliver Sacks). *Mystery Bruises* in turn had its own companion piece in Campbell's fifth solo show, *Theatre Stories*, which premiered in June 1996 as part of the Barclays New Stages Festival at the Royal Court, the first time Ken had returned there since *The Great Caper* in 1974 and a production he directed in the Theatre Upstairs of Heathcote Williams's *Remember the Truth Dentist* (with Dave Hill in the cast) two months later. He wrapped up a few of the old stories – the RDC hoax, the third-act detective (yet again!), Angus in *Macbeth*, David DeNil – and he recounted his experiences in transcendental meditation and with the Science Fiction Theatre of Liverpool. It was pretty tired, overfamiliar stuff: he needed a few new jolts.

The death of George Harvey Webb in December 1994 could have provided one of them. Ken had revisited his old Newfoundland friends in St John's several times and had no idea of one of the most fascinating real-life connections of all. It turns out that Harvey Webb's mother was a Newfoundlander and that one of his uncles owned the Neuf equivalent of Harrods, the Hudson Bay Trading Post. Not only that: Harvey Webb had actually been born in St John's but had emigrated with his family to Southampton at the end of the First World War; he had spent a lot of time over there playing the fiddle – which is a national pastime, especially in The Ship Inn, an explanation of why he was so very good at it. Ken had no previous idea about all this – Harvey Webb was merely his teacher, his mentor, his satanic conspirator in *Illuminatus!*, the main cause and facilitator of his going into the theatre in the first place – until Harvey Webb's daughter, Boo Oldfield, rang to say her father was dying and would he go round to see him. In his notebooks, Ken recounts how he paid that visit on the day before George died. The old boy was out of it and was jabbering on about being an honorary Neuf, and how, one night in St John's, in The Ship Inn, off Duckworth, he'd more than doubled his address book: 'And George opened his eyes and said, "That's where I'm from!" and he reminisced lucidly for half an hour or more, about life in St John's in the 1920s and early 1930s, and in our minds we walked along Water Street together and up the steps past The Ship Inn and up into Duckworth – and along Duckworth until we could see Signal Hill, with the sun setting over the snow – and then George lapsed back into the sleep from which he wouldn't wake.'

12

Relative Values in a Daisy Chain

Daisy Campbell remembers the best part of her adolescence and young womanhood as living around the Lea Valley during the Watermint Quay years. Ken first lived at number 34, sharing with a jolly black lady called Maxine, a platonic friend who later bought and sold clothes in Camden Market, before moving along the same quayside terrace to number 74, which had four bedrooms, always available to friends and colleagues. Daisy remembers the sight of auditioning actors assembling in the café, and being rowed across the river by a little old man; improvised performances under the Avroe arches; messing about on a boat – a four-berth job called *The Snark* – that Ken kept moored virtually outside the front door; and the first time she saw her dad on a stage, in *Furtive Nudist* in Chalk Farm.

It was always likely that Daisy would end up in the entertainment business. At the age of six or seven she and Ken had a comedy act called Silly and Sausage with a running gag about who was Silly and who was, actually, Sausage. This was performed in countless front rooms and kitchens around the place, never professionally, but there was a big red suitcase full of jokes, funny noses, plastic turds and strange gooey things. As she said in a *Sunday Times* 'Relative Values' interview in 1993, putting it mildly: 'My dad isn't a father like my friends' dads, more like a live-in funny chum. When my friends come round he'll pop in wearing strange masks and robes as though it's nothing out of the ordinary. They think he's a bald-headed loony who's very wacky: I'm so pleased I don't have a run-of-the-mill dad!' She was lucky with Prue, too, she reckoned: 'My mum's pretty different, too. For me, being different is very important. She wanders around naked when my friends are there. She strikes them as the sort of mum you'd have if you could choose one in a shop.'

Aged eleven, Daisy was packed off to Bedales, a liberal public school in rural Hampshire with a relaxed attitude towards sexual behaviour, although she was suspended when she was fourteen for drinking excessive amounts of alcohol; she had a few rough years, like her mother, later on. There was never any ideological dispute between Ken and Prue over the rights and wrongs of 'private' fee-paying education, and they split the cost between them. Ken thought it was a good adventure for his daughter, while Prue had taken to the place the minute she saw that the pupils, unlike those at her old school, Benenden, could rush off to class or the playing fields without making their beds. Although rebellious at first, Daisy came to like Bedales and stayed until she was sixteen, filling her English essays with some of the weird stuff her dad would talk about all the time – the Cathars, the original heretics, for instance, who had all been burnt at Montségur in 1244, was a recent project and part of his next show – and developing an original argument in Geography essays by suggesting that there was a public toilet situated at every crossing of the ley lines. She did exceptionally well in her GCSE exams, getting an A in all eleven subjects, several of them starred.

But parallel to this, there was an ongoing programme of personal schooling that Ken had devised for her called the Tilly Matthews Academy of Bizarre and Adventurous Education (Matthews was a London tea broker committed to Bedlam in 1797 and believed to be the first documented case of paranoid schizophrenia). On these courses, Daisy was sent to learn about neurolinguistic programming, German language and literature at the Goethe Institute, Punch and Judy techniques, scuba-diving with friends in Egypt, and computer science. She'd been attending the McKee group, having done *that* course, from the age of eleven, and remembers being taken to Germany a lot, where Ken's clown plays were always being done, and she'd be told to find props for the show that night, or the best sorts of slime and squirty juices. It wasn't so much that Ken was moulding her (well, he was, really), but that his instinct for sharing his own interests and obsessions was incorrigible.

And in 1994, Daisy's first play, *School Journey to the Centre of the Earth* (the full credit was 'co-written by Daisy Campbell with Ken Campbell'), was produced as part of the BT Connections programme at the National Theatre, although she'd written the first version aged eleven in school. Taking the outline of *Clowns on a School Outing*, a madcap escapade on a school bus, she remodelled the trip as an outing to the Alton Towers amusement park, during which one of the children, Tricia, believing they are instead heading towards the centre of the Earth, and that their teacher is a Russian spy, takes control – and the bus crashes. The children rise up and attack the teacher, the coach driver, and the audience. So, even his own daughter was turned into a protégée, and her ultimate Tilly Matthews task was the revival of *The Warp* that she put together with her father in 1997. This came about for two reasons: a new theatre generation was trying to find a way of recycling a sense of anarchy that was linked to the new rave and party climate in the hippy-zippie movement of those years; and there was a new, younger convocation of unaccommodated artists who loved the solo shows and wanted to have a piece of Ken Campbell for themselves.

One of the many extraordinary characters in Ken's life emerged at this time, and was promptly spellbound. The tiny Vietnamese violinist Thieu-Hoa Vuong was standing in a field in 1994 when Campbell came along playing the title role in a small educational film warning children to steer clear of funny old men. Thieu-Hoa (pronounced as if you're asking someone in stage Chinese if they would like a drink of 'tea, or wha'?') was a stand-in for one of the kids and, although aged twenty-two, easily mistaken for a child herself. It was, she says, not love but 'hilarity at first sight', and not just because Ken was in character wearing a tea cosy on his head and his 'Mellors' in his mouth. Almost instantly, Ken asked her to be his comedy partner – she was excellent at gurning and making pig noises, a rare thing in a woman – and her fiddle-playing talents were a bonus he felt he could exploit. He thus ticked another box on a list he had come back with as a result of a recent visit to Newfoundland to see Andy Jones and his sister Cathy, a leading comedienne on national television by this time. He'd owned up to feeling a bit lonely, and to being half in love with Cathy, too. She had told him he should try 'affirming' someone into his life by writing down everything he sought in a person; that person should then come into his life within eight days. Cathy did this all the time. Andy had done it, and on the eighth day had seen a woman passing a café window, had run after her, and asked her out. And over the next few dates he'd been secretly ticking off the affirmation list: she'd seen the right films, read the right books, and so on. 'Wow,' said Ken, 'So Andy's still with this woman, is he?' 'No,' said Cathy. 'He'd forgotten to put on the list that she would have a positive attitude towards his drinking and smoking, and she didn't.'

So Ken started writing his list, but he was really just writing about Cathy: that she could pull faces, had a background with pirates, that she was the toast of St John's. At which point, Cathy asked if her playing the violin in the middle of the night bothered him. Not at all, no it didn't. But Cathy, large and fair-skinned, didn't play the violin, so he deliberately added a few attributes that she didn't possess: that she was small, dark and played the violin. Eight days later he met Thieu-Hoa in the field. And of course she satisfied all the requirements on the affirmation list, including the one about pirates (as we shall see). She helped out a bit on *Mystery Bruises* at the Almeida and went with him to the Belgrade Theatre in Coventry to assist on *Fungus the Bogeyman*, adapted from the Raymond Briggs novel by Mike Carter and directed by Ken as 'a plop opera even more revolting than the book', full of lovely pus and piss-takes but not the most deliriously successful of Campbell's comedy shows. Their association would be cemented on his sixth solo show, *Violin Time*, which opened at the National Theatre, another Richard Eyre commission, in October 1996.

Thieu-Hoa – also variously dubbed Tea Wa, Tilly Warp, Tilly Wah and Tiddly Wah by Ken in his letters to her – was a Vietnamese boat person. She was born in 1972 and grew up in Haiphong, the second largest city, one hour or so from Hanoi. She and her family (mother, Chinese father, three brothers) fled the country in 1980 in a junk, had a brush with pirates along the Chinese coast, and made it finally, after three months at sea, to Hong Kong. There, the family lived in a refugee camp for a year before boarding a plane to Britain, where they were granted asylum and ended up in Alloa, north of Edinburgh, on the banks of the Forth. She doesn't even remember first picking up a violin, but was soon playing to a prodigiously high standard, right through convent school in Edinburgh, completing her studies at Dartington College in Devon. After their meeting, and first working together, she and Ken travelled to Scotland to visit her old haunts and made a trip to the Isle of Wight to catch up with James Nye, who lived there. A party at Nye's gaff ended in some very bad, very drunken, antisocial behaviour on Ken's part. But Nye says Ken was being torn apart by his obsession with Thieu-Hoa, whose reluctance to sleep with him was driving him mad. It was while stitching Thieu-Hoa into his working life that Ken at last addressed the years of mounting alcoholism.

In October 1994, Ken performed one of his lesser solo gigs, really a rejig of familiar material, *Knocked Sideways*, at the Queen Elizabeth Hall on the South Bank, in a co-presentation by the producer Michael Morris (who had succeeded John Ashford as theatre director at the ICA) and the London International Festival of Theatre, LIFT. There was a lot of drinking after the performance, says James Nye, and this continued when he and Ken went on with John Joyce to the latter's flat in Upper Tollington Road and continued imbibing until the dawn came up and beyond. Around midday, the three of them – who must have resembled Toby Belch, Andrew Aguecheek and Feste in their midnight cups – lurched back to the South Bank to collect the stuff they had stashed there the night before. Ken and James then headed for Prue's place in Highgate. At some point that evening, Ken asked Prue: 'When should a chap think of going along to Alcoholics Anonymous?' And Prue said that the time had probably come when the chap in question should ask that question. He did go along to AA, but not all that successfully, and not for an extended amount of time. Although there would be lapses in future years, mostly with the whisky bottle, this definitely marked his start-recovery point: and he had achieved complete sobriety as the new century clicked round.

Thieu-Hoa simply didn't comprehend, nor could she deal with, the drinking. She was far happier joining in on the McKee course and, especially, the big enthusiasms Ken had contracted from Jeff Merrifield for the Cathars and for the artistic community at Damanhur, near Turin. The founders of Damanhur, led by Oberto Airaudi, had settled in a valley with the highest concentration of different minerals in the world, where three synchronic lines meet and intertwine; it was a centre for self-improvement, they reckoned, and for the evolution of the whole of humankind. It was also a post-hippy hippy commune. The enormity of the project is what got Ken going, says Merrifield. Over sixteen years, and in secret, the cultists had dug four thousand cubic metres out of the mountain, developing, over an underground length of thirty metres, the equivalent of an eleven-floor building. There were frescoes on the walls, a hall of spheres covered in twenty-four-carat gold leaf, metal and spiral concoctions based on an ancient Egyptian science of energy, and a circular earth hall dedicated to the memory of past reincarnations, with stained-glass doors representing the sun and the moon. And it had all started for Ken when Merrifield gave him a copy of Theodore Roszak's *Flicker* (1991), an apocalyptic thriller and a secret history of film which veers off into the occult tale of the Cathars and their medieval heresy. Merrifield was down in the South of France before you could say 'Burn, baby, burn'. As for Damanhur, while Merrifield was something of a believer, Campbell was, as usual, a keen truffle hound after the amazing and slightly ridiculous that would make good material for a new show.

Thieu-Hoa must have wondered what had hit her as Ken wrestled this diverse and bizarre material into their show together, while also trying to unlock her own expressive muse. He arranged an outing to see Abel Gance's great *Napoleon* epic at the National Film Theatre and wrote, in April 1995: 'Don't arrange anything for immediately afterwards. It's so inspiring that you need to talk for at least two hours afterwards. I am sure it will spark off in you your ideas for your film. And I'd like to help you start to put those down on paper right there and then. It's all so much easier when we've just shared something major and astounding...' He also writes to Ken Dodd about her, after he's taken her to a recorded performance of *An Audience with Ken Dodd* at London Weekend Television, adding a Pidgin translation of a few of his jokes (Dodd's reaction to this is not known) and declaring his undying devotion first to Thieu-Hoa and then to Dodd himself: 'There may be as big a fan of you as myself, but I haven't the mental equipment to conceive of a bigger. I remain in awe and wonder of you.' And he raises money for Thieu-Hoa's impoverished family, or tries to, and buys her a return ticket to visit St John's, where she promptly falls in love with someone else in one of the pubs Ken tells her to visit.

Places, Ken believed, were also states of mind, and he liked the idea of 'mystic geography', another theme of *Violin Time*, and indeed a working title for the show in the first place. 'We could say about the British,' he wrote in another letter, 'that they have quite a well-developed America but have been a bit lazy with their China... I have an English friend with a very nice Amsterdam, but he needs to pay more attention to his Munich.' And as a preface to her visiting St John's – she was still to be 'affirmed' as the toast of that town – he explains that it's one of the best places in the world to buy weird books, pride of place on a recent visit going to *Last of the Moe Haircuts: The Influence of the Three Stooges on Twentieth-Century Culture* by Bill Flanagan. Instead, Thieu-Hoa concentrated on her violin-playing and catching up with Ken's friends. One she made on her own was Chris Darlington, a film-maker, and their subsequent marriage was promptly adopted by Ken as part of the show, at least in Newfoundland. This seemed of a piece with the oddity and general happenstance of life in St John's. As Campbell had explained to Michael Billington in their National Theatre Platform conversation, the Newfound-landers are not Canadian, exactly, nor do they speak in a dialect: it's a mixture of Scottish and Irish, and a bit of Bristol. Place names are often crude pirate slang like 'Shove-me-Tickles' or 'Up-yer-Chimney'. He had taken a car trip with Andy Jones to have pictures taken under these odd signs: they came to the little village of Dildo. 'We went into this bar and the largest pirate I've ever encountered came up and said, "What brings you here, me hearties?" We said that we were attracted by the name of the place, and he said, "We call it that in the hope it'll keep the real pricks out."'

Within three weeks of receiving the commission, Campbell had written a draft and then had about six months to rewrite and revise it while on tour before opening in the Cottesloe. The world premiere of *Violin Time* was presented in the Longshoremen Protective Union Hall in St John's on 15 July 1996 with, according to the playbill, the marriage of Thieu-Hoa, described by Ken as 'a living storyline', to Chris Darlington onstage during the performance: 'Sure to be unlike any theatre you've seen before.' 'My job,' Ken had written to her, 'isn't to write or rewrite your story. It's to help you FIND it. Stories are quite like life, but you cut out all the parking of your car (except when you back into someone – and then WHO? – and what happened then?), and also you cut out all the washing up (except that one night when a handsome stranger MATERIALISES behind you, and gently takes you in his loving arms, and...).'

In the week of the premiere, Ken had to fulfil his obligation to the *Guardian*, for whom in 1996 he was writing a weekly column, 'The End', in the Friday review section. He filed from St John's a piece about the interpretation of farts as the utterances of the famous Fart Man of Innu Religious Ideology, Tseknan Issishuen Matshishkapeu. The subject arose from a conversation he'd had with a singer, Melody Lane, in The Ship Inn about her forthcoming album of songs and one in particular hymning the sphincter ani: 'No matter how clever you think you are, you couldn't hold in your hands a mixture of solids, liquids, gas and then just let the gas out. The sphincter ani can.' Surprisingly, this gobbet did not work its way into *Violin Time*. Instead, at the October premiere in the National's Cottesloe, I was surprised to hear my own name crop up when, in the preamble – well, the preamble to the whole preamble – Campbell recounts Richard Eyre's gentle taunt that he'd have to do a lot better this time round and that only my own advocacy had secured him the Evening Standard Award for *Jamais Vu*. 'I know,' says Ken, 'he and I were both in the same amateur dramatic society in Ilford years ago – he always looks out for me when he can – there's no money involved.' He looked more like a madcap Magwitch than ever, complete with shopping trolley, tea-cosy headgear and 'Mellors'.

His journeys to Newfoundland, France and the Temple of Mankind in Damanhur came to pulsating life in *Violin Time* as Thieu-Hoa fiddled elegantly on the sidelines, grinning conspiratorially but still remaining a mysterious presence, while Campbell allowed the ambiguity of their relationship – was she his colleague, or his lover? – to hang there unresolved. (Answer: she was never his lover.) He was only prepared to admit that he now thought one-man shows might be improved by having one or two more people in them. The most remarkable aspect of *Violin Time*, though, is the cascade of information (the twelve pages of densely packed footnotes in the printed text are as entertaining as the play itself), as if Campbell is unleashed on the Niagara of his own devising and stays afloat only by paddling so fast. There's an especially revealing passage in his notebooks where he explains to Cathy Jones that while he's 'alone' he's not lonely: 'I'm extremely used to my own company... See, I have no fabricated ego, loud with answers – nor no Buddhist egolessness bonged out by gongs... I feel the same now as I did forty years ago: just running round like a dog in the wrong house – I haven't got the talent the others have got for belonging together.' These others, he says, know where to go, what to do, who to vote for, how VAT works, what the Footsie Index is... All he bothers with are those who *radiate* but don't seem to know it.

Trevor Nunn, who had been appointed Artistic Director designate in succession to Richard Eyre, wrote to Ken in November, having forgiven, apparently, if perhaps not forgotten, the RDC hoax, congratulating him on a show that was 'labyrinthine, touching and hilarious' and expressing a wish to maintain a dialogue in the wake of his special relationship with Eyre. Ken replied, typically, thanking him for the usable 'quote', enclosing a couple of 'crank *Guardian* columns' – possibly the one published that month about how he'd learned to 'blast-read a book at 25,000 words a minute with a tangerine impaled on the handle of a medium-sized sink plunger on his head' – and urging him to visit Damanhur: 'I can alert them to your arrival... It is the centre of all art in our sense of the word. When? Ken.' (Even this letter still sounds like a spoof.)

One person who seemed to *radiate* was the actress Nina Conti, who entered Ken's life by chance when she saw him pull up in a white van at a traffic light in Hampstead High Street. She had seen *Violin Time* and found herself running up to the window: 'I think you're amazing,' she blurted out and he replied, 'I like you too!' Then there was a kerfuffle as the lights turned to green and he stalled the car in order to continue the conversation. The next thing she knew, she was doing *The Warp*. And she became Ken's last major girlfriend, appearing in all versions of the new *Warp* and helping on the long-simmering 'wal wantok' (one-world language) project of *Macbeth* in Pidgin English, which ran parallel. She went with Ken and the Pidgin *Macbeth* in one of its try-out phases to St John's, but had a dire falling-out before picking up with him again after *The Warp*. Her life was completely turned round by Ken, not only on these productions, but in the reaction she had to them and what she later saw as the inevitable renunciation of his all-consuming, full-on amatory attention. Rehearsals were held in Buster Bloodvessel's hotel in the seaside resort of Margate, Fatty Towers, which catered specifically for larger customers, offering huge beds and greasy food (it closed in 1998). Nina didn't find Campbell nearly as affable as she'd thought him in *Violin Time*: 'He was really scary, cracking the whip. But you couldn't take your eyes off him because everything he said was funny, and he was an amazing director. I played about five of the women and maybe a man or two, and I got bumped up because people kept dropping out and I kept getting their roles.'

Daisy made the decisive break. Ken had sent her scuba-diving in Egypt while he started work on *The Warp* revival, but she couldn't bear not being there: 'So, after a week or so with these people all three times my own age, I got myself to the airport and begged them to put me on a plane home. So I turned up, much to Dad's surprise, in time for the whole Fatty Towers adventure.' She helped out with line-coaching and scene-running, just as Mike Bradwell had done at the ICA. As someone who'd been there, done that, got the T-shirt, I never felt impelled to see this revival of *The Warp* in any of its three reincarnations at Three Mills Island in the East End, the Albany in Deptford and finally the Drome near London Bridge. But it's possible that the new version was so far plugged into the heart of the turn-on, drop-out ethos, especially as part of a non-stop rave in the Drome version, that its value as 'theatre' was finally ditched. It became a cult, participatory phenomenon, not dissimilar to what had happened with another 1970s fringe freak-out, *The Rocky Horror Show*. For the 'believers', the new *Warp* was at least as valid as the old one. Certainly Neil Oram himself felt this, though most of the old *Warp* cast steered well clear; exceptions were Mitch Davies, Bunny Reed, Claudia Boulton, who was heavily involved, Maya Sendall and John Joyce, who helped out 'on the book' at the first of the three new versions, at Three Mills Island, an old warehouse and converted film-studio complex on the Stratford and Bow side of the River Lea.

The May 1997 weekend performance at Three Mills lasted nearly thirty hours, with Alan Cox, a really fine actor, and son of Brian, as Phil Masters, surviving heroically through the first seven plays but faltering badly, and half-relying on a script in his hand, with heavy prompting, for the last three. At the end of the show, Campbell brought John Joyce onto the stage, with the script, for a bow, and Joyce, a sweet and sentimental man, said that he felt as though he was taking a curtain call for all the unacknowledged prompters in the history of world theatre. Ian Shuttleworth reported an audience of 150 dwindling to a mere three dozen or so by the end, which sounds a bit sad after the sell-out history of the epic, while comedy critic Adrian Turpin, who saluted Cox's characterisation of rampant egotism touched with warmth and affection, clocked out after a mere fourteen hours, shortly after discovering the author snoring loudly under one of the stages. But still there was a mood to keep the show on the road for some more ten-play cycles.

Ken went away on a job in America and left Daisy and Thieu-Hoa in Watermint Quay to look after the dogs and, according to Daisy, get totally stoned while Daisy learned the role of Phil Masters in order to prove that she could take part in the cycle properly. She performed the first seven plays, as Cox had done, in a makeshift production in an old Portakabin round the back of The Old Bull in Barnet; it was, she said, the only time Ken ever said he was proud of her.

Together, Ken and Daisy started work on translating and adapting the Pidgin *Macbeth* – or '*Makbed* blong Willum Sekspia' – with students at LAMDA, creating a South Pacific environment of poles, face paint, grass skirts and bare torsos. As Campbell had explained, the lingua franca of the islands only has about fifteen hundred words, and whatever his motives in adopting it, the effect was of putting the original play into some kind of magical setting as well as relief. You can see, too, from some recordings made at the MacOwan Theatre at LAMDA in February 1998, that the actors are liberated joyfully into the play in a way that is unimaginable in, say, the RSC. Campbell also used the process to extend his experiments in role-playing and improvisation, as he insisted on all the actors learning all the lines, and then allocating roles at the last minute. Here are the seeds of what became his final area of work in improvisation, gathering everything he'd learned together in what we can now see as one last push towards a kind of unscripted, authentic, subversive theatricality.

It's as though he's refining each minute in the theatre right down, so that nothing is allowed to be seen as a preparation, or a recap, or a disguise, or a delaying tactic. The external exoticism of the performers is no more a cultural ploy than are the costumes of the clown or Harlequin in *Commedia dell'Arte*; the costume is what you have become, it's your definition and not some exotic send-up of those Zulu-dance Shakespeares that occasionally visit London. There was also something haunting and beautiful about the performance of this shadow-play to the real thing. Lady Macbeth's cry of 'Come you spirits that tend on mortal thought, unsex me here' sounded hilarious as 'Saten, tekem me hambag!' while Macduff's triple cry of 'horror, horror, horror' became 'bagarap, bagarap, bagarap'. But there was genuine poetry, too, in a rendition of the 'Tomorrow and tomorrow and tomorrow' speech: 'Naradei mo naradei mo naradei, Wok abaot snel spid de long dei long laswan tata tok, Mo olegeta yestedei blong yumifala, Oli laitem krangke haf madfala long griri finis.' It's like hearing Shakespeare in an approximate, not-too-distant language, like German or Danish. It makes the original sound new again in your mind's ear.

There were just two performances at the Cottesloe later in the year with a professional cast (including the McDevitt brothers, Niall and Roddy, a Polish mime artist and a visiting didgeridoo-maker from Newfoundland), followed by a three-week stint at the Piccadilly Theatre in October, sponsored by producer Bill Kenwright, in which both Ken (who prefaced the performance with a first-act demonstration of Pidgin and its properties, marshalling his actors and assigning roles with the aid of the audience) and Daisy appeared alongside Thieu-Hoa, Jeff Merrifield and Josh Darcy, a key colleague in Ken's last ten years: you couldn't really say that the 'wal wantok' idea took off.

Ken revived his *Theatre Stories* at Trevor Nunn's invitation in the Cottesloe in October 1997, a wittily generous move on Nunn's part as the RDC hoax figures large in the script. An old school friend whom Campbell hadn't seen for years came along with his wife, who'd bought tickets as a birthday present, and over a drink afterwards talked about their son, Oliver Senton, who'd trained as an actor at the Bristol Old Vic School and had been working professionally for a few years. On their instruction (from Ken), Oliver rang him and was summoned to report to the Irish Centre, where the LAMDA Pidgin *Macbeth* was in rehearsal. Ken pointed to his shopping trolley full of ring binders and VHS screeners – it was *The Warp*, *in toto* – and said, 'Right, go and have a look at that. If you like it, learn it, and if you learn it you can do it.' Out of vanity, and the thought that pulling off such a role – the longest ever written in the history of theatre – would stand him in good stead with casting agents in future, Senton learned it over a six-week period, while appearing in a touring production of Alan Ayckbourn's *Season's Greetings*. Like Russell Denton many years before, he took Christmas Day off, then told Ken he'd learned it. Ken sent John Joyce over to test him, a process that took two days. Joyce reported back, 'He can do it!' Ken said, 'But is he any good?' Joyce, exasperated, replied 'He's bloody learned it; being any good wasn't part of the deal.' So the actors were gathered and the new company rehearsed in the basement at Watermint Quay, which had been painted exactly as if the walls were the cavern walls of Damanhur. 'Ken would bake bread for us in Watermint Quay,' says Senton, 'then he'd drive off to a market somewhere and come back with boxes of vegetables, bananas and apples, and he'd make big tureens of soup. I always thought it was wonderful that, when he couldn't pay you, he would feed you.'

There was one trial performance of the complete cycle at the Albany in Deptford on 28 March 1998, then, because that went well, there were five more cycles on successive weekends through April and May. Daisy Campbell was in charge. There were later performances without Senton – a self-financed American called Johnny Stallings turned up, word-perfect, to do one show in Brentwood at Jeff Merrifield's arts centre and two at the Roundhouse – and then Colin Watkeys booked two shows at the Hoxton Hall, each one broken up into five sessions over a weekend, then another one in an upstairs venue in Old Spitalfields Market in the City, followed by the first show at the Millennium Drome near London Bridge in April 1999.

The Drome was a facility for the new-generation party crew masterminded by the alternative entrepreneur Fraser Clark, founder of the Megatripolis and Heaven nightclubs, and it was geared to the approach of the new millennium. *The Warp* returned – now with a new Phil Masters, the fresh-faced Etonian and country squire, Nick Marq – and played on alternate weekends, starting 16 October 1999, for twenty-four hours from 9 p.m. on a Saturday, as part of a bigger festival with hot tubs and string quartets, dance floors and art galleries. The show was a big hit all over again, playing to audiences of two thousand people. The poet John Constable, who was reading poetry in one of those other spaces, turned up one night halfway through to find Neil Oram, looking like an Old Testament prophet, holding forth in front of a bunch of confused-looking ravers: '*The Warp* you are about to see is not the true *Warp*. I wrote it as an allegory of the love of Jesus Christ, and Ken Campbell is not a Christian; he's an atheist, and what's more, he's never dropped acid...'

What was the difference between the first and second *Warp*? Claudia Boulton, who worked as an assistant director and *Warp* 'captain', says, simply, 'Lycra. Everything wrinkled back then. But it was the perfect time-gap, really. It became the story of your parents.' Daisy had appeared at the ICA in the first *Warp* as Meg's baby. Meg was then played by Claudia; and Daisy, who'd hooked up with Roddy McDevitt, playing Billy McGuinness among other roles, had given birth to Dixie, who now, at the Drome, played the baby her mum had first played at the ICA. This trans-generational resonance carried through in the overall casting, which included Alan Cox (son of Brian), Nina Conti (daughter of Tom), Benedick Bates (son of Alan), Kate Alderton (daughter of John and Pauline Collins), and Morganna Lake (daughter of Alan Lake, another of Ken's RADA contemporaries and husband of the iconic 1950s blonde film star Diana Dors). The actress and film-maker Jaqueline Genie, who joined the cast after the Albany run, sees it slightly differently, even though she, too, came from an unconventional middle-class background like Claudia: 'The thing about the old hippies is that they were in the vanguard of a lot of ideas that have become rather mainstream. Now, it really is like the second summer of love. *The Warp* is so strong, still. In the middle of one scene at the Drome, a woman rushed in with a baby from the hot tub next door, squirting breast milk all over the audience. Even we couldn't compete with that. Everyone is on drugs now. In the bohemian arts world, ketamine is massive. They call it "rape smack". It's like heroin and you can inject or snort it. We did a show of monologues from *The Warp* at the National and someone had to be with Neil every time he went to the toilet so he wouldn't inject himself again. That was the big thing in *The Warp*: people from the cast went up to his place in Scotland to be injected in the arse with ketamine. It's not my idea of a good night out.'

In a neat, barely credible echo of Ken's dad failing to take advantage of his friend John Moores starting the family pools business, Genie is creating some big events at the Liverpool Biennial of contemporary art with someone from that same Moores family whom she happened to meet (and then go out with) at a posh party. 'And I'll bring all *The Warp* people up there again... it's all come full circle.' Genie with the dark-brown hair lived in Watermint Quay for a year and became a good dog-minder. She takes full credit, as a conscientious dog-walker, for Gertie finding frisky friends on the towpath and thus having a whole lot of puppies, one of which, Max, remained 'in-house'; Gertie and Max were joined by the unpredictable Bear. Like Nina, Genie continuously took Ken's eye in rehearsals, for her beauty as much as her talent, and she later discovered that he'd taken a lot of Polaroid pictures of her and stuck them in one of his African voodoo boxes, with a candle and a calendar: 'He did make a slight manouevre but I said I wanted just to work with him and he never did anything ever again and was the complete gentleman. He looked after me.'

✧

Thieu-Hoa and Nina both appeared onstage at the Drome, but each was having trouble sustaining her relationship with Ken. Thieu-Hoa finally did find her own story, and it didn't involve Campbell, though she remained good friends. She struck out on her own in pursuit of an ambition to run her own school, studying to become a workshop leader at Goldsmiths College, where she can use what she's learned from Campbell. 'Without him, I'd just be a boring fiddle player. I'm grateful he took me out of that box. What he puts you through is hardcore military training which prepares you for everything, so you're never afraid... and you learn never to worry about money.' Thieu-Hoa divorced Chris and has since remarried. Ken's affair with Nina survived their bust-up over the Pidgin *Macbeth* in Newfoundland but it was a close call. He was anxious about the production and worried about Daisy's drinking. 'Daisy's alcoholism has to be faced,' he wrote in his notebooks, 'and what also has to be faced is that all Nina offers on this jaunt is her talent which turns out to be beyond believing...' and he dubs her Nina 'Batty', first leading lady of the world: 'I told Batty about coping with losing her but losing US I might never get over; she had same thing, she said, there was an US but it was me who destroyed it here in St John's.'

Back in London, Nina walked out of the NT version of the Pidgin *Macbeth*, hid away in her Hampstead turret opposite Belsize Park Tube station and auditioned successfully for the RSC. Cicely Berry, the veteran RSC voice coach, had said something to her about an actor having two kinds of voices, 'one she could listen to and one she couldn't, and I had to decide which one to use'. As luck would have it, Campbell had lately picked up a book on ventriloquism in the Offstage Bookshop and, typically, looked into the subject, having found out about the annual vents' convention in Kentucky. He'd then gone there ('I like going on long trips for a short time and seeing what emerges'). 'He rang me up,' says Nina, 'and said, "You've got to find out about ventriloquism because they're the experts on voice, not Cis Berry." But I had to put the hours in. Was I willing?' Two days later, a package arrived for her at the stage door in Stratford: a huge dog puppet and a teach-yourself-ventriloquism kit. She thought it was a great present, but didn't do anything about it; ventriloquism, she thought, was weird, and not at all funny. 'Then I decided to give it a go. I bought a video camera and filmed myself unpacking the box, to show him that I wasn't worthy of this and he should give it to somebody else. But when I watched it back it wasn't too bad and that puppet was coming alive in the picture. And I ended up talking to more puppets, and he got really excited, and sent me even more puppets.'

The result was a unique collaboration that launched Nina on a whole new career. And for Campbell, as always, the challenge was unleashing something new and unexpected... and, in this case, renewing a love affair. He always believed good acting came from the bowels, not the oesophagus and, in ventriloquism, which is a technical trick of projection, he could find an explanation of, and method of reproduction for, gastromancy – the dark art of the summoning of spirits from below the earth, not above. He developed this skill, and a discussion of it, in the new solo show he had offered Trevor Nunn at the National, with a title Nunn couldn't refuse: *The History of Comedy*. But there was an addendum: *The History of Comedy, Part One: Ventriloquism* opened in the Cottesloe in early 2000. In it, he dovetails his accelerating interest in ventriloquism, 'the oldest art known to man, and it indeed precedes man', with a ragbag of schoolroom and Pidgin stories, dog studies and an explanation of 'real gastromantic acting': what Judi Dench does, apparently, is 'dramatic portrayal', something quite other. Linking gloriously, he explained that ferrets possessed highly developed ventriloquial skills: he had once thrown a piece of meat into a batch of ferrets and discovered that one ferret could eat a morsel while simultaneously making the noise of a ferret eating the same morsel – over there! 'This fools all ferrets, and all ferrets can do it,' he beamed triumphantly, and who is there who can contradict him? He then explained the technique of voice-throwing with a model mouth, palate and teeth, bringing the sound we make right from the deep gastromantic interior to the front, the whole process taking on a weird tribal ritual in which he compelled the audience to join in the mass recitation of an exercise sentence to be recited without moving the lips: 'Who dared to put wet fruitbat poo into dead mummy's bed; was it you, Verity?' The sight of Campbell screaming at us, as we corporately muttered this absurd line back at him, cheeks straining, mouths pouting, was either a new high, or a new low, in the annals of audience participation, I'm not sure which.

Either way, it explained what was going on with Nina. Together, they wrote an X-rated farce for one woman and her puppets and took it to the Edinburgh Festival Fringe in August 2001. *Let Me Out!* was Nina's farewell to the legitimate theatre as she frolicked with her knee pals and explored the 'bi-locative vocalic delusion' of finding voices in her nose and backside. There was a luvvie gibbon, an inflatable Scottish bear, a lurking predator called 'Blob Hoskins', and a little Jack puppet she took along to her (failed) audition to appear on *Topless Snooker*. Best of all there was a little monkey, Monk, who was extremely foul-mouthed and stuck in unrequited love for his mistress. Nina adopted Monk as her number-one knee pal, partly because he was so portable. She booked herself into a 'new act' night in Balham and won the competition. Dates proliferated and in 2002 she won the BBC New Comedy Award. She's now one of the top vent acts in the country – to see her 'possessed' by her own little chap as he breaks her up with an operatic aria having roundly abused her for sticking her fist up his posterior ('How would you like it?') is a very special experience indeed. Now settled in East Finchley with a young son, Nina knows how much Ken changed her life: 'It was a difficult love story, really, and because of the huge age difference I never thought we could be properly together. He had some very special women in his life, and I was one of them for that time and we all loved him dearly and closely and did everything he said; and then suddenly when we realised we couldn't do anything else, it would all blow up. But we survived it, actually. I never thought I would.'

For many people who were closest to Ken, Prue says, it never really resolved itself, this question of 'How you live with, or live without, Ken Campbell?' Daisy tried constantly to escape his hold over her, but she finally succumbed in the second

Warp. Then she went slightly mad. After the Drome, she decided she needed another *Warp* altogether and that she would write it. There was a project to occupy the abandoned cinema (now a Marks and Spencer) at South End Green in Hampstead, but that collapsed, so she went with her daughter Dixie to Spain to stay with friends. She started, she says, drinking absinthe 'big time'. She returned to England and ended up living in a squat on the Bishop's Avenue – Hampstead's 'millionaire's row', curiously – in an abandoned home for survivors of the Holocaust (the last one had just died). She was writing her own new *Warp* on Post-it notes all over the walls when Ken – who was well advanced on his own retreat from alcohol – turned up and took her away to the PROMIS Recovery Centre in Dover, Kent. From there, she made another wrong move by joining a farming community on the Surrey and Sussex borders – recommended, with the best of intentions, by Claudia Boulton – which turned out to be, she says, 'accommodation for psychonauts'. She was on her own now with Dixie, and it was only after a conversation with Ken about the possibility of taking Dixie away that she came to her senses, left the farm and got sorted. She met another addicted actor, Greg Donaldson, 'while I was still bats, with pink hair in little bunches', and they got sober together in 2003, living happily together since and raising Dixie (with Roddy McDevitt, Dixie's father, still very much on the scene for her) alongside their own second child, little Django. It was a long and winding road to recovery, but there were so many excitements on the way that the last few years of Ken's life were blessed with a stronger domestic fabric, and a renewed relish in whatever it was Daisy and Dixie got up to; at the same time, his own work seemed to include a new function as he grew in stature as a wicked old grandpa of the fringe and guru figure for a whole new generation.

The Impro Years

The new millennium started for Ken with something of a flourish: he made a West End appearance alongside his oldest champion and mentor, Warren Mitchell; he applied to the National Theatre to succeed Trevor Nunn as the Artistic Director (and instantly turned his rejection into a fizzing new solo show); he moved house because of his dogs; he stayed sober; and he embarked on a rich new phase of improvisational theatre. Some of his older colleagues saw this as a period of decline and falling away, and there's no denying there was sometimes something doleful about the figure who turned up at an arts centre in his pork-pie hat and oatmeal overcoat, spinning out the same old stories for a dwindling audience. But there was something heroic, too, something akin to his idol Ken Dodd, battling undefeated round an endless circuit of one-night stands in places like Stockport, Dudley, Warrington and Leamington Spa.

The bookings were beginning to dry up at the time of Ken's death, Colin Watkeys admits, but Prue insists that bitterness was simply never part of his life. He'd talked at length to her about his marginal status, his outsider-ism, but he always came out fighting. Mike Leigh, no mean outsider himself, says of Ken that he was 'the outsider's outsider'. He made light of the fact that he was so highly regarded by the leaders of his profession: 'They call me a genius so they don't have to give me a job,' he quipped, but the truth is that three successive National Theatre bosses accommodated him whenever they could; the whole point of Ken Campbell, anyway, was that he didn't fit in properly. That was the joy of him. His role in life was genuinely alternative, adversarial, raspberry-blowing.

In the ventriloquism solo, he cut across one of his own riffs with an exultant cry: 'People think I go home to my real life after this. There is no real life! Nothing else matters! This! Is! What! Matters!' Michael Kustow hailed the Apollonian structure of this show, as well as its Dionysian abandon, and argued that Ken's gastromantic theory about the origins of theatre in the belly is something even Nietzsche overlooked when he wrote about the birth of tragedy. He added that Ken should get the next Nobel Prize for Literature if it was ever again awarded to a theatre person. It was. But it went to Harold Pinter, in 2005. I've often wondered whether Ken Campbell, like Joan Littlewood, would have been so extraordinary had he been given everything he might have wanted in terms of state subsidy. Not that he ever asked, really. Alone among his contemporaries on the fringe, the whole idea of enslavement by subsidy – 'hush money' as Charles Marowitz called it – was genuine anathema to him. He hated most of what he saw as 'Arts Council-approved'. Poverty, abrasion, anger and downright cussedness all defined his contribution. But he wasn't above earning an honest bob or two – he had to, really – by batting every now and then for the commercial 'other' side. At each end of his career, for instance, there are utilitarian cameos: in 1967 he was a desk receptionist in Ken Loach's landmark film, *Poor Cow*; and in 2000 he popped up as a cheery postman in Nigel Cole's comedy *Saving Grace*, in which a suburban widow played by Brenda Blethyn tries to pay off her debts by growing marijuana. And he appeared in several television advertising campaigns, notably one for Kit Kat chocolate bars, in which he took a break (took a Kit Kat) at the gates of hell dressed up as a sweltering devil with 'the stately homo of England' Quentin Crisp as an even unlikelier whiter-than-white member of the seraphim; and one for Citroën cars, in which his rather-too-pleased-with-himself salesman might have been more of a turn-off than a come-on, though he always gleefully claimed that a Citroën executive had told him that his campaign had shifted more cars than supermodel Claudia Schiffer's.

Then there was the West End... At the beautiful Wynd-ham's Theatre, Yasmina Reza's *Art*, translated from the French by Christopher Hampton, and then in its fifth year, had been kept fresh by repeated changes of cast. The producers' policy was to cause a surprise where possible, since its premiere with Albert Finney, Tom Courtenay and Ken Stott. The seven-teenth cast change, in November 2000, ushered in Warren Mitchell as the aeronautical engineer who loathes modern art, John Fortune (a gloriously deadpan revue performer from the David Frost satirical era and a regular comedy partner of John Bird) as the dermatologist who has bought a blank white can-vas for 200,000 francs – and Ken as their shell-shocked chum. All of them were too old for the roles they played, but it didn't matter. In a play about friendship and a painting, they were referred to by more than one critic as three old masters of comedy, and the sight of Campbell and Mitchell locking eye-brows like a pair of demented cockney gremlins was delightful (Fortune was a smooth man, much posher). Campbell's char-acter, Yvan, worked in stationery: he delivered the line 'I'm groping my way into the world of vellum,' Michael Billington said, 'as if it were some arcane, Masonic mystery.' He also dis-charged a torrential monologue about the complicated etiquette of his wedding invitations with the despairing fury of one crying for help in the wilderness – and for the instant obliteration of his future mother-in-law.

Trevor Nunn was always only going to serve five years as head of the National (Richard Eyre had served ten), so the feelers were out for his successor as early as May 2001, when Ken made preparatory notes for a meeting with the NT Chair-man Sir Christopher Hogg. He jotted down ideas for the repertory that included Neil Simon's *The Odd Couple*, Bob Hoskins in Eugene O'Neill's *The Hairy Ape*, Steven Berkoff's *Kvetch*, John Arden's *Serjeant Musgrave's Dance*, *Mary Poppins*, Jim Carrey as *Hamlet*, *Measure for Measure* 'translated into Eng-lish', and projects involving Terry Pratchett, Brian Eno and Ken Dodd. He later received a letter from Hogg saying that Nunn's successor was about to be announced (this was Nicholas Hyt-ner, who took over in 2003) and that they'd decided not to call him back for the final interviewing session. But Sir Christopher thanked Ken 'for all the material' – one can imagine the deluge of crazy, brilliant suggestions – and said how much he'd been enjoying reading the Keith Johnstone book (*Impro*, which evidently Ken had recommended to him). Ken's immediate response was to throw on another solo show – *If I Ruled the National Theatre* – at the ICA in September 2001, making a curiously compelling case for *Anne of Green Gables*, which he claimed had been used as a set text to teach English to the Japanese after the war. There would be circuses and year-round children's shows, Sunday openings (much of which has come to pass) and a musical version of Jack London's *Call of the Wild* with a chorus of singing dogs (which hasn't).

Maybe it was the dogs that gave the NT Board pause. Dogs were central to Ken's life, so much so that it was to suit them that he moved house around this time. Werner and Fred were gone, but not forgotten. The incumbents now were Gertie, her mongrel son Max, and Bear, a dangerous cross-breed of Pyrenean Mountain, Irish Water Spaniel and Shar Pei, who could attack without warning, as Chris Taynton found out to his cost at Ken's funeral. Max was in danger of being put down because, at some time in 2002, he had bitten a Watermint Quay neighbour who happened to be a policeman, and allegedly 'gone for' the policeman's child. The case involved a court appearance in which, under the Dangerous Dogs Act, Max was almost certainly doomed. Ken turned for inspiration to the famous eulogy for a dog delivered by a nineteenth-century American politician and lawyer, George Graham Vest, in a trial in which damages were sought for the killing of a dog in Missouri:

> The best friend a man has in this world may turn
> against him and become his enemy. His son or
> daughter that he has reared with loving care may
> prove ungrateful. Those who are nearest and dearest
> to us, those whom we trust with our happiness and
> our good name, may become traitors to their faith.
> The money that a man has, he may lose. It flies away
> from him, perhaps when he needs it the most. A
> man's reputation may be sacrificed in a moment of ill-

> considered action. The people who are prone to fall
> on their knees to do us honour when success is with
> us may be the first to throw the stone of malice when
> failure settles its cloud upon our heads. The one
> absolutely unselfish friend that a man can have in this
> selfish world, the one that never deserts him and the
> one that never proves ungrateful or treacherous is his
> dog... If fortune drives the master forth an outcast in
> the world, friendless and homeless, the faithful dog
> asks no higher privilege than that of accompanying
> him to guard against danger, to fight against his
> enemies, and when the last scene of all comes, and
> death takes the master in its embrace and his body is
> laid away in the cold ground, no matter if all other
> friends pursue their way, there by his graveside will
> the noble dog be found, his head between his paws,
> his eyes sad but open in alert watchfulness, faithful
> and true even to death.

Ken's solicitor told him that only five per cent of dogs got away with Max's kind of transgression, so in the six months before the case came to court, he signed on the dog at a heavy-duty training school in Brentwood. Making rapid progress, Max soon won a cup in a competition. Ken gave a demonstration on proper behaviour with dogs to the local Hassidic kids in Springfield Park and arranged some publicity in the *Hackney Gazette*. Meanwhile, he and the dogs had found a Swiss chalet on the edge of Epping Forest that seemed ideal for further activities, and he arranged to exchange contracts on the day of the trial. He took along all the publicity, and Max's rosettes, to the courtroom and pleaded guilty. The lady magistrate asked why the dog should have bitten the policeman, Mr Davies. The solicitor replied that perhaps Max thought Mr Davies was behaving in a threatening manner. 'Why should he have thought that?' 'Far be it from me, ma'am, to understand the reasoning of dogs, but maybe the dog thought that he was an enemy of Mr Campbell.' 'Why should he have thought that?' 'He is a policeman, ma'am!' Furthermore, the solicitor submitted that, if spared, Max was due to appear at Earl's Court in two weeks' time with the Essex Dog Display Team. This clinched it, and the magistrate spared Max his life. 'I wouldn't have gone to all that trouble for a human being, not even Daisy!' said Ken later.

The new home was on Baldwin's Hill opposite The Foresters Arms, overlooking the Great Monk Wood part of Epping Forest, a couple of miles from Loughton town centre. There had been an argument in the local historical society about the exact location in the forest of the woodman's hut where some monks of Essex had hidden in order to avoid being beheaded in the Reformation. The argument was won for Baldwin's Hill as a result of someone importing a Swiss chalet by boat and horseback early in the last century, and plonking it down right there: this was the hut. No one lived in it until forty years ago. For the last five or six years of his life, Ken became the woodland sprite, or troll, of the neighbour- hood, mellowed now beyond the alcohol years. He would walk the dogs for hours on end through an enchanted forest, arrange elaborate chases and games through the undergrowth for his grandchildren's birthday parties, and knock out tables and odd bits of furniture in the tiny scrub of a back garden (Prue tells me that the first book she remembers Ken having was *Carpentry without Joins*). He screened his Jackie Chan movies and DVD box sets for friends – *Buffy the Vampire Slayer*, *The X-Files* and *24* were firm favourites – ran work- shops and classes and sallied forth in his rattling white van to fulfill the odd booking, often with Jeff Merrifield, Tim Fiddler or Josh Darcy for company. He never slept in his own bed, dossing down on the sofa each night with the dogs, so that vis- itors could sleep in sheets without dog hairs.

And then there was Doris, the African Grey parrot. Once Ken was settled in Loughton, Daisy had suggested he might like what the internet had to offer and might consider buying a computer at last; so he headed into Hackney with a laptop in mind. But in one of those multiverse moments he had dis- cussed with David Deutsch in *Reality on the Rocks* (and a bit like the Gwyneth Paltrow character in the film *Sliding Doors*) he went into – not the computer shop – but the one next door, a pet shop, and bought a parrot. Doris was his destiny, his final girlfriend, and he devoted much time in his last years to arranging her droppings into framed artworks and teaching her to speak her own autobiography. He first coached Doris on her origins: 'I used to be an egg and then I hatched out, didn't I? All fluffy at first, then the feathers...' This progressed to her next common utterance: 'I was in a pet shop for a while, then Ken bought me...' This tuition was painstaking but rewarding, though Ken said that 'Sometimes things came out quick: "I'm up 'ere, you're down there! Shall I do my silly noises? I think I will... whoops!" And she does a formidable impression of the telephone. I don't answer it for a while because it's probably only her. She only does three rings and then she says, "Hello!" Parrots live for ever so she'll live way after me. So at least I know my voice will ring on long after my death: "I'm up 'ere, you're down there!"'

The workshops that he'd run concurrently with his productions throughout his career became more central in this period. And this led to a surprise renewal of his relationship with Chigwell School, which he'd never much worked on till now. He began teaching at East 15 Acting School – the Joan Littlewood-related drama school, bankrolled initially by George Harvey Webb and his wife – and he liked Chigwell's splendid new theatre, which had lately forged an affiliation with E15. He said, too, that his old dad would have liked the fact that he now lived at the end of the 167 bus route that Ken had used as a schoolboy. So there is a sense in which Campbell's life achieved a sort of completion, however sudden and unexpected in its ending, and in that at least I think he was fortunate. His manager Colin Watkeys felt that improvisation was not the Holy Grail but never once advised him not to continue. Not that Ken would have listened anyway. He was caught up in a new wave of experimentation, developing skills in young actors in the pursuit of long-form, narrative improvisation, rather than just the short form popular on television programmes like *Whose Line Is It Anyway?* or onstage at Jongleurs and the Comedy Store.

The impro years began when Ken was asked to do something for the Liverpool Everyman's fortieth anniversary in 2004. He didn't want to do an old show, so Josh Darcy, who'd been in the Pidgin *Macbeth*, brought along a couple of friends and they threw something together. At the same time, the actor and producer Adam Meggido had gone along to some of Ken's 'eccentric' acting classes 'and got the full force of Ken', while another actor and teacher, Sean McCann, was asked by Ken if he'd like to come along to some workshops. McCann had seen *Jamais Vu* on its West End transfer to the Vaudeville ('It still remains the most extraordinary thing I've ever seen a person do on a stage'), and had worked on a Horror Theatre Festival at the Union Theatre in Southwark with Meggido in 2004. He arranged some meetings in the South Camden Community School where he was working: it's a school specialising in performing arts with a fine small theatre.

These three – Darcy, Meggido and McCann, three brilliant musketeers of impro, certainly in the same class of talent as Keith Johnstone's Theatre Machine that Ken so admired in the early days – were central to everything Ken did in the last years of his life. Having found them, he pressed them immediately into service on a gig that Mark Rylance, then Artistic Director of Shakespeare's Globe at Southwark, had booked him for on Shakespeare's birthday, 23 April, 2005. The Liverpool improvisers were up for this, as were another group in Gateshead on Tyneside called the Suggestibles. Campbell had organised a competition between these two teams, with comedian Phil Key as one of the judges, whose job was to hold up placards with points on them. This was all done in the spirit of Keith Johnstone's 'theatre sports', which were always more to do with 'good nights out' than spawning great performers.

The upshot for the Globe evening was *Shall We Shog?* (a line of Pistol's sidekick Nym in *Henry V*), a vaudeville of Shakespearean skills played out against the supposed pomposity and grandeur of Shakespearean theatre in general (and especially, perhaps, at the RSC) under such sketch headings as 'best use of pillars', 'best first entrance of Richard III', 'running out of breath and injured entrance with news of the battle involving

high-speed use of confusing geography and reference to people who we're not sure who they are,' 'best pitch-black-night
acting', 'hearty laughter at fuck-all', 'most unfunny funny scene'
(it comes to an end if it gets a laugh), and the 'hey nonny song'.
'The skill of the evening was remarkable,' says Rylance, 'much,
much better than I was expecting.' Oliver Senton did some
freestyle iambic improvisation in the interval and also performed 'To be or not to be' without using the letter 'e' (it
started: 'To do, or not to do') – a challenge suggested by
Georges Perec's 'e'-free novel *La disparition*, translated into
English by Gilbert Adair as *A Void*.

Another of Sean McCann's specialities was the improvised sonnet, composed while counting backwards from one
hundred. His own expertise in this changed McCann's life, literally. Ken used to make him improvise a sonnet to a woman
in the audience. At the Hay-on-Wye literary festival, he picked
on the writer and film critic Antonia Quirke, who, he says,
chased him down a street afterwards and dated him for a
while. Later, he was told by Ken at a conference of Newfound-
landers in Harlow, Essex, to direct a sonnet at a beautiful girl
at the back of the hall. ' "Oh no," I protested,' recalls McCann,
' "these sonnets get me into trouble." But Ken was gripped by
the excitement and said, "Go on, do it to her... yeah, you want
to sonnet her!" So I asked her a few questions about herself
and did the sonnet, then she asked me to show her round
Oxford, where I teach at the drama school. I did, and we ended
up married.'

There was something in all this that was tapping new
sources of energy in acting that had been submerged in years
of 'correct' performances in the anodyne repertory theatres
and the control areas of the RSC and the National. Gastromantic acting went deeper, into the bowels, and claimed
disciples down the years from the great Victorians to Olivier
and Joan Littlewood, Steven Berkoff, George Robey and Ken
Dodd. The Seymour Hicks advice about having a yard of
meaningless verse up your sleeve to cover a 'dry' was part of
this embedded rich vocalisation, and was enshrined in the art
of 'nubbing', or improvising in iambic pentameters to escape

potential disaster onstage. Campbell auditioned three times for the RSC in the 1960s, 'and three times they had the wisdom to turn me down'. On one of these occasions, eschewing his preferred route of the noble nub, he offered his 'pick a sausage, any sausage' routine, in which, eyes closed, he invited someone in the front row to choose any one from a bunch of bangers, then shuffled it back into the pack and successfully (always) identified the selected saveloy. 'My secret dream, though,' he confessed, 'was not to score with the sausage routine, or to impress anyone with my Shakespearean interpretations, but rather to dry up and launch into a formidable nub!' The actor Tom Wilkinson – a regular in the Richard Eyre Nottingham company – had passed on a useful 'nub' line to Mark Rylance when at RADA. He reckoned you could proclaim – 'O to be a king and ride naked through the gates of Hypernium' – and create enough space and wonder in the audience (and your fellow actors) that it wouldn't seem odd for you to either leave the stage or consult with the prompt corner.

'There will always be someone like Ken cropping up,' says Mark Rylance, 'though it's hard to see anyone like him right now. For as long as we carry on the tradition of Burbage to Garrick to Kean to Olivier, there will always be the Will Kemps. I talked a lot to Ken about Kemp, he was very like him; Kemp would improvise for twenty minutes after a great tragedy, take a story prompt from the audience – often about a husband being away and the milkman paying a visit – and make up a song with that story while he was dancing. He was the Billy Connolly of his time, and of course the audience was longing to know what was happening in his mind as he acted the great comic roles like Touchstone. I remember Ken saying to me that he thought the writing-down of Shakespeare plays was only for rainy days, or when they weren't particularly feeling up to it; but that when they were really on form, they just channelled it... The real Shakespeare was channelled, whereas what we are left with is really just the dull shadow of the plays themselves. And he would say these things with such marvellous credibility. There was always poetry behind his apparent foolishness, something philosophical at the back of it all. He never demanded anything less than enormous skill from his performers, and he had this fantastic relish for language. I see now that I really should have got him to do Ben Jonson at the Globe.'

Towards the end of this year, Campbell began talking more about the long-form Canadian soap-improvisation group Die-Nasty (the antidote to *Dynasty*) whom he had seen in Edmonton, Alberta. Their trademark format is the fifty-hour improvathon, which breaks down into twenty-five two-hour episodes over one weekend, or a couple of days. The actors improvise within their characters, playing out scenes barked at them from the sidelines by the director, Dana Andersen, who is flanked by an electrician controlling the lights, a production assistant and a musician or two.

Campbell sent Sean McCann over to investigate further; McCann ended up playing a grumpy chef and Mick Jagger for fifty hours with four hours off in the middle, which he spent asleep on a sofa. 'It was the most glorious thing I've ever done,' he says. Ken decided that he had to do one of these sagas himself, though he didn't like the word 'improvisation' and for a time used the term 'extemporisation' before settling on 'hard bardics', or 'opening the bardic tap'. 'This meant,' explains Adam Meggido, 'tapping into "the other", in whichever form it took, whether it was glossolalia, channelling flights of lyricism, touching the muse, or glimpsing the gods... It could be musical, verbal, physical. He was the goader and we were the rhapsodes.'

Meggido, McCann and an extremely hirsute Darcy, as well as Oliver Senton, all appeared in a series of one-night impro shows at the Royal Court starting in November 2005 as part of the theatre's fiftieth-anniversary celebrations, under the title *Décor Without Productions* (a staple of the early Royal Court days was Sunday-night productions without décor). These were batty, enjoyable occasions marked more by Campbell's impatience with the actors than any particular intrinsic theatrical merit, although the speeded-up skit on *Look Back in Anger* was a hoot on home territory, and the improvised *Odyssey* had its moments ('Why did they wear masks in Greek theatre?' Campbell had asked: 'Because they already had them on.') The actors were pushed and prodded round the tiny stage while Campbell rummaged in his trolley for exemplary literature and tried to induce a form of abusive fury that only he could possibly manage. There were seeds of something here, but nothing to rival memories of the Road Show. The gusto seemed enforced rather than spontaneous.

In the following month, December 2005, Watkeys helped Ken organise the first Die-Nasty-influenced thirty-six-hour improvisation at the Inn on the Green fringe and community theatre in Ladbroke Grove. (Watkeys remained sceptical: 'They all say there's no point in doing it unless it's as good as something that's written down, and it never is.') Adam Meggido, meanwhile, worked with Ken on a brand-new show for Edinburgh in August 2006. This was to be the reinvention of Shakespeare's lost play, *Cardenio*; or, rather, Shakespeare and John Fletcher's lost play, according to scholars who have pored over an eighteenth-century Drury Lane play called *Double Falsehood; or, The Distrest Lovers* by Lewis Theobald who, in turn, claimed to have based his play on three (lost) Shakespearean manuscripts. In the end, *In Search of Cardenio* became not an academic exercise using the now generally agreed textual fragments but the launching pad for the School of Night company that Meggido now runs. When they were researching the authorship question, Ken decided that, like Sir Walter Raleigh, he wanted a school and that these guys should be the scholars. 'So for a time,' says Darcy, 'we improvised-up plays in any style. The main thing that modern playwrights should do, the thinking went, was not write plays, because that wouldn't get them anywhere; what they needed to do was become famous. And then their plays would get put on and people would want to see them.'

The School of Night segued into Showstoppers, a companion troupe which improvised on musical plot lines suggested by the audience, until the last ten minutes when the musician Dylan Emery sat at the piano to suggest what might happen if this really was a musical. 'This opened up one of Ken's bardic taps,' says Meggido, 'but he wasn't sure what to do with it.' They took the process further at a series of workshops at the Actors Centre in Covent Garden in 2007, and were ready to launch the full musical Showstopper experience at the Edinburgh Festival Fringe in 2008. On one night, in three successive weeks, the actors improvised a complete musical based on a review of a non-existent show written by a national newspaper critic (Ian Shuttleworth, Dominic Maxwell and Robert Dawson Scott).

I'm not sure if Ken ever thought that this work led anywhere. A lot of it became a way for him to get through the day: Josh Darcy certainly felt there was a mood of semi-retirement about him. And he hadn't been well. 'He had been to the doctor about a minor prostate problem,' says Darcy 'and then he decided to go on this radical fruit diet. He was on it in Edinburgh, just before he died, and it was giving him horrendous headaches. And he was getting a bit morbid. On the last night, he actually did say, "If I go in the middle of a show, you'll just have to carry on." And I said, "What do you mean?" and he said, "If I go to the toilet..."' Despite this sense of slowing down – and Jeff Merrifield thinks that the prostate problem might have been a bit more complicated than was generally thought – Ken's death still came as an absolute shock to everyone. He never bothered with doctors much, and his physical default system was usually one of cheerful ebullience. He may have been sixty-six, clickety-click, years old, but he was Peter Pan, eternally mischievous and bright-eyed. He was found dead in the chalet by Daisy on Sunday 31 August 2008 around lunchtime. The dogs had been recently fed and there was no sign of any other disruption. He had keeled over on the living-area floor between the kitchen and his improvised platform. As the cause of death was a heart attack, there was no further autopsy.

'Everywhere he went,' says Meggido, remembering Ken a few months before he died, 'was a theatre, a place of performance, and everyone he met was a member of the audience. He, Sean and I were on our way to that Hay-on-Wye Festival to improvise sonnets. He got all his books out, and told us to start "sonneting" to an elderly couple sitting near us on the train. He asked them for a style. They thought they recognised him, but they weren't sure. The woman was delighted with this, but the man looked incredibly suspicious and, after a while, with us improvising and doing requests, he leant over to Ken and said, "Why do you do this?" And I noticed something Ken always did when he was being amazingly truthful – it was like a poker tell; he would just nod his head back – and he looked at this fellow and said, "For the good of man. For the collective soul of mankind." There was utter silence. And I thought – yeah, you really do believe that. That is why all this stuff happens. Good on you.'

Just how far this new strain of work could go was demonstrated posthumously in the three London Improvathons to be staged since Ken had brought the Canadians and his guys together. The last of the three shows, in January 2010, was a Victorian soap, *We Are Not Amused*, at Hoxton Hall in Shoreditch, an appropriate music-hall setting for a tale of skulduggery, lost children and vivid, almost operatic, tableaux, with a cast list including the Queen and Prince Albert, Charles Dickens (with a Klezmer band called Dizzy and the Rallies), explorers, cowpokes, a violent nurse and a media mogul called Francis U Cund, which he was quite often. Alan Cox popped up as both Dante Gabriel Rossetti and Willy Wonka in a chocolate-factory chorus. Josh Darcy dealt with bowel demons as Ebeneezer Grimes, the Peckham gastromancer. Maya Sendall, veteran of all the *Warps*, hoisted her skirts and bawled for England as a lady of ill repute. Prince Albert took leave of Ruth Bratt's luminous and hilarious Queen Victoria in an astonishing scene of surprising pathos. And the entire cast filled the stage as orphans, pimps, gamblers and adventurers to improvise full-bodied chorales which, bathed in glorious lighting, were as moving and melodic as anything in *Les Misérables*. The actors appeared to enter another zone of concentration. The level of performance and ingenious scene-moulding was extraordinary. And as the audience and actors mingled after the marathon show on a bitterly cold night in East London, in that curious cloud of exhaustion and elation more characteristic of the end of a sports tournament or an election campaign, the bearded director, Dana Andersen, raised his cap and raucously invoked the spirit of Ken Campbell. The roar from actors and audience alike must have carried as far as Epping Forest.

Epilogue

A year after he died, Ken's friends and family gathered once more in Epping Forest to mark the anniversary. Tales were told and songs were sung. Josh Darcy ventriloquised part of the George Graham Vest oration with a dog puppet. Nina Conti did the 'pick a sausage, any sausage' routine. Mitch Davies placed a wooden profile, made to last in resilient elm, on the earth mound. Granddaughter Dixie, now ten, read a poem she had written:

> So bald a head
> So strong a will
> That many have fled from Baldwins Hill
> But those who knew him extremely well
> Knew this was merely his outside shell
> So bald a head
> So strong a will
> That many have fled from Baldwins Hill.

Ken made his last, posthumous appearance on British television as a strange alcoholic butler in the new Miss Marple series starring Julia McKenzie. The butler himself probably wasn't strange, but Ken certainly made him seem so, giving people odd looks for no apparent reason. 'There's something funny going on here,' he leered, sidling along corridors and suddenly singing 'Pack up all your cares and woes... bye, bye, blackbird' straight down the camera's throat. The real mystery in the mystery was: if the butler hadn't done it, why was Ken Campbell's extraterrestrial performance so criminally over the top? Answer came there none.

Five weeks later, on 12 October 2009, the National Theatre hosted a tribute in the packed Olivier stalls that was a
delicious ragbag of capers, including one I'd never seen before:
mime artist Toby Sedgwick playing a rasher of bacon as it sizzled in the pan, flipped over, then sizzled again. Sedgwick
curled up into a crispy foetal ball, somehow reducing the
length of his body into that of a well-fried rasher. We also relished the sight of Nina Conti proceeding to the back of the
Olivier stalls with a fifty-foot length of knicker elastic that she
was stretching from the mouth of her 'husband' in order to
pang him out of his dangerous invasion of his own posterior.
Hubby gripped the lethal device in his teeth. Was he ready?
'Yes.' Knicker elastic rebounded at top speed in the wrong
direction... Two extended extracts from *Illuminatus!* and *The
Warp* gave a good idea of the epic bagginess of those ridiculously ambitious play cycles, if not the full flavour and
impromptu ingenuity of their original stagings. But the whole
show, devised by Daisy and directed by Richard Eyre,
reminded us not only of what a great spirit Campbell was, but
also what a great writer. There were three long episodes from
Pigspurt performed by Toby Jones, Alan Cox and Chris Fairbank. Each of these different actors confirmed that there
might indeed be a real theatrical future for this marvellous
material performed by people other than the master himself.
The writing is simply too good to languish between book covers. It demands to be channelled.

John Sessions compèred proceedings with a languid,
anecdotal brilliance, Daisy led a hilarious distillation of the Pidgin *Macbeth*, and Warren Mitchell touchingly took the stage,
very frail now, to tell us that he was the one who doesn't talk like
Ken Campbell. The last twenty minutes by the impro group the
School of Night was a digest of great stuff that, given it was by
now getting on for midnight, began to outstay its welcome and
the odd seeker began creeping away to the outside world of dull
normality. In this respect, the event took on the atmosphere of
a Ken Dodd show, testing the audience's patience by the simple
expedient of refusing to give in or shut up. This, of course, would
have delighted the other Ken no end. But the chasm of his

absence was tangible, although when Chris Fairbank interrupted the first half from the auditorium with a torrential rant of Campbellian rage and abuse, screaming and waving his arms and storming towards the exit, most people were mightily relieved to realise that this wasn't the real thing after all.

The impact Ken Campbell made on so many people, their careers, their attitude to their work, their dreams of what they might achieve, is incalculable. As an ephemeral art form, the theatre lives in the moment and seizes it: that was his greatest gift, an ability to enliven the here and now, electrify the current between artist and audience, making both sides feel fuller and funnier and friskier. In his own way, he was as dominant a character as Orson Welles, only more down-at-heel, and less grandiose, fearsomely in charge, voracious in his appetites and enthusiasms, often doing too many things all at once, perpetually strapped for cash and seeking always to be the perpetrator of the perfect hoax. The telling of an incident was the business with him, not so much the incident itself.

This is why he was such a fantastic theatrical fabulist: the truth of what happened mattered less than the manner in which it was transmitted, and the transmission was all. Everything, in the end, was theatre, a conduit for describing, understanding, supposing. 'If you can meet with Triumph and Disaster, and treat those two impostors just the same... you'll be a man, my son,' wrote Rudyard Kipling in his most famous poem. This ability to embrace whatever happens to you in life, let alone make something creative and artistic of it, is rare. Chris Langham talked to me about what he called Ken's 'black-belt spiritual approach, of treating what happens as being the next remarkable – and who'd have guessed it? – event in a wonderful series of events... What are you going to do? You've got a front-row seat to your own life, what's the point of complaining about it? The only sane approach is to say, goodness, I didn't expect this to happen, I wonder what will happen next...'

Prue's family have owned, since the late nineteenth century, an old Welsh farmhouse that sits on the shore at Rhosneigr on the Isle of Anglesey. She and Ken and Daisy spent most summer holidays there together. Ken loved the place as much as he loved Epping Forest, unleashing his dogs over the endless miles of white sand, scouring the bird life with his binoculars, going on boat trips, making picnics. Prue and Ken had a good time together in Anglesey before his last trip to Edinburgh. Anglesey is almost on the same latitude as the Wirral, where the Campbell clan gathered a hundred years earlier, perhaps when the Gees were settling on the island peninsula. The degrees of separation get smaller by the decade.

Poignantly, just one year after Ken died, John Joyce died, too, of an oesophagal cancer which was too far advanced to be treated successfully. He had stuck by Ken from the start of his adventures at the Nottingham Playhouse, right to the end, always game for a caper and up for a laugh, and glad to be of service, like the loyal Earl of Kent in *King Lear*. At the end of Shakespeare's play, Kent is invited by the Duke of Albany to 'rule in this realm and the gored state sustain'. He is unable to do so and retreats on the enigmatic line, 'I have a journey, sir, shortly to go; my master calls me, I must not say no.'

There are several Ken capers I'm sorry I missed, one of them a puppet show about the great turn-of-the-eighteenth-century clown Joseph Grimaldi, which he wrote with the composer Richard Kilgour for the Little Angel Theatre in Islington in 1995. He recreated the scene of Grimaldi's over-bearing father – known as 'Grim-all-day' – playing a pantaloon at Sadler's Wells with little Joey as the monkey. The action develops as a riot of adventure and mishap, and silly songs, in search of the rare oonga-boonga bird, a cross between an ostrich and a starling. 'Old clowns never die,' sings Joey in the graveyard in the beginning and at the end, with a chorus of ghosties and ghoulies, 'they only lose their pom-poms... I'm dead, I'm dead, I'm just not in my bed, I'm somewhere else instead... Most often, you will find me in my coffin; and there again most often... you'll find me laughin''.

Select Bibliography

Ansorge, Peter, *Disrupting the Spectacle* (Pitman, 1975)

Billington, Michael, *One Night Stands* (Nick Hern Books, 1993)

Bradwell, Mike, *The Reluctant Escapologist* (Nick Hern Books, 2010)

Callow, Simon, *Being an Actor* (Methuen, 1984; new edition, Penguin Books, 1995)

Campbell, Ken, *Old King Cole* (Eyre Methuen, 1975)

Campbell, Ken, *Jack Sheppard* (Macmillan Education, 1976)

Campbell, Ken, *Skungpoomery* (Methuen Drama, 1980)

Campbell, Ken and Waechter, F. K., *Clown Plays* (Methuen Drama, 1992)

Campbell, Ken, *Furtive Nudist* (Methuen Drama, 1992)

Campbell, Ken, *The Bald Trilogy* (Methuen Drama, 1995)

Campbell, Ken, *Violin Time* (Methuen Drama, 1996)

Eyre, Richard, *Utopia and Other Places* (Bloomsbury, 1993)

Findlater, Richard, ed., *At the Royal Court: 25 Years of the English Stage Company* (Amber Lane Press, 1981)

Goorney, Howard, *The Theatre Workshop Story* (Eyre Methuen, 1981)

Hall, Peter, *Peter Hall's Diaries: The Story of a Dramatic Battle*, ed. John Goodwin (Hamish Hamilton, 1983; new edition, Oberon Books, 2000)

Hicks, Seymour, *Twenty-Four Years of an Actor's Life* (Alston Rivers, 1910)

Johnstone, Keith, *Impro* (Faber, 1979; new edition, Methuen Drama, 1981)

Jung, C. G., *Memories, Dreams, Reflections* (Fontana, 1995)

Kustow, Michael, *theatre@risk* (Methuen Drama, 2001)

Lee, Gwen and Sauter, Doris Elaine, ed., *What If Our World is Their Heaven? The Final Conversations of Philip K. Dick* (Duckworth, 2006)

Littlewood, Joan, *Joan's Book: Joan Littlewood's Peculiar History As She Tells It* (Methuen Drama, 1994)

Merkin, Ros, ed., *Liverpool's Third Cathedral* (Liverpool and Merseyside Theatres Trust, 2004)

Oram, Neil, *Spy for Love, 87 Raps from the Warp* (Oberon Books, 2002)

Roszak, Theodore, *Flicker* (Bantam Books, 1992)

Shea, Robert and Wilson, Robert Anton, *The Illuminatus! Trilogy* (Dell Publishing, 1975; collected trilogy, 1984)

Spolin, Viola, *Improvisation for the Theater: a handbook of teaching and directing techniques* (Northwestern University Press, 1963)

Wright, Nicholas, *99 Plays* (Methuen Drama, 1992)

Index

Index

Index

Index

Index

Index

Index